Jane Caro wears many hats, including author, lecturer, mentor, social commentator, columnist, workshop facilitator, speaker, broadcaster and award-winning advertising writer. Jane runs her own communications consultancy and lectures in Advertising Creative at the School of Communication Arts at the University of Western Sydney. She has published four books: *The Stupid Country: How Australia Is Dismantling Public Education* co-authored with Chris Bonnor (2007), *The F Word: How We Learned to Swear by Feminism* co-authored with Catherine Fox (2008), *Just a Girl* (2011) and *What Makes a Good School* co-authored with Chris Bonnor (2012). She has also appeared on Channel 7's *Sunrise*, ABC's *Q&A* and ABC's *The Gruen Transfer.*

DESTROYING THE JOINT

WHY WOMEN HAVE TO CHANGE THE WORLD

Edited by Jane Caro

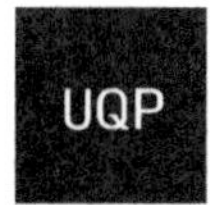

First published 2013 by University of Queensland Press
PO Box 6042, St Lucia, Queensland 4067 Australia
Reprinted 2013 (twice), 2015, 2016, 2017

www.uqp.com.au
uqp@uqp.uq.edu.au

Cataloguing-in-Publication entry is available from the
National Library of Australia
http://catalogue.nla.gov.au/

ISBN (pbk) 978-0-7022-4990-7
ISBN (ePdf) 978-0-7022-5177-1
ISBN (ePUB) 978-0-7022-5178-8
ISBN (kindle) 978-0-7022-5179-5

Typeset in 12/17 pt Bembo by Post Pre-press Group, Brisbane
Printed in Australia by McPherson's Printing Group

Contents

Introduction: Sometimes You Just Have to Laugh

Jane Caro

On the evening of Friday, 31st of August, 2012, I was sitting around, sipping a glass of wine, keeping one eye on the telly and the other on Twitter. Twitter began to command more of my attention as I saw women responding with understandable hurt and outrage to the comments made by Sydney radio shock jock Alan Jones on his top-rating show that morning. In response to an announcement by Prime Minister Julia Gillard that Australia would donate $300 million to train women in the Pacific region in leadership, Jones declared women leaders were doing enough harm already. He named two – Christine Nixon, the ex-Victorian Police Commissioner, and Clover Moore, the current lord mayor of Sydney – and said that women leaders were 'destroying the joint'. Jones clearly accepted the all too common view that while the failure of male leaders reflects only on themselves, any mistakes on the part of a female leader – whether perceived or actual – reflect on the capability of all women to wield power.

As I watched the storm brew, I tweeted the following: 'Got time on my hands tonight so thought I'd come up with new ways to destroy the joint, being a woman and all. Ideas welcome.' I hit send with no end in mind except a desire to model how we could respond to Jones's remarks without going on the defensive.

What followed was extraordinary, entirely spontaneous and hilarious. Women and men took up the challenge in droves. Jill Tomlinson (clearly more savvy about Twitter than I am) added the now famous hashtag, Jenna Price created a Facebook page, Yvette Vignando whipped up some t-shirts, wristbands and other collateral, and a tweet became a phenomenon. By the end of the first weekend, #destroythejoint was trending worldwide and I was being interviewed by the BBC World Service!

How it developed from there is explained in Jill's, Jenna's and Yvette's essays later in this book, and by the collective who have turned Destroy the Joint from a cheeky tweet into a powerful and effective agent for change. But we must give Alan Jones his share of the credit. As I described him in a later tweet, he was the gift that just kept on giving. Not content with slagging off women as leaders, he then famously 'joked' a few weeks later that the prime minister's recently deceased father must have 'died of shame' because of her supposed lies. As you will discover as you read this book, that's when Destroy the Joint really showed its muscles.

But why did my original tweet hit such a nerve? Why, at this stage in human history, do women still feel they have to justify their right to be taken seriously?

When Egyptian dictator Hosni Mubarak was ignominiously bundled from power in early 2011, the world's press went into paroxysms of ecstasy. This was the kind of destroying of joints the West wholeheartedly supported. Headlines around the world declared that people power had sent a tyrant packing. Like most of the rest of the world, I watched the events in Tahrir Square with fascination and excitement, but I am a feminist and that helps me see things differently.

The day after Mubarak fell, many news outlets carried headlines about people power and pictures of the jubilant crowds in Tahrir Square on their front pages. My feminism meant that I automatically scanned those photos for female faces. I found very few. I doubt they'd have made up 1% of those pictured, to be honest.

Just imagine for a moment if the genders of the protesters in Tahrir Square had been reversed; if those pictures had shown 99% women and 1% men. There is no way on earth the headlines would have called it a victory for the 'people'. And that's because, as Jones revealed in his original response to Gillard's donation, men can be people but women are still only ever women.

Not that we're actually supposed to point that out or complain about it. No, we're supposed not only to cop being considered second rate, but collude with those who'd rather pretend that it isn't how we're thought of at all. This form of mass gaslighting has very effectively kept women more or less in their place for millennia. If you are not familiar with the term *gaslighting*, it comes from the 1944 film *Gaslight*, in which Charles Boyer tries to make Ingrid Bergman believe she is losing her mind. Women have adopted the term to describe how they feel when their perceptions and responses to their differential treatment are dismissed or belittled by others, particularly men. Done skillfully enough, it can make women doubt their own senses.

Well, perhaps it is more accurate to say that it used to be able to make us doubt ourselves. Since the advent of social media, the ability of patriarchal societies to isolate and control women by dismissing their perception of the world has been seriously undermined. The reason for this is simple: social media bypasses the old gatekeepers. The people who used to decide who could get access to the public conversation and what they could discuss – the vast majority of whom were men – are losing their stranglehold. Some are hanging on grimly, of course, as Wendy Harmer points out in her essay on the almost exclusively male world of commercial radio.

But women and other previously marginalised groups now have unmediated access to the public conversation for the first time in history. They are able to post their perceptions of an event, an article, a discussion, a policy, a crime or a stupid remark and instead of being mocked, ridiculed or even just ignored (though they can expect those responses too), they can find common ground with others. As #destroythejoint powerfully demonstrated, the way they see the world is not crazy or illegitimate.

Post Tahrir Square, women began to tell their stories about why they were not demonstrating in greater numbers. Turns out, it was grossly sexualised bullying by what appears to be organised groups of men that kept them away. In India, after a horrendous rape and murder, Dalit women, the most despised people in that country, found the courage to take to the streets in droves to protest. Emily Maguire explores the way marginalised and silenced women are beginning to fight back all over the world in her essay. In Australia, the rape and murder of Jill Meagher – followed obsessively on social media as it unfolded – brought 30 000 people onto the streets of Melbourne. In Russia, the trial of Pussy Riot was watched and discussed by millions. And social media was quick to point out how comprehensively the mainstream media had missed the point of Julia Gillard's now famous sexism and misogyny speech. All over the world, women are mad as hell and refusing to take it any more. Hashtags like #destroythejoint, #everdaysexism and #shoutingback are giving women the courage to speak up and speak out. This is not bullying, it is not fascism, it is not a conspiracy or even very organised. It is spontaneous, real and profoundly democratic. Indeed, we may at last be seeing the emergence of real democracy and freedom of speech.

As Leslie Cannold, Paula McDonald and Abby Cathcart point out in their contributions, this resurgence of women's voices is shaking the joint to its foundations. If the most conservative leader of an Australian political party for decades now has to identify as a feminist to have a realistic chance of winning government, women are powerful. American Republicans are still scratching their heads over the way women have deserted the grand old party. They appear to think that you can want to remove a person's right to decide what happens to their own body and make fatuous remarks about rape to back up your right to colonise someone else's uterus, and the owners of those organs won't mind. That's serious dehumanising, right there. Britain's David Cameron is also struggling to attract women voters: the gender gap between Conservatives and Labour in the UK has now hit 26%.

The women who have contributed their responses to this book represent a wide cross-section of backgrounds, ages, beliefs, experiences and biases. Feminism is a broad church. Catherine Fox writes about the difficulties facing women who aspire to rise to the top of the joint. Stella Young fulminates about her inability to even enter most joints. Clementine Ford dissects a comedy joint and Krissy Kneen ends the collection by bringing all the joints tumbling down. Politicians Penny Wong and Christine Milne shine a political lens on the joint while Carmen Lawrence wonders if we really will end up destroying the whole joint, aka the planet. We also approached women from the conservative side of politics but, for various reasons, none were able to contribute. Nevertheless, you will hear from young women and old women, middle-class women and working-class women; women with all sorts of different experiences of life. Some of their stories will make you laugh. Some will make you cry and some rage with fury. The following pages include polemic, satire and impassioned arguments. The one thing they all share is a desire to change the world and make things fairer: for women, for men, for children, for the disabled, the indigenous, the migrant, the poor, the gay, the straight, the despised and, not least, the planet. Some people call that destroying the joint.

For myself, my abiding and most precious memory of that wonderful weekend when one cheeky tweet hit a nerve and started something important is when, in the midst of the general hilarity and wit that made up #destroythejoint, a woman tweeted: 'This is the most fun I've had with feminism in years.'

Me too.

A Complex Problem

Monica Dux

So I was driving to the zoo with my two-year-old daughter one morning in September 2012, listening to the local ABC radio. Jon Faine was discussing the whole 'destroy the joint' thing with one of the chief destroyers, Christine Nixon.

Naturally, Nixon and Faine weren't too sympathetic to the gentleman who'd started it all. 'One of the great privileges of living in Melbourne is that you don't have to listen to Alan Jones,' said Nixon, and I chuckled along, a contented member of the choir she was preaching to.

There was another reason that I was enjoying this discussion, other than the pleasure of having my politics affirmed. When we left home, my daughter Mila had made a huge stink about the fact that I hadn't put her *Play School* CD on, most particularly 'The Rainbow Song', a sweet ditty that I had heard approximately 34 000 times. Baulking at the 34 001st rendition, I turned the radio on instead. 'Mummy's going to listen to this today, darling,' I explained firmly, while she convulsed in her baby seat, literally turning crimson with rage. Yet as I gripped the steering wheel and cranked the radio up, Mila slowly calmed down, eventually falling uncharacteristically quiet.

Mummy: 1; Two-year-old: Nil.

Of course, I knew that she was probably busy cooking up plan B, likely involving her screaming 'I NEED TO DO POO!' just when I was trapped in some really heavy traffic. But I decided to enjoy the peace while it lasted, focusing on the radio, not on the poo forecast. It never occurred to me that my daughter might be quiet because she was doing the very same thing.

When we got to the zoo, Mila failed to spark up, remaining morose as I pushed her around to visit the equally sad animals. Then, as I struggled to induce a red-spotted jezebel to land on my finger, in direct contravention of the Butterfly House do-not-touch-the-butterflies rule, Mila suddenly spat it out.

'Mummy,' she asked, her little face filled with worry, 'why women on radio wreck? Why women wreck the joint?'

Like most small children, my daughter is fascinated by gender difference. Mila had recently worked out that Mummy is a 'woman', and that she would one day join me in that club. To Mila, the only qualification for membership is having boobies and a 'fluffy' vagina, both attributes she eagerly desired. Yet now, looking at her troubled face, it suddenly occurred to me that while I'd been enjoying an intelligent, nuanced, occasionally ironic discussion of the broader social issues surrounding Alan Jones's misogynist outburst, Mila had homed in on the one phrase that had been repeated again and again, and she had taken it quite literally. The busty, fluffy team are just a bunch of no-good wreckers!

I was about to launch into an elaborate explanation of what Faine and Nixon had actually meant when I remembered my friend Annie, whose son Charlie had expressed a fear of death. Annie had attempted to remove the sting by explaining that, while death is final and absolute, it is also quite beautiful, because you rot into the ground and become food for all the worms and bugs, thereby closing the great circle of life. Following this account, Charlie screamed himself to sleep for a week, proving that, when it comes to small children, honest explanations of complex concepts are not always in order. Instead of attempting one with Mila, I just gushed, 'Oh no, no, no, darling, women don't wreck, those people on the radio were just joking!' Then I cranked 'The Rainbow Song' up loud as we drove home. Mila was more than satisfied, and it seemed that the incident was forgotten.

Yet there was something about the whole business that still bothered me. That night, with baths and bedtime stories behind us, I told my husband about the Butterfly House outburst. Not only was my normally neurotic spouse unconcerned, he found it quite funny. 'It was one silly phrase that stuck in her head!' he said as he scrubbed at the dishes. 'How is that going to do any harm?'

I thought for a moment, still uncertain about why it bothered me. Then, watching him scrape at some baked-on grease, it came to me. 'I guess I'm worried that it might give her a complex.'

It's a strange thing when you open your mouth and hear your mother's voice come out. My husband was just as surprised.

'God, I haven't heard that expression in years,' he said.

Neither had I, I admitted. So why had it popped into my head now?

As a child there were many things I feared. Forgetting to do my homework, turning up to school without any underwear, and not graduating from pencil to pen were all terrors that loomed real and large in my pre-adolescent world. I didn't become any less anxious as I grew older, but my fears did become more lurid. Inadvertently deflowering myself while riding a horse was high on my teenage list, as was being visited by a divine harbinger bearing the news that I'd been chosen by God to birth the Second Coming. No surprises here, just the usual worries of a well-adjusted Catholic girl. But perhaps greater than either of these terrors, and certainly more enduring, was my fear of growing up and discovering that I had a 'complex'.

My mum and my aunties talked a lot about complexes, and about the unfortunate women who had them. Cousin Sarah dressed badly and never got married because of hers. Mrs Bernstein who lived up the road was a nasty piece of work because her lazy-good-for-nothing husband had given her one.

These were damaged women whose lives had been poisoned, but complexes could also be more specific and focused, impacting on one aspect of your psyche while leaving the rest intact. Aunt Edna, for example, developed a driving-related complex after my Uncle Bert criticised her skills at the wheel. Aunt Vera insisted on wearing a wig for 50 years, because of a complex of uncertain origin that made her think her hair was unfashionable.

Given this extensive list of casualties, a sensitive lass like myself could be forgiven for concluding that we were in the midst of a complex epidemic. Even my own mum had one, acquired in her youth, she said, when she was engaged to the semi-legendary cad Jimmy O'Leary.

But what were these malevolent things that stalked the good women of East Ryde and surrounds? My childish understanding of the matter was that a complex was a chronic mental condition that you caught when people or events undermined your confidence. Once the seed of self-doubt was planted it would spread in your mind like cancer, mutating normal healthy thoughts into twisted, misguided ones until, before you knew it, you were wearing a bad wig, rejecting all offers of marriage, and taking a bus to bingo. This could happen without you even knowing it, and once you caught a complex they were almost impossible to shake off.

Women seemed far more likely to suffer with them than men, and when blokes did get them they manifested quite differently. Women usually put up with theirs in noble silence, as they might a case of urinary incontinence, while a man with a complex was to be feared, and definitely never dated. Because a man with a complex could be a source of complex contagion.

Jimmy O'Leary was a case in point. Jimmy had spent a few years training to be a priest back in the 1950s, but had jumped ship in order to pursue his true calling, which turned out to be seducing good Catholic girls. Looking at the current state of the priesthood you'd expect that Catholic seminaries in the 1950s and '60s would have been complex hotbeds, but Mum always insisted that it was the men who *didn't* finish their priestly training that you really needed to look out for. Such men, Mum warned me, were all 'mixed up', and should be avoided as suitors. And, presumably, prime ministers.

My mother's generation was the last to talk so enthusiastically and earnestly about complexes, although the term has lingered in common parlance. We still occasionally hear about Napoleon complexes, Cinderella complexes and god complexes, although the most common varieties are the 'inferiority complex', essentially meaning that a person has low self-esteem, and its mirror image, the 'superiority complex'. Yet there was a time when the idea of the complex was not mere pop psychology, but an important part of serious, mainstream science.

The concept was invented and elaborated by the heavyweight fathers of psychoanalysis, Sigmund Freud, Carl Jung and Alfred Adler. Jung was perhaps the foremost champion of the complex (or at least a close second after my mum), but it was Freud who first postulated the Oedipus complex, still the most famous complex of them all.

My friend Professor Nick Haslam, an academic psychologist at Melbourne University, explained to me that Freud and friends understood complexes as 'amalgams of thoughts, emotions and desires', which could form symbolic clots or fault lines in a person's unconscious. A complex could be seeded in a variety of ways, often quite subtle, and because they were submerged in the unconscious mind the victim might suffer from one without even realising it. Yet its impact on his or her behaviour could be far-reaching and profound.

It may seem silly, but back in the day it never occurred to me that the complexes my mum spoke about were the same sorts of thing that Oedipus had lent his name to. Suddenly seeing Mum's psychiatric diagnoses in an entirely fresh light, I phoned her up to see what she would make of the Butterfly House Incident. 'It's all Alan Jones's fault,' she said, without hesitation. 'He's another one, you know, just like Jimmy O'Leary. Thinks he's the greatest. Your father can't stand him either.'

I was stunned. So, Alan Jones and the Notorious O'Leary were of an ilk? Who'd have thought it!

'No, no,' said Mum, frustrated with her slow-witted daughter. 'What I mean is, they've both got superiority complexes. And the way they make themselves feel big is by making other people feel small. That's why they're so dangerous.'

When I was in high school in the 1980s, feelings of superiority and inferiority were also widely discussed but the language had changed since my mum's day, so that now we spoke of self-esteem, or a lack thereof. To help fend off this threat, my classmates and I were encouraged to love ourselves, and to affirm this love regularly. To this end we were given classes in 'Health', a coy name for a very Catholic subject that covered everything from menstruation (use pads, never tampons, as they will deflower you) to drugs (just say no) to sex (say no, or you'll go to hell). These classes were conducted by Sister Bernadette, a well-meaning little nun with remarkable calf muscles. According to Bernadette, there were all sorts of ways a girl might affirm herself, but the very best way was to do it in song. Judging by Bernadette's enraptured expression whenever we listened to her records, I suspect that she had a passionate crush on the Catholic folk superstar Sister Janet Mead, yet Bernadette's very favourite song of affirmation was Whitney Houston's 'The Greatest Love of All'.

Almost every week we were invited to listen and reflect upon this song, as Whitney crooned what was to become the central message of my years in Health – that loving yourself was not only the greatest thing you could do, but that it was 'easy to achieve'. Hardly a subtle lyric, yet still I found it rather confusing, not least because we'd always been taught that it was Our Lord Jesus Christ whom we must place first on our love list. But even putting this theological conundrum aside, 'The Greatest Love of All' never sat easily with me. Because if the greatest love you can have is for yourself then, by implication, the greatest failure is *not* mastering self-love. And if it's so easy to achieve self-love, then those of us who don't manage it have only got ourselves to blame.

Yet as my high school years progressed, Whitney's warblings proved to be a perfect reflection of the times. With the rise of neo-liberalism 'personal responsibility' became a virtual catch-cry, in economics, politics and, eventually, in the wider social world. If you were poor, we were told, it was probably because you didn't work hard enough. If your dreams remain unfulfilled, it was likely due to you not wanting them enough. If you suffered from low self-esteem, it was surely because you didn't say your affirmations with sufficient gusto. Of course, it wasn't just Whitney delivering this message. In the USA there was Reagan, in the UK there was Thatcher, and on the TV there was the most powerful and influential one of them all, Oprah. And from time to time, of course, there was also our Alan.

Ideological fashions have changed, but this way of thinking has never really gone away. Today it impacts particularly on women, as even our personal lives are subjected to the nasty finger pointing. If you have no partner, it's sure to be because you were too fussy. If you have no children, it's because you were too focused on your career. And if you don't love your body, then maybe you should just stop hoeing down all those carbs, fatso.

To someone who believes all this garbage, the idea of a complex really must seem very old-fashioned and quaint. Yet I feel a warm wash of nostalgia for my mum's way of talking. Because I think she was essentially right about the women who populated my childhood. Over the course of a long lifetime, many of them had been more or less crushed by the profoundly sexist world they lived in, and this was in no sense their own fault. There was not a thing they could have done about it.

Even today, women are subjected to all sorts of shit that men never get. Throughout our lives we are told that we're ugly, fat, hysterical and irrational, that we can't drive or read maps, that we don't deserve promotions because we're more interested in making babies and that our worth can be measured by the dimensions of our bodies. In the modern world, most of these messages are subtle and coded; occasionally, as with Alan Jones's rantings, they are still overt. But either way, they are constant, and they do wheedle their poison into our psyches, eventually mixing up the way we see ourselves, and our place in the world. If you doubt this just listen critically to the way women talk about themselves: teenage girls talking about their bodies, new mothers about their guilt, or successful professional women apologising for their achievements. In their words you'll hear the blockages and the fault lines, created over the years by the constant drip of sexist poison.

Alan Jones's Destroy the Joint rant was not unusual in its content, only in its honesty. Instead of encoding his message, disguising it or wrapping it up in pleasantries, his words were basic and crude and unashamed.

And maybe that's why the whole thing with Mila bothered me so much, because it was the first time that she's actually *noticed* a negative message about women. It triggered a realisation in me that my smart, powerful little daughter was going to spend her whole life getting hit with the sort of rubbish that Jones was peddling, only most of the time it was going to be too subtle to notice, sneaking into her unconscious without me or anyone else even realising it.

A week later I found myself driving Mila to the zoo again, and on the way I asked her if she remembered what we'd heard on the radio last time, about women wrecking the joint. She said yes, she did remember. So I explained to her that the man they'd been talking about that day, he has what's called a complex. 'And Mila,' I told her, 'best keep away from men with complexes. They really do wreck the joint.'

Destroying the Joint Is About More Than Being a Woman in Power

Senator Christine Milne

What did Alan Jones mean when he said 'women are destroying the joint'? Was it, as some have characterised it, nothing more nor less than a howl against the rise of women into positions of power and influence? Was it purely and simply an angry man's general tirade, steeped in misogyny? Or was it a deeper fight back against the slow but sure progress towards a fairer, more compassionate, more forward-thinking society?

Pondering that raises a perhaps more important question: What do we mean when we talk about 'destroying the joint'? Are we happy simply to see women occupying powerful and influential positions in increasing numbers? Or do we need to go further? Is it not enough unless we use those positions to drive deeper change?

For me, destroying the joint means challenging the power structures that say that might is right and that today is more important than tomorrow. Destroying the joint means building a new system in which it's not OK to allow people to be marginalised, exploited and discriminated against; it's not OK to ignore the needs of future generations; it's not OK to wreck this extraordinary, beautiful, fragile planetary environment that sustains us – our Mother Earth.

We don't want power and influence just because it's time for men to share. We want power with a purpose.

All my life I have been challenging the status quo. I can't help myself – if something seems really unfair to me, then I just have to become involved in trying to fix it. I've often wondered why some people feel that need and others don't. To what extent is it innate and how much are we the product of our upbringing?

I grew up in the 1950s and '60s, in a conservative farming community in north-west Tasmania. My sister Gaylene and I were brought up on the family dairy farm before we were sent to a Catholic girls' boarding school, St Mary's College, in Hobart. It was the story of many other girls of my generation who went on to be resigned to, happy with, or successful within the status quo. So what made some of us want to rattle the cage and why did we do it?

Looking back, I realise that, while the seeds of my passion for destroying the joint were sown then, it was not the intention of my parents or the nuns at St Mary's to turn out radicals. It was certainly their intention to give us the skills to get to the top, to achieve our greatest potential. But, looking deeper, they made it clear that getting to the top was never just for ourselves; it was for the betterment of all people and of society at large, now and into the future.

That is the gift that has driven some of us to keep on trying not to just get to the top for ourselves, but also to remove the barriers that prevent other women, and other marginalised people, from getting there. Therein lies the rub.

Getting to the top makes you a role model for other women and girls, regardless of what you do when you get there. And fair enough too. Women are half the population and deserve half the representation regardless of the views we hold. But being at the top does not automatically make you a role model for advancing women's rights.

Some women in positions of power and influence have found ways around or through the barriers to entry but, because of an unwritten law not to upset the apple cart, have deliberately or inadvertently denied similar access to women who come after. By reinforcing the foundations of the status quo, they have effectively held back women's rights. I would go so far as to say that, in many cases, they have been preselected, by both men and women in factions or on preselection committees, specifically for that purpose.

Frequently it has been a religious perspective that has overridden a women's rights perspective. How many female MPs, for example, voted against RU 486, or against equal marriage, or against funding women's reproductive health programs through overseas aid?

Frequently, the way through has been dynastic succession. How many women in countries where there are now quotas for women MPs are the wives, sisters, daughters or mothers of the powerful men already at the top? Are they role models for women? Yes, of course they are. But are they advancing or stalling women's rights? That depends on what they do when they achieve their position.

But often, particularly in the Westminster countries and in the USA, it has been simply the gravitational pull of the status quo that has held back progress despite the rise of individual women.

Take Margaret Thatcher, for example. The Iron Lady learned the rules of the joint and played them harder than the men in British conservative politics for over a decade. Thatcher did nothing to improve the chances of women in Britain or anywhere else in the world, and she plunged Great Britain into the Falklands War. But she remains undoubtedly a role model to this day, in the sense that she proved a woman from a working-class background could be a successful prime minister.

Getting to the top is destroying the joint to the extent that it shows that women can do whatever we set out to do and take our place on the road to equal representation, even within the existing framework and structures.

Women of all political persuasions – Julia Gillard, Bronwyn Bishop, Rachel Siewert, Julie Bishop, Larissa Waters, Tanya Plibersek, Connie Fierravanti-Wells, Lee Rhiannon, Nicola Roxon, Sarah Hanson-Young, Penny Wright and I, together with all female MPs – have this much in common. We share stories of how hard it has been, of how what we wear or how we look is criticised when it's not the same for men. Remember how Joan Kirner was always mocked in cartoons for spotted dresses, and how Julia Gillard's jackets are constantly under scrutiny. We've seen the same in newsrooms, where women have historically struggled to maintain positions as they have aged or become pregnant.

Just as those who have been destroying the joint in politics have had some successes, so have those in the media. It would have been unheard of once for a pregnant woman to read the evening TV news, or to be preselected in politics, but that has now happened in Australia on more than a few occasions, and it is fairly common for women in politics to become mothers as sitting MPs.

Parliament, its buildings and its sitting hours have historically been family unfriendly. When I was first elected to the Tasmanian Parliament in 1989, there was no place to take children who came to the parliament to visit sitting members, especially since the offices we occupied were like broom cupboards. So I argued for 7pm adjournments and the setting up of a spouses' room in the parliament as a family lounge room. We succeeded in both, but sadly the spouses' room was rarely used. It was ahead of its time in terms of the number of members with young children, so it was eventually converted to another use.

Preselection for winnable seats is changing for the better in all political parties, but that is a relatively recent phenomenon and an indication of the power of women voting for women and organisations within parties, like Emily's List. The Greens have always had a proud record in this regard and we remain the only party in federal parliament with more than 50% of our representatives being women.

In some ways, the language of politics has also changed for the better, hard though that might be to remember, given the standard of our current debate. Back in 1989, when it was unusual for women to be in Tasmanian politics at all, let alone in the balance of power, my colleague Dianne Hollister and I were shouted at and abused by prominent Liberals across the House of Assembly as 'political sluts' because we dared to support a Labor Government. There were five Greens MPs, but it was we two women who were accused of prostituting ourselves for political power. The recent examples such as Prime Minister Gillard being referred to as Bob Brown's bitch are just as offensive, but thankfully would no longer be accepted inside the parliament.

Nevertheless, the description of women's behaviour by the media and by male politicians still demonstrates the discriminatory overtones women endure to this day. How many male MPs are described as 'shrill', or as stamping their feet when making a strong speech in the parliament? Former Tasmanian Premier Michael Field used to start sentences with: 'Christine Milne can stamp her feet as much as she likes, but Labor will … ' It is and was a put-down, suggesting that women are unable to debate the point but rather resort to temper tantrums. The irony is that it is often the failure of men to be able to argue the point that leads them to make sexist remarks instead. The same goes for references to female MPs as witches – the none-too-subtle idea being to drown them for their blasphemy, their daring to challenge accepted mores.

I was very lucky to grow up with role models willing to take on the status quo through their actions.

My life's experience was of both parents working, both parents cooking and growing food, and both parents running the farm, as Dad did the physical work and Mum did the books. Having two daughters meant that there was no discussion about boys inheriting the farm or questions as to what the girls would do or get. All options including farming were on the table for my sister and me, but it was as hard to make a living on a family farm then as it is now and my mother was passionate about her girls getting an education. She had been a St Mary's girl, sent by her parents from a farm at Sheffield to board in the 1930s. She subsequently went to teachers' college and, quite radically for the 1950s, went back to work as a Home Arts teacher the year I started school in 1958, in large part to pay for Gaylene and me to have the education she so ardently valued as the key to life's opportunities.

At St Mary's, the teaching staff were overwhelmingly nuns of the Presentation teaching order. In word they never challenged the mores of the male-dominated Catholic Church to which they had dedicated their lives, but their actions did challenge accepted wisdom about gender roles. Historically, and to this day, it has been the women's orders who are the most passionate advocates for social justice and environmental stewardship within the Church. Nuns did everything in the day and boarding school. Not only did they teach in the daytime, but they marked books, cooked and cleaned, taught piano before and after school, not to mention looking after the boarders.

When I was there, nuns got drivers' licences for the first time. Some also enrolled in university and drove themselves there dressed in the full black and white garb. They set up missions in developing countries and we were read the letters from nuns in what seemed then exotic and dangerous places. These reinforced the martyrdom stories we were told of people who had paid with their lives for standing up for what is right – 'our fathers chained in prisons dark were both in heart and conscience free'. So, when nuns told us 'girls can do anything', it was pretty obvious that we could. They inculcated the idea that you must have the courage of your convictions, that there is no such word as can't; it simply means you are not trying hard enough.

But all this was nevertheless meant within the strict rules of the Church.

It was a hard life, and I used to envy the day scholars going home after school, but there was no tolerance for tears. How many times, as our letters home were torn up to be rewritten, did we hear that our parents had not made sacrifices to provide us with a good education to be rewarded with complaining letters? Tears were a weakness, an indulgence in self-pity, not to be tolerated. They were also an outward indication of vulnerability and it was made pretty clear that, to make it in a tough world, one didn't wear one's feelings on one's sleeve.

This is one of the many lessons of those years that I find fascinatingly reflected in politics. Since the assumption is that men are strong, when male politicians such as Bob Hawke or Peter Beattie cry, it is applauded and rewarded. They are deemed to be sensitive, caring and empathetic. But because female MPs are assumed to be not as strong as their male counterparts, when they cry, they are deemed not to be coping, not up to the job. Equally demeaningly and utterly unfairly, if they don't cry, it is because they aren't caring or sensitive enough, they are somehow lacking in femininity, 'unsexed' like Lady Macbeth.

A similar disparity applies to disparaging references to Julia Gillard's 'empty fruit bowl'. Parallel references to Joe Hockey's basic digs in Canberra, and those of so many other senior male MPs, are made as gentle jibes, rather than a question of their competence to hold the job. Clearly a lack of domestic homeliness is a criticism of a female MP but appealing in a male. Apparently it is heart-warming to think he needs a woman to look after him!

When I started teaching in high schools on the north-west coast of Tasmania in 1975, sexism was pretty well entrenched in teaching career structures. There were some very female senior mistresses but virtually no female vice principals, let alone principals, and it was not compulsory for female married staff to contribute to superannuation. Thanks in no small part to teachers' unions across the country, this has now changed. Indeed women in the union movement have been front and centre of campaigning for better pay and conditions for women in the workforce.

But, at the time, the different values and expectations regarding long-term career prospects placed on male versus female participation in teaching was stark. One example was that the male staff from some schools used to drink on Fridays after work at the Devonport Gentlemen's Club, where a sign at the door said 'No Ladies Beyond This Point'. Since prospects for career progression without relationship building were limited, this held women back. Equally, at the athletics carnivals, it was the open boys' 100 metres that was the prestige event, and it was the boys' cricket and football that commanded the greatest kudos in the school communities. Needless to say, my female teaching colleagues and I took this on in various ways. It soon became a thing of the past for senior male staff to socialise in men-only bars, and we ended once and for all the staff versus students tug of war being for males only.

When I became the spokesperson for the Wesley Vale farmers in the campaign against North Broken Hill's billion-dollar pulp mill, it was both a strength and a weakness to be a female leader. Part of the strength was that, as a young mother campaigning against corporate greed and pollution, the message about organochlorines and health and children cut through particularly visibly. Woman, wife, mother, full-time unpaid campaigner – it said it all, really. But when the serious conflict and campaigning got underway, I remember going to Hobart to meet Environment Minister Graham Richardson. Door-stopped by media outside Wrest Point casino, I will never forget the local ABC radio reporter (a man) asking me why I thought as a housewife from Ulverstone I would be able to influence the federal minister. Little did he know, or even think to ask, that I had already met the minister privately to discuss the next steps of the campaign. His prejudice cost him a scoop.

All of these experiences from before and after politics are common to female MPs across party lines. Such anecdotes and stories together form the narrative of what it's like for women in politics – and I dare say in the media, the law or most professions. It is the ongoing story of the sisterhood, and it is why women everywhere cheered when Prime Minister Gillard took on Tony Abbott when he tried to lecture her about misogyny. There was a collective roar from women who had been itching to say that to a man and hadn't found the courage or opportunity to do so. It was the political 'I am Woman' Helen Reddy moment.

But to destroy the joint, we need to do more than just defy the odds and make it in spite of the ongoing sexist frames through which we operate to this day and more than just stand up and give male counterparts a blast.

If we are really to make a change, we need to challenge, restructure and rebuild society's foundations so that marginalised people or ideas, excluded from serious consideration for structural reasons when we achieved our positions, are no longer so regarded. I hasten to add that this will only lead to a better society if it is driven by justice and fairness, and not by populism or fear. After all, fascism and totalitarianism were marginal ideas that were made mainstream by those who succeeded in destroying the establishment of the day.

This is why I was not as impressed as many by Julia Gillard's misogyny speech.

Powerful and necessary and inspiring as it was, it would have had immensely greater power if it had been backed by considered and consistent actions of the prime minister born of a conviction to improve the lot of all women, rather than a political strategy. It was a speech designed to appeal to the basic role model case of a woman's right to be in power, and it was ready to be delivered at a politically appropriate moment: to blur the inconsistency between the prime minister calling Tony Abbott out on sexist language, but not equally condemning Peter Slipper for his sexist text messages. It was not a speech timed or motivated by a desire to advance the cause of women, it was a speech delivered to hold on to power.

While much has been written in the mainstream media about the political context of the speech, what is far more troubling, as highly regarded feminist Eva Cox said at the time, is that much of the commentary failed to recognise that Prime Minister Gillard made the speech on the day she slashed support for single parents. Surely the bigger issue is that the speech is out of alignment with a series of decisions that entrench the marginalised position of women.

How much better would the speech have been if it had not come on the very same day as Prime Minister Gillard's decision to cut support payments for single parents – who overwhelmingly are women – putting a political surplus ahead of women struggling with poverty? How much more impressive would it have been if it had not come after her decision to extend the Northern Territory Intervention and income management, denying many vulnerable and Indigenous women agency over their limited financial resources? What does her decision to deny equal marriage to same-sex female and male couples say about her commitment to genuine social change? How much more power would her speech have had if it hadn't been preceded by her decision to abandon guardianship for unaccompanied refugee children so that they could be sent off shore to detention centres, or her decision to stop family reunions, leaving men in refugee camps with no hope of reuniting with their wives and children and family members?

The Gillard Government has cut Australia's foreign aid program, much of which goes to programs to lift women and children out of poverty, including through women's reproductive health programs. Childcare remains a key element of ensuring women can access the workforce equitably, yet the government has failed to tackle the structural changes needed to make childcare more affordable and accessible. This government has cut over 4000 Commonwealth public service jobs in the last two years, job cuts which tend to disproportionately affect women. Australia's low female workforce participation rate and growing gender pay inequity mean that many older women struggle to find the financial resources to live well in retirement. The government has failed to make our superannuation system fairer by increasing tax on the superannuation of higher-earning (usually male) employees to pay for measures to assist workers with low superannuation accounts, usually women.

For me, destroying the joint means more than just saying it's not OK to see women, children, refugees, Indigenous or LGBTIQ people marginalised, discriminated against or subject to violence; it's not OK to destroy the physical world in which we live and to drive species to extinction; and it's not OK to ignore the needs of future generations.

We must take consistent political action to deliver on these goals. That is the point of political power: not for its own sake but rather for a purpose, for justice, for now and for future generations, for Australia and for the world. That's why women need more than female role models in politics; they need role models who get there and take on the status quo. That's why I'm a Green. That's why it is also wrong to discount the roles of men who clearly don't qualify on the first level as role models for women, but sometimes are stronger role models to advance the cause of women than some women in power. Bob Brown was by far a stronger advocate to empower and advance women than Julie or Bronwyn Bishop have ever been.

At the height of the campaign to save the Franklin River, I remember smiling in the police van on the way to Risdon prison and thinking: I wonder if this is what the nuns at St Mary's expected to reap when they had sown the idea that, above all else, we girls needed to stand up for what we believed in, to stand up for justice's sake, to use our god-given talents to improve the lives of others because we had been afforded so many opportunities denied to millions around the world, not least in the missions.

I know many of them would have been proud to see us destroying the joint then and to this day.

A Fairer Country

Michelle Law

There are several things that my mum dislikes. A strong tasting cheese is one of them. Cold weather is another. Lilies and other flowers that shed pollen are a no-no. And she finds wearing shoes indoors or in bed unhygienic. But what she dislikes above all else is when people who are not stay-at-home mothers call stay-at-home mothers 'lazy' or '*just* homemakers'. She believes that parenting is a full-time, unpaid job that is often underappreciated, but she's always enjoyed motherhood and is proud of how she raised us.

And yet, there are occasions – usually when she is upset with my siblings and me, or she is drinking wine, or philosophising after drinking wine – when she will tell us that if she could go back in time, she might not have had children. Well, two children, maybe, but definitely not five. If she had her time again, she would have been much more progressive, and she would have gone to university.

'I'd want to put my career first,' she'll muse in Cantonese.

'Yes, I'd definitely be a career woman … actually, that's funny because you would never call a man a "career man".'

When I graduated with a degree in writing, Mum told me it was good that I knew what I wanted to do with my life. I didn't tell her that because I had an arts degree I was qualified to do little more than pace around my apartment deconstructing literature and having panic attacks while clutching paperwork for Newstart.

'I don't know if I want to write forever,' I said. 'I'd like to do other things too.'

'Like what?'

'I don't know. I like the idea of being a pastry chef. Or a florist … but I've heard that floristry really fucks up your hands.'

'Ai-ya,' said Mum, slapping my wrist. 'Don't swear. Besides, at least you have options. Women these days have so much choice, especially in Australia.'

Having migrated to Australia from Hong Kong more than 30 years ago, Mum can't help comparing Chinese and Australian values. Nowadays, she identifies as being more Australian, and when it comes to the treatment of women, she believes that Australian culture is fairer. But I know that in some small way, my birth would have influenced that belief.

I was born in autumn during a week of incessant rain. Mum had booked herself into a private room in a private hospital, a luxury she felt she deserved for her fifth and final baby before having a tubectomy. She was scheduled in for surgery the following week because she couldn't physically handle another pregnancy. Technically, she shouldn't have even had me; her calcium stores were low and she was becoming anaemic. And throughout the entire pregnancy, she felt completely alone.

Dad worked long hours at the family restaurant and then stayed out late playing mah jong after twelve-hour shifts. When Mum did see him, he was usually catching up on sleep; she understood that he was overworked, but so was she. Running a household with four kids under eighteen was difficult enough and she was heavily pregnant and didn't have time to unwind. The only time Mum had to herself was in the early hours of the morning when my siblings were asleep. She would sit in the hallway listening to them snoring and rub her belly in the dead of the night.

When I was born, Dad took my grandmother to visit Mum at the hospital. They found Mum sitting up in bed with her eyes closed, deeply asleep, with me cradled in her arms. My grandmother leaned over Mum to get a good look at my face and then sighed deeply.

'It's a girl,' she said, crestfallen.

Dad rested a hand on her shoulder. 'Girls are … OK too,' he whispered.

Both Dad and my grandmother had been hoping for another boy despite already having two boys, my brothers, in the family. They had probably already chosen a Chinese boy's name for me, something like my brother Andrew's name, *Tin Cheong*, which means 'flying free in the sky'. Otherwise, it could be something along the lines of my sister Candy's name, *Ngar Yee*, parts of which mean 'in hope for a son'.

'Come on,' said Dad, shooing my grandmother out of the room as Mum began stirring. 'Let her sleep.'

Mum, who had been awake the entire time, overheard the whole conversation and relayed the story to me years later when I was old enough to understand. In Chinese culture, she explained, boys were desired and girls were tolerated. Girls menstruated, which meant that they cost more to rear, and when they married they didn't carry the family name. And once the one-child policy was introduced, people started drowning their newborn daughters and throwing them from their apartment windows. Sure, things weren't perfect in Australia, and girls were treated differently from boys wherever you went, but at least things here were a lot more equal.

But during high school, a time when everyone becomes hyperaware of their own sexuality and their interactions with the opposite sex, I realised that Mum might have been wrong – when it came to gender, things were anything but equal, even in the lucky country. The sexism I saw and encountered during school was of a different breed from what Mum had experienced, because it was unspoken. It was subtle and slipperier because no one ever verbalised their negative feelings towards women; it was simply evident through their actions that they believed women should be treated differently and unequally to men.

Awful things happened to the girls I knew – to my friends, to my classmates, and to girls at other schools – and they happened every day. There was the teacher who asked a student who modelled part time if she also modelled lingerie. There was the party where a girl was forced to perform oral sex but didn't report it because the boy was popular and whose side would everyone take? There was the boy who told his girlfriend that the only good thing about dating her was that she was on the pill. There was the Blue Light Disco where a girl was sexually assaulted on the dance floor. And there were the girls who called other girls sluts in messages they scrawled across the toilet cubicle walls.

During university, the good times continued to roll. My sister Tammy and I moved in together, into an apartment that was prized for its location; it was situated on a main road in Brisbane's south, near a dining precinct, local schools, and within walking distance to all forms of public transport. The building's greatest downfall was that it didn't have a parking space, so we used a permit for the neighbouring streets. The street we frequented most often was a narrow road parallel to an old but well-kept church and a newly renovated block of apartments. It was brightly lit from the road works happening down the street, was connected to the main road, and generally felt safe.

One afternoon, we turned into this street and parked a few metres down from a group of men talking on the footpath. A few of them were drinking, but they weren't drunk. When we stepped out of the car they started verbally abusing us, unprompted, in a chummy, smug kind of way – the way friends might share a joke. There was a lot of laughter on their end, and a lot of rage and pant-shitting on our end. From the moment they called us 'Asian bitches', there was a steady progression of: Tammy and I defending ourselves; the men recovering from the surprise that we could speak English; Tammy and I locking the car; the men unleashing an arsenal of racist and sexist insults ('cunts', 'bitches' and 'fucking Asian bitches'), the men following us as we walked down the street;

Tammy and I breaking into a jog; and then Tammy lamenting that the men were probably going to scratch the car.

When we got home, we locked the front door and paced around the living room for a while, fuming and venting aloud to no one in particular. We were shaken, but we weren't shocked; we'd both had similar things happen to us before, and something like it would happen again.

Afterwards, I shared the story with my friends and discovered everyone had a personal bank of horror stories. Someone had been chased on the street in broad daylight. Someone else had been drugged at a nightclub. Most people I talked to had been wolf-whistled at from a moving vehicle. Everyone had been leered at on public transport. One person told me they had 000 on speed dial when they walked home alone at night, or they just sprinted the entire way. Other people were pissed off at the small things, like choosing a glossy magazine at the Coles checkout. Why was it so difficult to find a woman's magazine that didn't feature articles like 'Smile Yourself Thin!' and 'Why You're Single and What You're Doing Wrong, Ya Dummy!'

Sexism and misogyny was so deeply ingrained in our culture and everyday lives; we'd all been taught how to accept it, live with it, and work around it to survive. But it was affecting women far worse than I realised. It was a reality that domestic violence was the greatest health threat to women aged 15 to 44. It was a reality that female workers earned $1 million less than their male co-workers within their lifetime, despite having the same qualifications. And in some sectors, that gap was widening. Gender inequality was innate and expected in our daily conversations and interactions, so that made it the norm. But that didn't make it normal.

There's only really one surefire way I know of fighting gender discrimination and that is to be a feminist. Here is the moment I realised that I was a feminist:

INT. FAMILY HOME/DINING ROOM – DAY

MICHELLE (9) and her BROTHER (18) sit at the dining table watching television and dissecting a piece of news that Michelle doesn't understand but would like to in order to gain the approval of her cooler, older sibling. Both are wearing Mango brand board shorts because their parents refuse to buy them real surf wear. They stare at the television intently, watching a group of protestors marching and waving banners.

MICHELLE
(confused)
Why are they so angry?

BROTHER
They're protesting because they want to legalise abortion.

MICHELLE
Why are abortions illegal?

BROTHER
It's really complicated. But this group is protesting because they think that women should have control over their own bodies.

MICHELLE
Isn't that normal? Like, shouldn't everyone be allowed that?

BROTHER
I think so. But like I said – it's a complicated issue.

Michelle nods. The news piece ends. A TVC for *SeaChange* starts playing.

BROTHER (CONT'D)
Do you reckon you're a feminist?

Michelle pauses, thinking.

MICHELLE
I don't know. I mean, I think women's rights are important and stuff, but I'm not all: 'RAH RAH RAH WOMEN!'

BROTHER
(laughing)
But do you believe that men and women should have equal rights?

MICHELLE
Yeah!

BROTHER
Well, then you're a feminist.

MICHELLE
!!!

Feminism isn't a club that I belong to. And it's not something I broadcast every day to any poor soul who will listen. I'm a feminist because each time I hear about an abhorrent action towards someone that is based on or influenced by their gender, it gives me courage to know that beyond just recognising something as wrong, people will call it out and try to make things right. I'm a feminist because without feminism I can't vote. I'm a feminist because I don't think a woman's worth should be determined by her appearance. I'm a feminist because feminism allows writers to take risks and create complex, flawed, intelligent female characters for girls to look up to.

I'm a feminist because I believe Bratz dolls are terrifying and will end us all.

I'm a feminist because every time my mum tells me the story about when I was born, I always get hung up on the conversation between my dad and my grandmother in the hospital. When I ask Mum what she did after overhearing them, she told me that she just held me, and then she cried and cried – in part because she felt disposable, but mostly because she felt sorry for me.

I'm a feminist because feminism gave my mum courage during my parents' divorce. I didn't want my parents to split up, but I'm glad my mum had the strength to end a marriage that wasn't healthy for anyone involved, despite the knowledge that she was being antagonised, judged and abandoned by her own family and friends, because divorce – especially when it is initiated by a woman – is strongly stigmatised in the Chinese community.

Being a feminist is not about despising men, or overtaking them. And it's not about despising Alan Jones. Feminism is about despising an idea. And the idea is that women are unequal to men. It is that they deserve or should expect the kind of sexism, misogyny and mistreatment that they receive. It is that they should receive this treatment and take it on the chin. It is that any woman who rejects this treatment will be met with aggressive, irrational and sometimes unintelligible scorn. When we are destroying the joint, we are calling out sexism and misogyny. When we are destroying the joint, we are helping establish gender equality. We are destroying the joint, because otherwise, we may destroy the rights women have fought hard to achieve.

Destroying the Joint Starts at Home

Leslie Cannold

> She [the prime minister] said that we know societies only reach their full potential if women are politically participating. Women are destroying the joint – Christine Nixon in Melbourne, Clover Moore here. Honestly … there isn't a chaff bag big enough for them.
>
> *2GB Radio Broadcaster Alan Jones, 31 August 2012*

> Got time on my hands tonight so thought I'd spend it coming up with new ways of 'destroying the joint' being a woman & all. Ideas welcome.
>
> *Tweet in reply to Jones, Jane Caro, 31 August 2012*

In this piece, I want to speculate about why the Destroy the Joint slogan – and the social media-based movement that flourished around it – has been so successful, and where it might go from here.

Second-wave feminism – the movement precipitated by older-edge baby boomers – was all about destroying the joint or, as they say in academia, 'achieving structural change'. This may be obvious to some, but so many reductionist or plain silly things have been said about feminism over the years – that it's about man-hating, or the right of women to dance around poles half-dressed or to wear their armpit hair long – that I feel compelled to spell it out.

Some baby-boom feminists wanted a more gender-equitable division of the pie; others believed both the size and composition of the pie must change. But whether liberal or liberationist, feminists were committed to destroying the very foundations of today's world so a better joint – or at least a fairer one – could be built in its place.

What's interesting about the current moment in Australia is the friction between those of Alan Jones's generation – men who've grown accustomed to the joint's showering upon them of the invisible privilege they kid themselves they've won on merit – and a younger generation of women and egalitarian-oriented men who rightly think gender discrimination is unjust and wrongly believe it's a thing of the past.

The friction comes from the collision of two different world views. In one corner stands the aging former rugby league coach and administrator Jones and his ilk, convinced that the rightful foundations of the joint – one run by and for men – are being eaten away. In the other, the bewildered and belatedly outraged daughters and (some) sons of the baby boomers, who thought the gender-emancipated world for which their mothers fought so hard had been won. When radically different views of how the world is and how it should be collide, smoke and fire result. The question is how we can fan a fire that leads to renewal, not scorched earth devastation.

THIRTY PER CENT

No ruler secure in his citadel takes pot shots at the peasants. Jones's decision to use the bully-pulpit of his popular 2GB talkback show to attack Australia's first female prime minister, first female police chief, first popularly elected female mayor of Sydney and one of the central contentions of contemporary feminism itself, suggests that on the gender relations front, he wasn't feeling relaxed and comfortable at all.

The source of his discomfort is 30%.

Feminist aspirations for women to participate equally in society were for 50%. They believed that a fair and equitable society would offer opportunities to all its citizens regardless of gender and, because women were just as capable as men, equal opportunities would result in equal participation.

We're not there yet. While Australian women's educational attainment is among the best in the world, the *Global Gender Gap Report 2011*, from the World Economic Forum, shows that we fell six points to eighteenth for economic participation and six points to 38th for political empowerment.[1]

Among the many things we've learned from women's slow progress is that there are critical waypoints along the road to equality. One of these waypoints is 30%.

Thirty per cent is the point of critical minority and therefore critical change. When 30% of any workforce or team is female, women become visible: they are seen by their own daughters and girls in general as an example of what's possible; they can influence how a work environment operates rather than needing to act like a bloke to fit in; they can sponsor other women into positions of influence and by so doing bring about lasting change.

None of this is to say that 30% represents equal participation for women. It does not. Nor is it to say that women must settle for 30% because in a world still run by men, this is the best they can realistically hope for. Rather, it is to suggest that 30% can serve as an effective staging post from which equality-minded citizens can consolidate and gather forces for the final assault on the male citadel and a true and total sharing of power.

There are ample studies to show the ways in which 30% constitutes a critical mass but for me the proof of the pudding has always been in the way the most terrible sexists start squawking whenever the 30% mark in their field of endeavour is approached or reached. I'm not saying they're doing the numbers, but rather that it's an intuitive thing. To sexist males, 30% is the point at which they start to feel uncomfortable because when they look around, the joint is no longer being solely run by and for them.

I'm a writer, so I first noticed it here. When male writers start claiming – as did Gerard Windsor in 1986 – that 'women writers get favoured status treatment … the worst position for a writer to be in is that of being a middle-aged, Anglo-Celtic male', I did some counting and discovered that women were by no means dominating among published authors but from humble beginnings had crept past the 30% mark.[2]

While I hesitate to call Jones a journalist, he does operate in the media world and the media is largely focused on happenings in the world of politics. A 2012 paper on female representation in Australian parliaments found that 30% of all parliamentarians in Australia are female. This figure breaks down to reveal that 31% of Australia's federal politicians are female and 25% of those in the NSW parliament are women.[3] A 2009 paper found that 23% of the Australian police – but only 8% of senior commissioned officers – are women.[4]

Moving on to the media world, Chrys Stevenson demonstrated in a 2012 *The King's Tribune* article on gender equity in Australia's fourth estate, women are at the 30% mark in most of the counts that matter. Percentage of female front-page bylines – 30%; percentage of stories about women or in which the main talent is female – 30%. Subjects of, or female talent for, the story – 30%. Percentage of women featured in front-page photos and cartoons – including Melbourne Cup hat and other glam shots – 36%.[5]

To Jones, the sudden visibility of women rubbing shoulders with the powerful, expecting – perhaps even feeling entitled to – the same opportunities for advancement as he has always enjoyed, is the sight of the barbarians at the gate. When men like him and Windsor gripe about being overrun by women, they are not making precise numerical claims about female dominance in their field of endeavour. Rather they are calling upon the language of fairness and justice to express their view that however much women have in a numerical sense, they have too much in a moral one. More – to be precise – than men like Jones feel they deserve.

THE BARBARIANS AND THE ELUSIVE QUEST FOR TRUE EQUALITY

To the feminist barbarians who clashed with Jones over the 'destroy the joint' comments, everything about what Jones said and what he represents rankled. The 30% aspiration for female participation distressed because everyone knows that true equality requires women to get half, while the struggle women face to achieve this reduced goal was plain depressing. Add to this Jones's threat of violence against the few women who have managed to fight their way past the old guard and get their just desserts – by a man who serves as a towering example of all that is wrong with the way the joint had been run to date, no less – and the ingredients were there for a riot. Or a revolution.

The groundwork for revolution rather than riot was laid due to the quick thinking and wit of Jane Caro and the good hearts and tenacious organising skills of those involved in Destroy the Joint: Sally McManus, Jenna Price, El Gibbs and others mentioned elsewhere in this book. Caro's 'Got time on my hands' tweet inverted the destroy the joint sledge with the prized Aussie quality of humour. It also urged feminists to externalise their dismay over Jones's comments rather than internalise it, which can lead to depression and feelings of powerlessness. Turned outwards in the form of tweets about how Caro and other women could destroy the joint, the Twitter hashtag #destroythejoint enabled feminists of both sexes to find both company and comfort in the anger and wit of fellow travellers.

Inspired by the runaway hashtag – which trended on Twitter for days – McManus started a Facebook page that at this writing has 25 000 likes, as well as a website where members of the public can report 'any public statements in Australia that demean or vilify people because of their gender, race, religion or sexuality'. Some have credited the Destroy the Joint internet phenomenon with giving Prime Minister Julia Gillard the courage to make her now famous misogyny speech. The prime minister had the confidence to lambast the sexism of Federal Opposition Leader Tony Abbott in parliament, the argument runs, because the Destroy the Joint phenomenon gave her the confidence she would be supported.

DESTROYING THE JOINT – WHAT'S NEXT?

Social media and the interweb more generally have proved effective tools in toppling unpopular individuals or political regimes. The effective use of social media is credited with toppling rulers in Tunisia, Egypt, Libya and Yemen and destabilising others in the Arab world.[6]

However, such tools have been noted as less effective in building capacity and the new structures, than in tearing down the old. This is commonsense: it is easier for people to agree on what they know and don't like, than on what first must be imagined, collectively agreed and then put into place!

For some, Destroy the Joint's public equality watch is in keeping with its origins, and an appropriately contained and important agenda for the group. Others may not like it, or may think it's a great idea but want to do more. For those in the latter camp, the question is: Given the difficulties feminists continue to face in changing the joint enough to give our daughters the same chances in lives as our sons, what should we do now?

The answer to that question could easily fill a book – indeed it has filled many – so I'm going to keep it brief by offering just a few nuggets as food for thought. Further detail can be found in my book on the social constraints on women's decisions to mother, *What, No Baby?*

In a nutshell, I think we must follow on from the success of Destroy the Joint by forming a gender liberation movement. This movement must have a real world and online presence, and advocate effectively for the end of sex-role stereotyping and constrained social and financial opportunities on the basis of sex. This movement would not replace the women's and men's movements, both of which have been extraordinarily successful and must continue to offer in-depth analyses of how sexist socialisation and social structures limit the life chances of females and males, respectively.

Instead, a gender-equality movement would work with both to assist in the work of creating a gender-equal world by focusing on the equal but different costs to men and women, and boys and girls, of sexism inside and outside the home. At the core of its activities would be the pursuit of gender egalitarian arrangements for the raising of children, as the basis for undermining limiting ideals of male and female, and the most effective route to challenging the social structures that limit men's and women's capacities to share the rights and responsibilities of financially supporting and caring for dependents.

Why must revolution start in the home? The 24/7 workplace is structured around a worker who has no home or family connections or has a wife at home tending to them. Gender socialisation has seen women rather than men remove themselves from the workforce, or work limited or part-time hours to manage the second shift, while men tend to work even more extended hours when children are born, to increase the security of their breadwinner wage.

Not only do women lose their financial independence in

this process, their career progression and lifetime earnings even when they do return to work rarely recover. These are among the reasons why motherhood is a well-known point of feminist radicalisation for women.

The cost of a gender-based labour-specialised approach to children and men is less recognised. Children miss out on the alternative socialisation provided by gender egalitarian parenting. Men miss out on the time required to build intimate relationships with their children; so much so that in the event of divorce, such father/child relationships may not survive.

Because men don't share the work of child-rearing with women, fatherhood doesn't raise their awareness about the child-unfriendliness of the 24/7 workplace, nor invest them in attempts to change it. Indeed, quite the contrary: men's increased immersion in the workplace, and their at least partial dependence for their own advancement on the disablement of half their competitors by motherhood, further invests them in existing workplace structures. Ironically, the consequent defence by some men of the status quo and their policing of their public power may increase the desire of women to police – rather than share – their power in the private realm, which in turn may lead men to jealously guard their own power unless and until they feel more empowered in the intimate realm – and on and on it goes.

The circuit breaker is to ensure that from day one, men are equal partners in the work of caring for dependents, while women share the financial responsibility for the household. Only when men care for children will they participate in public debates about the quality and funding of childcare; only when men struggle to balance work and family will they help women question the sustainability of the 24/7 workplace; only when men's careers are being downsized and daddy-tracked will they contribute to discussions about the social value of children and the fair valuing of part-time work. And when men are home caring for kids and the household, more women have more time to continue progressing up the career ladder, inspiring their daughters to believe they can be anything they want to be, and changing the way their workplace operates to be more friendly to, and promote more, women.

It's the most radical elements of the second-wave feminist program that have been hardest to achieve. Sure, there was some kicking and screaming, but ultimately it wasn't too hard for the powers-that-be to come around to the idea that women could work 'too'. Consistent with this is the view that a woman's wage must cover the cost of the care required when she abandons her rightful child-caring role.

The radical change required – and one we need a gender-equality movement to achieve – is a rethink of children as a social good and paid work as a right and a duty for all. Given that men and women will work, and may also choose to contribute by having children, the question becomes how can they be facilitated to support each other – and we to support them – to do a good job? When posed this way, gender egalitarian answers to the problem flow naturally.

But no one ever hands power over willingly. As a university lecturer explained to me once, 'it must be taken'. Years from now, we may see the Destroy the Joint phenomenon as the progenitor to the gender-equality movement that changed the world for women, men and children by finishing the work the feminist and men's movements had begun.

Girl Talk

Lily Edelstein

'Nah, I wouldn't call that rape,' she says, rummaging in her bag. 'Like, if you're with a guy and you're already making out and stuff, and you're enjoying it, and you don't say no or something – I don't think that's rape.'

I'm in my cabin on Year 12 camp, with seven or eight other girls, munching on chocolate and flipping through magazines. We're all testing the water here – how much can we ask about sex and drugs and skin cleansers? We do this, naturally, with the aid of the sealed section in a *Girlfriend* magazine.

The dismissive remark about rape throws me. I start frantically arranging thoughts in my head, just as I hear from beside me, 'That swimsuit is SO. CUTE.'

'Ohmygod, it would look *great* on you!'

Over the next ten minutes I try in vain to explain what it felt like to be sexually coerced in ways this girl might not deem 'rape'. But my stories are continually interrupted by a photo in the magazine, or disinterest. I would be given far more attention were I talking about some crush, or a dress I'd bought.

This was not entirely unexpected. Just as society often brushes aside or minimises the issue of rape, teen girls have learned to do the same. We internalise our experiences, and wave away violence and intimidation as 'just a boy thing'. And until there is proper discussion about our experiences, we are forced to believe that sexual assault is 'just one of those things', a rite of passage.

About a month before the Year 12 camp, I was sexually harassed on a bus for the second time that year. A man – on the first occasion, it was a boy – had aggressively masturbated at me. For most of the year, I'd had trouble sleeping, and suffered from increased paranoia not just on public transport, but everywhere. I began to really wish that girls were taught more about how the world treats us and how to cope when we encounter sexual harassment and abuse. I had read an article on the *Rookie* magazine website about street harassment – 'It Happens All the Time' – and spoken to my family and friends about my experiences with complete honesty.[1] I'm healing. But not every teen girl who is harassed or abused has the capacity or the knowledge they need to cope in the aftermath.

Most girls aren't taught that the scary and disgusting way a man talks to you on a bus or that thing that happened the time you stayed over at your boyfriend's house can cause months of emotional backlash. We aren't told that these things are *sexual harassment* or *sexual assault*. We don't discuss what to do when we are touched inappropriately or made to feel uncomfortable, and how incredibly brave and frightening it is to stand up and yell. These things certainly aren't given time in schools. We are given seminars on self-esteem and self-defence, but no time is given to the wider reality of being a girl: that we are constantly taught to feel weak and afraid, and that we aren't given reason to talk about this or what we're feeling. For these reasons, and many more, I worry.

That's not how it should be. That night in the cabin, there was so much that I wanted to tell my friends. Later, I wrote an open letter to teen girls. In it I said all the things I wished I could have said in the cabin:

> *The body's reaction to being threatened (not just flight or fight, but also freezing in the face of danger) is something that can influence the way each of us deals with being threatened, especially in an intimate setting. If you don't know your limits, and thus can't articulate them, your body gets the message across however it can. That can mean lying completely still, numbed, and waiting for it to end. I have been there.*
>
> *'Sexual assault' is defined by personal experience, which means that however the victim feels is valid, and no one has the right to pass judgement on them. I didn't have time to tell my friends how hurtful and scary it was for me to encounter this attitude from them – that when they talked over me and dismissed what I was saying, what I really heard was, 'Just get over it', or, even scarier, 'That hasn't happened to me before … Has it?'*
>
> *Sexual abuse is a very, very broad spectrum, ranging from abusive relationships to being harassed by a stranger, and any sort of situation where a person feels uncomfortable sexually can have very serious repercussions.*

Basically, I want you to know that what you feel is valid. Even when you don't know exactly what it is or why you're feeling it. If you feel scared, uncomfortable, sad, guilty, confused – I urge you to explore this feeling. We need to talk about all the little things that happen on a daily basis, the things society tells us we shouldn't make a fuss about. Just by saying things like: 'I can't really remember what it felt like when we were doing that … But I feel kind of sick when I think about it', or, 'I wish I hadn't done that for him, because it makes me feel really scared when I think about it', or, 'One time this guy on the bus came up and sat really really close to me. He touched my leg. And now … I find catching buses kind of stressful. I always sit up the front', we can begin to break down the stigma of talking about our experiences.

Know how you feel. Be honest about it. There is nothing to be ashamed of, ever. That thing that was a bit you and a bit your boy/girlfriend, or that thing that happened on the train, doesn't have to be your secret. Moving seats because you feel uncomfortable isn't rude, it's your right. 'I don't want to do this because it makes me feel weird' is a very important and valid reason not to do something. Even something like asking your friends, 'Guys, can we get a taxi tonight instead of the train home after the concert?' can make a big difference to how we start conversations about sexual assault.

And finally, don't let anyone give you shit for how you feel. Don't take it from your friends, or your family, or someone you just met. Stand up for yourself. Walk away. And tell your story, even if you didn't get up and walk away when the danger was there. Saying, 'Yep, that happened. I let it happen.

And now I am hurting in a way I can't articulate and am shit scared', is powerful.

What you feel is VERY important.

GROWING UP GIRL

Teenage girls are constantly sent messages that tell us we are both vulnerable and the adult object of everyone's desire. Our interests are devalued because of the ways we show excitement – Justin Bieber and One Direction are inexplicably linked to teen girl excitement, their passionate fanbase ensuring that both artists are untouchable outside of this age group, dismissed as a tween fantasy. Our mistakes are capitalised on and commodified – *16 And Pregnant*, *Brat Camp*. We are fetishised and shamed, often in the same sentence, for conforming to the role that is sold to us, as are role models like Katy Perry, Taylor Swift, Nikki Minaj and Rihanna.

One of the biggest problems we face as teenage girls is that we aren't encouraged to discuss how others frame our lives, not with adults and not with each other. Completely aside from 'feminism is a dirty word', teenage girls aren't given power to define themselves without society telling them how they should be.

And most disturbingly, one thing every woman learns from adolescence is that we are expected to pander incessantly to the delicate male gaze. There have been multiple occasions when teachers at my school have made announcements at assembly about the state of our school uniform. At the most recent assembly, and indeed the one before it, no explanation was given other than, 'Please lower your hemlines. We have male staff who are feeling uncomfortable.'

What does this teach us? In context, I took this to mean that the male teachers' 'discomfort' was sexual arousal, and that it is up to us – as teenage girls – to keep the inappropriate behaviour and attitudes of our teachers in check. The responsibility lies with us, not them, as it is our bodies that are so obviously at fault: we *know* that we are fetishised by all of society, so can't we keep our legs hidden? Gosh, be a lady.

A few months ago I took a trip to the hairdresser that resulted in a short haircut. It was on a whim and I'm used to changing up my hair every few months. In fact, this trivial change began to weigh heavily on my shoulders: I had butterflies at the thought of how my friends and family would react. I secretly feared that my boyfriend would be confronted by the change and wouldn't find me quite as attractive. I was expecting the disapproval of my father and the shock of my girlfriends. It was making me uncomfortable and nervous, emotions I had never associated with *a haircut* up until this point.

My worries were, of course, baseless. The people I actually care about happen to like me for who I am, not my haircut. How had I completely misjudged the ways all these people would react to a small display of 'masculine' aesthetic on the top of my head?

A week later, still adjusting to my new look, I waited for a train in my school uniform. I was in regulation stockings, blazer and below-the-knee skirt (ahem), with no make-up. I looked fairly conventional, which is of course the point of a school uniform.

As I waited for my train, I smiled at the strangers around me, as is my habit. I generally get a positive reaction; from thirteen years old, I have been regularly waved on to buses free of charge, called 'love' by the drivers, and subsequently been gawked and smiled at by other passengers. But on this morning, something happened that made me realise I could categorise and predict the reactions people had to me based on their gender. Men who used to smile back indulgently at me or give me compliments now looked at me in mild horror or at least with a lack of understanding. My status as cute, sexy or attractive to the average man up and left with ten centimetres of my hair. I had become an anomaly, outside the range of females conforming to the mainstream, male-driven expectations of 'attractive', and processing what they saw did not leave them with enough time to decide on a smile.

By contrast, a young lesbian couple were laughing and holding hands as they walked down the platform. I smiled at them, and one was clearly flattered. She grinned back, and kept turning around to look at me and giggle. I smiled at a girl picking up rubbish on the platform and she beamed back, visibly warmed by my friendliness.

What was going on? I felt even more visible than I usually did, more scrutinised than I typically felt in my school uniform. It began to dawn on me that my smiles with this new aesthetic meant something different. I was used to mostly neutral reactions from women around me, but today they seemed much more enthusiastic. I now appeared to offer them unthreatening flattery. In a world where women compete with each other for male attention, from the way we dress to the way we speak to one another, I clearly wasn't there to swindle them out of their fair share. They were courteous enough to swing a smile back at me. On the other hand, the men I smiled at saw in me a renegade: I didn't exist for their own appeasement, and in fact, I might be there for myself. By cutting my hair so short, I had broken the rules.

Once again I had learned that as a girl, and indeed as a woman, I must be effortlessly beautiful and loveable, and only through prescribed femininity. To take it a step further, I also knew now that the only criteria for *loving oneself* is in how other people perceive you.

FIGHTING BACK: GRRL POWER ONLINE

The truth is, teen girls are powerful. We have carved out avenues in which to express ourselves and have found healthy role models. I'm not the only feminist in my school.

The feminist society at my school, Collective Voice, was started in 2010 by our teacher Ms Fajou, in response to a lack of discussion with our peers about the sexism teens receive from the media and each other. We discuss what feminism means to us – how we feel about body image, violence against women, homophobia, politics. We have a very active Facebook page that we use to share videos, articles and current events connected with feminism. We are building skills of productive dialogue, knowledge and opinion. We aim to provide girls with supportive environments in which to be themselves, encouragement to be curious and passionate, and validation of their experiences.

One big thing we're working against with Collective Voice is widespread online sexism; a lot of online spaces have been claimed by a boys' club of anonymity, obscenity and oppression. Girls have found and created communities online, on websites like *Rookie* and Tumblr, where they feel welcomed and can discuss their real-world experiences, and where sexism that otherwise surfaces online is minimised.

Rookie, an online magazine written by and for teenage girls, was launched in November 2011 by American teenager Tavi Gevinson. It has authors from around the globe and publishes articles on politics, television, feminism, fashion and being a teenager. There are whole articles written about intersectionality, personal accounts of and advice on toxic relationships, and, significantly, a lot of space given to friendships and how to manage them. As girls, misogyny is ground into us; we internalise it so much we feel threatened by each other and attitudes like 'I'm more of a guy's girl, like, I don't really hang out with girls' are rife. Opening up a dialogue about dealing with friendships as relationships and respecting each other is hugely important and hugely undervalued.

Readers of *Rookie* chat with each other in the comments, and have organised *Rookie* Meetups in cities dotted around the world. Rookie Meetups encourage girls to create and unite and the *Rookie* 'flower crown' – made by hot-gluing fake flowers and knickknacks to headbands – is celebrated alongside zines, handmade magazines filled with art, opinion and creative writing. These objects and rituals help *Rookie* culture do two things: embrace girlhood and accept that being feminine is positive and strong, while simultaneously encouraging us to be confident thinkers and creators, learning, especially, how to express opinion. There is a generation of teenage girls out there writing, drawing, painting and being loud about their feelings.

Another online avenue teen girls use to express themselves is Tumblr, the proclaimed micro-blogging platform. It provides a place to record and celebrate your own thoughts and life as well as providing a community through reblogging – posting and commenting on things other people have made. Images, writing and quotes are shared and discussed and teen girls make connections with like-minded people around the world.

Although statistics show that the demographic of Tumblr users fluctuates between being slightly male dominated and slightly female dominated, I have met very few teenage girls who don't use it. Conversely, I have met very few teenage boys who don't condemn it. In any discussion about Tumblr where boys are present, I am forced to remind them: 'Look, buddy, just because there's one portion of the internet which isn't *aimed at you*, doesn't mean it's bad or wrong or boring. Go run along to the rest of the world you own.'

Tumblr is a powerhouse for young women: it has made it possible for girls all over the world to learn, connect and experiment in a safe place, especially in terms of social justice blogging. I am part of communities of young feminists across continents, who write together, laugh together, and learn together. The age group of women who are connecting with each other through this website ranges from early teens to mid-twenties, creating a space where girls are respected, mentored and challenged in a way that is not offered to us through the strictly regimented social circles of high school.

Tumblr may hold pockets of consumerism and hatred, as does all of humanity, but it is where we are finding healthy role models and a space to be ourselves. In 2012, Tumblr user grrrlfever – Sarah McClelland, a seventeen-year-old Australian – uploaded The Teenage Girl Manifesto.

TEENAGE GIRL MANIFESTO

We are teenage girls and **our emotions are valid**.

We are teenage girls and we cry and feel pain and joy and anger and have complex emotions; **we are not 'drama queens' or 'crazy' or 'just looking for attention'**.

We are teenage girls and we have our own interests, hopes and dreams. **We're not your two-dimensional stereotype.**

We are teenage girls and **society teaches us to hate ourselves and each other**.

We are teenage girls and **we're sick of being treated like a joke**.

We are teenage girls, and **sexism hurts us**.

We are teenage girls and we're angry and **we fight back**.

The manifesto has been embraced on Tumblr by teen girls all over the world. This is the strength that comes from our community! It is important for teenage girls to feel empowered and to feel that our experiences matter. If Tumblr is the platform where we are comfortable enough to stand up for ourselves, it is a space that should be nurtured.

There is a future for feminism in teenage girls, and right now it is being built through cables, wires and computer monitors. The criticism that is thrown around about the way girls use technology, about how the photos we publish and the 'messages we send' are issues in themselves. Let's be honest here: we're the generation that grew up with the internet, and yes, we're doing things that haven't been done before. In fact the new, positive spaces that we are building are giving us the skills and networks to make changes in our own lives; we are educating one another, supporting one another and taking these skills into the real world. These online spaces will continue to grow and are helping to stop conversations like the one I had on camp from happening. More girls are aspiring to be great women, stopping their friends from developing damaging attitudes and standing up for their rights. We're tired of being treated as incompetent and irresponsible. We deserve spaces where girls are heard, respected and valued. We are not weak.

Women Destroy the Joint

Tara Moss

Women have been informed they destroy the joint in many ways, over many centuries, from a variety of sources – radio announcers, ancient books, academics, and legislation designed to control these destructive abilities of ours for the moral safety of society.

Pandora, the first woman on earth, created by a male god (Hephaestus) on the order of a male god (Zeus), as a wife for a male (Epimetheus), destroyed the joint when she opened that box – in fact a jar – back in the days of ancient Greece, letting all the evil into the world.

> From her is the race of women and female kind: of her is the deadly race and tribe of women who live amongst mortal men to their great trouble, no helpmates in hateful poverty, but only in wealth.
>
> Hesiod's *Theogony*

Eve, the first woman on earth, created by a male god from a man's rib as a gift for a male (Adam), destroyed the joint when she sought the Tree of Knowledge and famously bit into that apple in the Garden of Eden, letting all the evil into the world.

> And the Lord God said unto the woman, What is this that thou hast done?
>
> *Genesis 3:13*

If only Adam had met some Greeks, he would have known what was coming.

It's been this way from the start, you see. Whether Pandora, Eve or Lilith, Hillary Clinton, Julia Gillard or Germaine Greer, the female gender – the creators of all human beings – are in fact the destroyers. They are dangerous. It's a matter of biology. Though men commit about 90% of homicides, are 400% more likely to commit an offence intended to injure and 28 times more likely to rape, women are the ones to really beware of.[1, 2]

Perhaps.

Or perhaps we should consider the common epithet of Pandora's husband, Epimetheus – 'the father of excuses' – and the concept at the centre of our centuries-old culture: that a male god birthed the world but it took a woman to introduce evil into it.

One of the great ironies of announcing that one particular gender in political power is 'destroying the joint', is that, as a group, women make up about 50% of the world's population but are only 19% of parliamentarians.[3] Outnumbered more than four to one even in these 'progressive' times, few if any of the most powerful women in history can really claim to have destroyed the joint, or even a small fraction of it, if 'the joint' can be understood to be the institutions that run human civilisation.

Women – so outnumbered in positions of power, yet so magically capable of destroying civilisation itself.

This latest declaration, springing as it did from the lips of a radio announcer in Sydney, is itself a small thing, a mere drop, if you will, in the long-running stream of statements perpetuating that centuries-old myth that power in the hands of women can only ever end in destruction. A simple statement like Alan Jones's doesn't matter.

Unless it does, to some, because there is a point at which enough is enough.

When *is* enough, exactly? The feeling that something is wrong rarely comes in a single blazing moment, like a lightning strike, but rather *accumulates* like rising water, drip by drip. For some people, enough is enough when discriminatory legislation is passed, like that in Aceh, which decreed women must ride motorcycles side-saddle to avoid arousing men, or the law in Ireland that led to the death by sepsis of a woman needing to abort her pregnancy. For others, it can be a statement or a slap on the rear, or discovering a friend isn't being paid what her male peers are. For each of us that moment is something different. For me, it's the stats.

Women working full time in Australia earn on average 17% less than men.[4] That is about a million dollars less in their working life. Twenty-seven per cent of Australian women have no superannuation whatsoever and the average superannuation for working women at retirement is less than one-third that of men.[5] Women have to make their savings last longer, too, as they live, on average, 4.5 years longer than men. And despite everything we hear about girl power and women's equality, women are still vastly underrepresented, even on issues relating to their own bodies. During six months of election coverage in the USA, across all major media, 81% of quotes about the issue of abortion were made by men.[6] The 80% male-dominated US Congress this year is being heralded as a milestone for gender equality, Congress having never had so many female senators. Only four women in the USA have ever become Supreme Court justices. In the UK's National Gallery, out of 2300 works, there are only ten paintings by women.[7] Out of 573 listed statues commemorating important people around the UK, only 15% are of women, with a large number of those being the queen and characters from Greek and Roman mythology.[8] A study carried out by Women in Journalism (WiJ) last year found that 78% of front-page articles in the UK are written by men and 84% of those quoted or mentioned are male.[9] According to statistics collated by VIDA Women In Literary Arts, in the most important literary publications around the world, male writers are up to 418% more likely to be reviewed than female writers, though men and women are published in about equal numbers.[10] These are just a few stats. I could list some more but I'm starting to feel unwell.

Either women, as a group, seriously lack merit, skill and opinions worth listening to, or there is something else going on here – a long-standing epidemic of underrepresentation and misrepresentation.

A paper recently published in the Proceedings of the National Academy of Sciences showed the results of a randomised double-blind study where half of a group of scientists were given applications with a male name attached, and half were given the exact same application with a female name attached. Results found that the 'female' applicants were rated significantly lower than the 'males' in competence, hireability, and whether the scientist would be willing to mentor the student, despite the applications being identical apart from the names. The scientists also offered lower starting salaries to the female-named applicants. Apparently the scientists who judged the applications were both male and female, showing that a bias against women exists in both genders.[11]

Perhaps when a major newspaper names a horse (Black Caviar) Sportswoman of the Year, we can finally admit that we do have some way to go in recognising the achievements of the 50% of the Australian population who are born female.[12]

If feminism is widely understood to be about achieving equal political, social and economic status for women, I see no proof that this goal has been achieved. Every statistic we have tells us there is still work to be done. I'm sure that's what Mr Jones *meant* to say: that women make valuable contributions to society and deserve equal opportunity, equal rights and representation, and a fair go like everyone else.

Perhaps the best way to destroy the joint, then, is actually to *de-story* it, by changing the tired old tale, one woman at a time.

Marie Curie destroyed the joint when in 1903 she became the first woman to win a Nobel Prize. Sri Lanka's Sirimavo Bandaranaike destroyed the joint when she became the world's first elected female prime minister in 1960. Rosa Parks destroyed the joint in 1955, when she refused to give her seat to a white passenger and go to the back of the bus. Lilly Ledbetter, of the *Lilly Ledbetter Fair Pay Act*, destroyed the joint when she refused to accept her lifetime of pay inequity.

The joint these women destroyed – or in truth, chipped away at piece by piece when they changed history – is not civilisation itself, but only the tired old status quo, with all its prejudices and limitations for minorities and women. The joints are the worldwide parliaments where women are still, on average, outnumbered more than four to one. The joint is the Australian Parliament that took 109 years to have a female prime minister, and where women are still outnumbered two to one, occupy less than one quarter of Cabinet positions, are labelled the 'handbag hit squad' by other politicians and as 'window-dressing' by columnists.

Honestly, if that is the joint, I say we smash it.

History's Footnote, or, a Wolvi Incident

Melissa Lucashenko

They say you inevitably turn into your parents, but bugger that for a lark, I'm galloping back a century, and turning into my great-grandmother instead. First I'll tell you her story. Then I'll explain why the texture and grain of her life, and how she lived it, matters in 2013, as Australia – or the half of it bearing a double X chromosome, anyway – has a conversation about fairness, equal pay, and the lofty ideal of not being raped on your way home on Friday night, nor beaten to a pulp when you get there.[1]

The name we have for her is Christina Copson.[2] She was removed, as the known Aboriginal world collapsed around her

1 Assuming you have a home in the first place, that is. It's estimated that 44% of homeless Australians are women, many of them with children who are also homeless. 'Counting the Homeless', Australian Bureau of Statsitics, 2006, http://www.ausstats.abs.gov.au/Ausstats/subscriber.nsf/0/57393A13387C425DCA2574B900162DF0/$File/20500-2008Reissue.pdf.

2 'Copson' is a white surname that no Aboriginal group in Australia can recognise. Her colonial kidnappers, by imposing this name on her, deprived her descendents of any hope of land rights, native title, or normal participation in Aboriginal social, political or economic life. Not that I'm bitter.

c. 1885, from northern NSW into child slavery in Queensland.[3] An illiterate eight-year-old Aboriginal girl, she was destined never to return home. As the twentieth century turned into itself, though, Christina had the strength and wit – and the luck – to secure her freedom and make a life for herself – a good life, even – in the cesspit of racist misogyny that was early Queensland. She lived beside if not within white society; she worked independently of so-called Protectors, and was even, in adulthood, permitted to own and use a hunting rifle.

Geography is destiny. But then so is biology, and history too. All three of these combined to form, for Christina, a decidedly pitiless crux where her Aboriginality, her femaleness and the fact of being born on the very brink of the Queensland assimilation era should have made her chances of a happy life laughably remote. Allow me to elaborate.

Item: Christina was removed into Queensland by persons unknown and remained there until she died in 1953. Technically a British subject, in early life she had few recognisable rights. In 1901, the year Christina's daughter, my grandmother, was born, the Australian parliament debated the issue of whether Aborigines were, or were not, human beings.

Item: Sometime in the first decade of the twentieth century: *They come.* They come to remove Christina's daughter, my grandmother, to Barambah mission, there to better monitor, control, educate, brainwash and assimilate her. Her brothers are not sought; it is the 'breeders' – the lighter-skinned Aboriginal

3 Technically, slavery requires the buying and selling of humans to other humans. I have no evidence that my mother's grandmother, an unfree, unpaid child lackey of white farmers whose children's socks she scrubbed, was in fact sold or paid for, but other Aboriginal people in her time and situation were sold for as little as sixpence, so to all intents and purposes ...

girls – who are seen as 'the problem'. There is strenuous resistance; my grandmother is, miraculously, not removed.

Item: In 1907, with Christina in her twenties and living free, but dangerously close to the Barambah Mission (later Cherbourg), the official policy states:

> If there are any complaints made to me about the blacks stealing jam tins, looking over the fence where sweet potatoes are growing, dirtying the river water, &c, I listen to the complaints, then remove all the Aborigines out of the town, and keep them out for about a week. By that-time all the housewives are very pleased to see them return again: and so things jog along smoothly until some poor old gin happens to steal another sardine tin, when out they go again.
>
> *Report of Queensland Inspector of Aborigines, 1907*

Item: Circa 1922. Some twenty miles from where Christina is living, the displeased mistress of a Kilkivan household one day takes steel wool in hand and attacks her Aboriginal servant. 'This is how you clean!' the woman lectures as she scours the dark cheek; Emily Williams wears the scar of the metal on her face for the rest of her life.

Item: The last recorded massacre of Aborigines takes place in the Northern Territory in 1928. It is the year Christina's oldest grandchild, my mother, is born. There is, however, much Aboriginal oral evidence of massacres into the 1940s. Christina lives most of her life knowing that Aboriginal people are vulnerable to attack by gangs of white murderers, frequently without penalty.

Item: By the early 1930s, my mother is living with Christina in a Tin Can Bay shack (possibly a humpy: Mum's lips are sealed on this small but interesting point) with three siblings. Times are tough. After a working life of more than 40 years, Christina finds herself ineligible for any child endowment or dole – all Aborigines are ineligible. She instead somehow manages to extract a tithe from local trawler fishermen down at the wharf: a mullet a day. This, plus what the family of five hunt and grow, enables them to stay alive.

My great-grandmother's life: the constant undercurrent of knowing that massacres of 'wild blacks' are happening, further north and further west. The very clear evidence that no Aboriginal child is ever safe from arbitrary removal should authority happen to look your way. Not to mention the likely prospect of being swept 'out of town' upon the mildest of complaints from whichever white housewife takes a set against you. Oh, come closer, my children, and don't you stray too far from home.

But then stories of women enslaved and of women scratching at the edge of town to feed their kids abound, many of them happening as I write and you read; why should this one matter?

It matters first because these stories always matter: their characters are real, they are human beings, every such story matters. It also matters because it happened *here*, never mind the starving children in Africa, I'm talking about events two hours from Brisbane, within living memory.[4] But my great-grandmother's life matters most, I assert, because it

4 Do mind the starving children in Africa, and everywhere else too: www.redcross.com.

demonstrates something valuable about the porous nature of oppression. It tells us that the (to some, very useful) institutions of sexism and its gibbering demented cousin, racism, can be fought. They can even, sometimes, be beaten back into the primaeval caves where they belong, allowing us gals to get on with something like the lives we wanted to live in the first place.[5] How so?

Christina Copson was an orphaned black child; a footnote, at best, to white society. Yet she understood the world she inhabited, and she lived long enough, and was smart enough, to ensure that her children, grandchildren and the first of her great-grandsons were kept from the corrosive misery of the government missions. In an era where Aboriginal lives were held by many to be utterly worthless, Christina rode a horse around the local district, acted as midwife for white farmers' wives, and once expertly guided a visiting American botanist around the local rainforests with her traditional knowledge.[6] It's not that she lived free of men's demands and of white men's prejudice; she didn't. I simply say that she was made a slave, but then she made a path to another, freer life.

We have only two photographs of Christina. Possibly more existed, but in 1953, in a last defiant flare of ancient culture, she burnt all her belongings shortly before she died.[7] In the first she is an old woman, with a halo of soft silver curls, looking directly at the camera. She looks steely but not hard. She is composed, amused even, and unafraid. In the other photo, the

5 AKA 'destroying the joint'.

6 Many still hold Aboriginal lives as worthless; the rhetoric about 'shooting cheeky fucking blacks' that can be heard in many a country town today should not be lightly dismissed, viz the brutal death in custody in 2004 of one Mulrunji Doomadgee, for which no cop has been dismissed, or even punished.

7 A common practice to foil sorcery in many tribal cultures around the world.

one I keep on display, she is much younger, perhaps 40, and is seated, laughing, beside a white friend who is also grinning as she raises an admonishing forefinger in fun. Christina's smile splits her dark and lovely face; she has been caught by the camera in a moment of utter radiance.

Most of what I've related here comes from family tradition. But Christina did make it briefly into the public record after an incident near Wolvi in 1907, when she would have been in her late twenties. The story is as follows: out in the scrub alone one November day, Christina is beset by a 'coloured' man, Fred Dunne, who accosts her. He throws her to the ground and attempts rape. She fights him, and fights him hard. The following day she shows police the place where she alleges the struggle happened; she, nevertheless, is the one charged with assault.

She defends the charge in court.

She wins.

But wait. It wasn't simple assault that Christina was charged with, for her would-be rapist was either very stupid or very inattentive. Remember the hunting rifle? Reader, when Fred Dunne attempted to rape my Aboriginal great-grandmother on the third of November 1907, she shot him in the leg. Then she beat the charge, and then – the glistening cherry on this particular cake of ancestor worship – she had Dunne charged and sent down for six months' gaol.

Christina was an Aboriginal woman – *a poor old gin* – who shot her rapist in Heart-of-Darkness Queensland in 1907 and lived to tell the tale. Can you imagine it? Her life matters today because of who she was and what she did: she said I refuse to be your slave, I refuse to be raped, and I will resist, I will not give in, I will fight for my dignity as a human being and as a woman and if you try me then you will meet my wrath. They took her from her home. They destroyed her joint and they decimated her people, but they didn't destroy her; my great-grandmother lived a long and good life with many friends, and when she died in 1953 we were a free family, and she was a fucking *hero.*

We *Are* Destroying the Joint

Carmen Lawrence

Without really knowing what he was saying, Alan Jones was right – we are 'destroying the joint'. Any dispassionate assessment of the state of 'the joint', both the corner we occupy and the planet as a whole, shows that we are making one hell of a mess of it. Increasing consumption and a growing population are accelerating the depletion of our finite resources, including our precious soils. We are polluting our air, land and water, destroying our heritage places and our communities, producing drastic changes to our climate and pushing out other species at an alarming rate. Human distress and inequality are on the rise, despite our increased material wealth. And all the while, most of us seem to be cheerfully – even wilfully – oblivious to the state we're in.

As the ecologist Jane Lubchenco said in her address as the president of the American Association for the Advancement of Science, 'During the last few decades, humans have emerged as a new force of nature. We are modifying physical, chemical, and biological systems in new ways, at faster rates and over larger spatial scales than ever recorded on earth. Humans have unwittingly embarked upon a grand experiment with our planet. The outcome of this experiment is unknown, but has profound implications for all of life on Earth.'[1] David Suzuki has often expressed a similar concern pointing out that, without anything like adequate knowledge, we are altering the life-support systems of the planet and pushing them to their limits. Our very lives depend on clean air, clean water, clean soil and biodiversity, yet we are extracting raw materials and pouring waste into our environment with little regard for the consequences. We are destroying the joint.

But the 'we' is not women, it's all of us. And as a matter of record, since most women have not, until recently, occupied significant positions of influence and power, we should be judged less culpable than men. Given that women are still in a minority in board rooms and executive positions, as well as in politics, I think it's pretty rich to blame women for the current state of affairs. It's fair to say that the responsibility for the mess we're in resides mainly with those who've historically made decisions about the way we manage our societies and economies – privileged, powerful, Western white males.

It's true, however, that many women now in positions of power appear to share the view that the planet's resources are inexhaustible and that the only serious policy objectives are those which promote economic growth and material acquisition, with little eye to the social and environmental costs. This was not what women of my generation campaigned for. While we were caught up in a global push to redesign the roles of women and to challenge the many barriers to our full participation in Australian life, many of us were also impatient with the broader values of our society. It was intrinsic to much of the early feminist debate, that in seeking equality, women were not looking to simply replicate the experience of men. Nor were we enthusiastic about embracing a capitalist ethic that regarded materialism, competition and selfishness as cardinal virtues. We did not think we could – or should – 'have it all'.

It is no accident that at the same time as we were questioning the nature of our society and our place in it, we were also beginning to probe our relationship with the natural world and disputing some of the benefits of technology. In the early '60s, when Rachel Carson released her ground-breaking book *Silent Spring*, on the cumulative effects of pesticides on the natural world, there was an immediate response, some bitter and derisive debate, but also action from the Kennedy administration. Underpinning Carson's approach was a strong rejection of consumerism; she placed spiritual values ahead of material ones. Her book was, as much as anything, an attack on the paradigm of material enrichment driven by scientific progress that was so central to post-war American – and Australian – culture. She also had a strong belief that the idea we can control nature is an arrogant one, which created, as her biographer Mark Lytle puts it, a 'deadly irony: in their determination to control nature, human beings posed a growing threat to all life on earth, including their own'.[2] *Silent Spring* is often credited with spawning the modern environment movement and has, as a result, been an object of scorn for those, then and now, who see the environment as a limitless sink. As a *New York Times* Editorial writer said in her defence at the time, 'Miss Carson does not argue that chemical pesticides must never be used, but she warns of the dangers of misuse and overuse by a public that has become mesmerized by the notion that chemists are the possessors of divine wisdom and that nothing but benefits can emerge from their test tubes'.[3] Substitute economists for chemists and models for test tubes and you get a more recent read on the problems we collectively confront.

At around the same time, Australian poet Judith Wright, deeply concerned about the increasing destruction of the natural environment and alarmed at the prospect of oil drilling on the Great Barrier Reef, helped found the Wildlife Preservation Society of Queensland. Wright was very influential in the fledging movement, encouraging a focus on educating Australians to embrace 'a deeper kind of belonging'. Wright, like Carson, was also unapologetically critical of excess consumption and waste. In her poem 'Australia 1970', she is scathing about exploitation of our forests and the application of European styles of farming to our dry, poor soils. Her visceral images evoke the idea of the land's brutal retaliation to its abuse: Australia is a vicious dying snake that invades its killers' minds with fear, a mighty tree that wrecks the bulldozers as it falls.

Later, Wright argued that the future of the planet depended on individuals developing a new relationship with nature that would require a 'reassertion of the values of feeling against the economic and technological Gradgrinds of our time'.[4] Wright often wrote of the need for Australians to see the country differently: 'Instead of "seeing the country"', she said, 'we despised it and dubbed it a "mere wilderness" … we are floundering now in the results of our lack of ability truly to "see the country" and its past and future.'[5]

While there has been a virtual revolution in women's education and working lives since these women wrote; while our choices have multiplied and we are wealthier than we have ever been, deeper, nagging doubts remain about just how much women's (and men's) lives have really improved. I suspect more than a few women question whether some of the objectives we've been encouraged to embrace do really contribute to our wellbeing. Does it actually improve the quality of our lives to spend endless hours at work, depriving ourselves of precious time with friends and family; time for leisure and creativity? Can we justify our ever-increasing consumption while others live in rank poverty and the world's resources are being depleted at an alarming rate? Have we forgotten the warnings of prescient women like Carson and Wright? Are we paying too steep a price for our materialism?

Despite renewed questioning of our economic circumstances during the current global financial crisis, most of those in positions of influence still buy the orthodox line that there are no serious limits to our capacity to exploit the planet's resources for our benefit; they ignore the reality that the economy is a sub-system of the environment. As eminent British economist Partha Dasgupta acknowledged, 'we economists see nature, when we see it at all, as a backdrop from which resources and services can be drawn in isolation ... Accounting for nature, if it comes into the calculus at all, is usually an afterthought to the real business of "doing economics". We economists have been so successful in this enterprise that if someone exclaims "economic growth!" no one needs to ask "Growth in what?" – we all know they mean growth in gross domestic product (GDP).'[6] Conventional economic theory takes nature to be a fixed, indestructible factor of production. The problem with this assumption is that it is wrong: as Dasgupta also points out, 'nature consists of degradable resources. Agricultural land, forest, watersheds, fisheries, fresh water sources, river estuaries and the atmosphere are capital assets that are self-regenerative, but suffer from depletion and deterioration when they are overused.'[7] We need look no further than the Murray-Darling Basin for a potent local example.

Consider, too, the world's fisheries. According to the World Bank, the global catch rose from 19 million tonnes a year in 1950 to 140 million tonnes in 2004, with the result that 70% of the world's saltwater fish are judged to be overexploited or fully exploited. Some fisheries have collapsed altogether and are unlikely to recover any time soon. In Australia, we like to pride ourselves that our fisheries are well managed, but there has been a decline in fish stocks, with state assessments showing that in Queensland, New South Wales and Western Australia, for example, the stock of the prized pink snapper is overfished. Similarly, many of the planet's mineral and energy resources are being used so rapidly that we are fast approaching – and may even have passed – the peak of production, the case of oil being the most often debated.

The dramatic loss of global biodiversity continues to accelerate under the pressures of urban and agricultural expansion. In Australia many ecosystems have been destroyed over the past 200 years: the Australian Museum reports that 75% of rainforests and nearly 50% of all forests, over 60% of coastal wetlands and nearly 90% of temperate woodlands have been lost. As a result, hundreds of species have become extinct. Acidification and erosion of our soils continue apace.

Despite optimistic pronouncements about the dematerialisation of advanced economies, the aggregate volume of material used globally (and in most regions) is also rising quickly and – apparently – inexorably; resources like fuels, wood, sand, minerals and biomass are being used at ever increasing rates. In 1980, we extracted and used 40 billion metric tonnes of such materials. Twenty-five years later, the figure had increased by 45% to 58 billion.[8] And while we might not be suffering the levels of pollution that are all too evident in the rapidly growing economies of the region – recent levels of air pollution in China are truly staggering – the fact is that we are effectively exporting our pollution, since we import vast quantities of cheap goods that are manufactured with little regard for the attendant contamination of air, soil and water.

These changes have human impacts too. The World Bank has highlighted the fact that a third of the world's population faces water scarcity, which threatens their health, that soil degradation affects a significant proportion of both irrigated and rain-fed agricultural lands and that every year at least a million people die prematurely from respiratory illnesses linked to air pollution. However, many of those who acknowledge that we are pushing the limits still look to technological miracles to avert catastrophe, invoking human ingenuity as our salvation, not seeing that it is such unbridled 'ingenuity' that has got us into this mess in the first place.

Increasingly, I find myself agreeing with the late historian Tony Judt that 'something is profoundly wrong with the way we live today'. In his book *Ill Fares the Land* Judt argued that we have come to make a virtue out of the pursuit of material goals to such an extent that 'this very pursuit now constitutes whatever remains of our sense of collective purpose'.[9] He suggested that this pursuit is now firmly entrenched in an orthodoxy that judges achievement and public policy in exclusively economic, rather than moral, terms. The result is that when we consider whether to support a particular development or initiative, we don't ask whether it's good or bad, whether it will help bring about a better society or a better world, but rather, how will it affect the economy, whether it is efficient, whether it will lead to increases in GDP and, if so, how much it will contribute to growth.

Most people do not appear to regard this as a problem; the equation of wellbeing with economic growth is taken as given and the identity of society with the economy as uncontentious. Indeed, they do not see any alternative to this construction; it is simply the way the world works. And the adverse consequences on us and our environment and our communities simply have to be borne. It remains the case that for many, especially those in a position to influence public policy, the economy and society are identical; if one grows, the other must be improving along with the quality of people's lives.

There are, of course, people who dissent from this orthodoxy, people who recognise that markets are part of a broader social fabric, human creations that come in a variety of forms, governed by rules and supported by agreed conventions and legislation and which do not always produce optimal outcomes for society. But for the most part, the goal of economic growth is clearly the touchstone for judging major public policy decisions and is the most familiar subject of economic commentary in the media. Economies and firms are judged not just by whether they are growing, but by how fast they grow. Some have described this as a 'secular religion' and the historian J R McNeill concluded that 'the overarching priority of economic growth was easily the most important idea of the twentieth century'.[10]

It is now obvious that there are two glaring omissions from current models and theories of growth: the planet and the human families and communities that live within it. These models neglect the fact that the human economy is embedded in the biosphere, which consists of living things, the products of living things and the necessary resources and conditions for living things to survive and thrive. When they are considered at all, such resources tend to be viewed as infinite. Often such consideration is simply omitted altogether, so problems are effectively defined out of existence. But as Nobel Prize-winning economist and *New York Times* columnist Paul Krugman reminded his readers, 'we're living in a finite world, one in which resource constraints are becoming increasingly binding'.[11]

Until fairly recently, few economists paid much attention to the costs of the near exclusive focus on economic growth; now the consequences of environmental degradation and rising CO_2 emissions – together with challenges to economic orthodoxy from within profession – are forcing some reassessment. As Nobel Laureate Joseph Stiglitz has argued, using the language of orthodox economics, 'pollution is a global externality of enormous proportions'.[12] David Orrell puts it more bluntly:

'the real credit crunch is not the one involving banks, but the one involving the environment'.[13]

Whether the focus is on pollution, biodiversity loss, resource depletion or climate change, the underpinning cause is the same: the human consumption that drives economic growth. Yet research shows that here, and in other developed countries, even when people obtain more money and material goods, they are not necessarily more satisfied with their lives or more psychologically healthy, especially if it has been bought by the destruction of cultural and environmental heritage.[14] Our levels of consumption are high and rising and, in the West, we are more affluent – and wasteful – than we have ever been. We no longer seem to have any understanding of the concept of 'enough'. And Australia has the uncomfortable achievement of sitting at the top of most of these lists of excess – house size, carbon emissions, species loss, inequality.

And the price we pay for despoiling our environment and trashing our heritage is high. Whether we are aware of it or not, we are connected to and influenced by our social and physical environments, our cultural landscape. People typically have strong emotional bonds to places and the communities in them. There is a now a great deal of evidence that our wellbeing depends in large measure on our relationship with our environment – broadly conceived, the relationships we have with the people around us and the natural and built environment we inhabit; if this cultural environment is destroyed or degraded or if people are prevented from enjoying it, their health and wellbeing deteriorate.

In Western Australia, for example, it has been found that the happiest and healthiest Indigenous Australians, with low arrest rates and good educational attainment, are those who have been able to retain a strong attachment to their country and a strong Aboriginal identity.[15] Conversely, the psychologically adverse consequences of destruction of people's familiar environment have been well documented. Interviews with people living in the Hunter Valley of New South Wales found that 'the transformation of the environment from mining and power station activities was associated with significant expressions of distress linked to negative changes to interviewees' sense of place, wellbeing, and control', a phenomenon philosopher Glenn Albrecht has described as 'solastalgia', a loss of a sense of place.[16] In the Hunter, millions of tonnes of coal are extracted each year, using open-cut techniques that blast away soil and rock and spread plumes of dust to settle on homes, crops and livestock. Sites are often permanently lit and trucks and coal trains provide a background of constant noise. Rivers and streams are polluted.

Some of the opposition to the construction of a major industrial gas complex in the Kimberley and to the proliferation of coal-seam gas sites on agricultural land in New South Wales and Queensland almost certainly stems from people's desire to avoid such experiences and to retain their familiar and aesthetically pleasing environments – not to mention the desire to avert dust and noise and traffic and pollution. Such sentiments are often derided as 'nimbyism' and given little weight, but they are an expression of the profound human need for connection with the natural world and cherished places.

We also know that people exposed to persistent noise, drought and unusual weather are more likely to report feelings of unhappiness and ill health – and, in the case of extreme heat in Australia, even to be admitted in increased number to emergency psychiatric care.[17] While it appears to be generally assumed that humans will simply adapt to warmer climates, in reality 'even modest global warming could … expose large fractions of the population to unprecedented heat stress, and that with severe warming this would become intolerable'.[18] We already know that heat waves increase deaths among the elderly and vulnerable.

In recent studies, the state of the environment has been shown to be an important predictor of national differences in general wellbeing. For 67 countries tracked between 1972 and 2000, climate variables had a highly significant effect and projections indicated that countries with very high summer temperatures, like Australia, were the most likely to suffer as a result of climate change.[19] In one of the few studies to examine the effects of environmental conditions in a developing economy, people living in Chinese cities with high levels of atmospheric pollution, environmental disasters and traffic congestion were found to have significantly lower levels of wellbeing – as well as poorer health.[20]

Economic activities that diminish the quality of the environment and increase pollution harm the communities that are supposed to benefit. Conversely, contact with the natural environment has been shown to reduce stress, improve children's behaviour and increase wellbeing. Indeed, patients appear to recover faster from surgery when they are able to see plants, flowers and trees. Although we might like to think that the natural environment is a tool at our disposal, that we are entitled, as the Book of Genesis suggests, to 'dominion' over 'all the earth', we are in fact part of the natural world and, for better and for worse, inextricably linked to and deeply affected by it.

In any case, there is now good support for the proposition that, beyond a certain point, the premise that more consumption and greater wealth improve wellbeing does not stand close scrutiny. On the contrary, it seems that the more material goals matter to people, the more unhappy they are likely to be. Research here and in other wealthy countries shows that even when people obtain more money and material goods, they are not more satisfied with their lives or more psychologically healthy.

At some level, people seem to understand this. Many people are uneasy about the fact that children today are growing up in a winner-takes-all economy where they are encouraged to see the main purpose in life as getting whatever they can for themselves. In popular culture, selfishness and materialism are no longer seen as moral problems, but as cardinal goals in life: 'more for me', as one TV advertisement boasts. Selfishness, once seen as a moral failing, is now depicted as desirable.

The influence of consumerism is pervasive and buttressed by an enormous advertising industry whose sole purpose is to drive consumption. The result is that many people have come to evaluate their lives and accomplishments not by looking to their relationships or community, but to what they possess and what they can buy. They act as if they believe that the consumption of things will confer real satisfaction and guarantee a full life.

At the same time, judgements about what is enough are not absolute, but relative to others; people judge their own worth by measuring their wealth and possessions against that of others – and since there is always someone with more, this is a recipe for dissatisfaction. In fact, research shows that merely aspiring to have greater wealth or more material possessions is likely to be associated with increased personal unhappiness. People who strongly value the pursuit of wealth and possessions report more symptoms of anxiety and less vitality, are at greater risk of depression, are more narcissistic and experience more bodily discomfort (aches and pains) than those who are less materialistic. They watch more TV, take more alcohol and drugs and have more impoverished personal relationships.[21]

Economies focused on consumption foster conditions that heighten such psychological insecurities: they fuel themselves. Parents work more and more hours outside the home, to acquire the buying power to obtain more goods that they have been taught they and their children 'need'. Attention to children, intimate time with partners and friends, and other satisfactions that cannot be bought are pushed to the periphery.

Materialism is also associated with more anti-social and self-centred behaviour. One of the effects of a materialistic disposition is a greater tendency to treat people as objects to be manipulated and used. Materialistic values conflict with making the world a better place and the desire to contribute to equality, justice and other aspects of civil society. Attitude surveys show that people highly focused on materialistic objectives show little concern for the wider world – they care less about protecting the environment and less about their fellow citizens.

We are all so caught up in this consumption spiral that it may sometimes seem that there is no escaping it and no way of reshaping our economies, but the passionate advocacy of those indomitable women, Rachel Carson and Judith Wright and others like them, serves to remind us that change is possible. Well known primatologist and founder of Roots and Shoots, Jane Goodall, for example, tirelessly travels the globe sharing her concerns about the state of the planet. She has observed that 'People now think, instead of "How will this affect future generations", [they think] "How will this affect me now, or the next shareholder's meeting, or the next political campaign?" We've lost something.' But she adds, more optimistically, that change is still possible; that 'small does make a difference'.[22]

And it is the dispositions that are more common among women that may be crucial in effecting this change. I'm not arguing that women are all virtue and no vice, or that no men share these characteristics, but we do know that women generally are more likely to see the need to protect the environment and to display more environmentally responsible behaviour. They are also more likely to exhibit strong attachments to place and to be less materialistic in a variety of settings. Women also generally show greater levels of cooperation and express greater empathy towards others. Psychological research also suggests that they are more altruistic.[23]

While the epithet 'tree huggers' is often hurled at those who seek to protect the environment with the clear intention of characterising them as soft-headed, it has its origins in a very powerful women's protest. During the 1960s, India's push for economic development resulted in more and more trees being cleared; soils were washed away, causing landslides, floods and silting of many rivers. Not only were crops and houses destroyed, but women had to travel increasing distances for their fuel, fodder and water. In protest at this deforestation, a non-violent protest movement called Chipko was born. *Chipko* in Hindi means to cling or embrace, reflecting the protesters' main technique of throwing their arms around the tree trunks designated to be cut and refusing to move, despite threats of violence from the woodcutters. These women literally put their lives on the line to stop the logging. This was far more than an emotional embrace – it was a powerful expression of opposition to rampant destruction of their life support system.

Why attributes like these appear to be more common among women is debatable. Some have suggested that it is the gendered socialisation that is still typical in most societies that is responsible for the difference: females are socialised to have a stronger 'ethic of care', to be more compassionate, nurturing, cooperative and helpful; it is also argued that their roles as carers reinforce these values. Whatever the accuracy of these interpretations, it seems clear that if these virtues were more highly valued and cultivated in men and women alike, we might have some chance of pulling back from the brink; if not for ourselves then, surely, for our grandchildren.

We cannot ignore the fact that high and accelerating levels of economic growth are generating serious problems of resource insecurity, environmental degradation and social dislocation, which produce distress and disease: there is a serious downside to growth. One of the reasons policy makers continue to be fixated on increasing growth as a pre-eminent objective in the face of these effects is that they believe there is no alternative. This represents a failure of the imagination by the political class, a refusal to take seriously and develop other possible models which have – somewhat tentatively – been proposed under the heading of steady state or no-growth economics.

Even Robert Solow, who won the Nobel Prize for economics for his work on growth theory, apparently now describes himself as 'agnostic' on whether growth can continue and told *Harper's Magazine* in March 2008 that 'there is no reason at all why capitalism could not survive without slow or even no growth. I think it's perfectly possible that economic growth cannot go on at its current rate forever … There is nothing intrinsic in the system that says it cannot exist happily in a stationary state.'

It is surely time for these ideas to be taken seriously so that we – collectively – can stop 'destroying the joint'.

Global Destroyers

Emily Maguire

> Fair dinkum, mate, this is borrowed money – $320 million to increase the number of Pacific women in leadership and decision-making roles, to increase women's access to financial services and markets, to improve the safety of women through better violence prevention. She [Prime Minister Gillard] said, 'We know that societies only reach their full potential if women are politically participating.' Women are destroying the joint!
>
> *Alan Jones*[1]

During the mighty, righteous furore that followed these comments, the context – the announcement of $320 million to help with the political participation and economic advancement of women in the Pacific – has been lost. Of course, Jones's reaction was all about the Australian context and what women leaders such as Clover Moore and Christine

Nixon were apparently doing to our society, but still, there's a world-shakingly important sentence in there right before Jones drops the DtJ bomb: 'We know that societies only reach their full potential if women are politically participating.' He's quoting the PM who was, on this, absolutely right. The society-transforming power of gender equality is something that has been shown again and again throughout our region and beyond.

Actually, Jones was absolutely right as well. When women participate politically, joints do get destroyed – joints that treat women as second-class citizens or property, that deny girls education, that claim democratic status while refusing women citizenship, that allow the elites to grow richer and stronger on the blood of the poor and the weak. It's marvellous, actually, the way this keeps happening: women start to lobby and agitate and suddenly all these violent, sexist, racist, unjust, repressive joints begin to crumble.

Let's get this clear up front: women deserve human rights because they are human and they deserve to play a part in political and civil governance because they are part of the polity. No other justification is needed.

But in light of claims that women in leadership are somehow wrecking things, it's worth putting the facts out there. According to the World Bank's 2012 World Development Report, improving a country's gender equality 'can enhance productivity, improve development outcomes for the next generation, and make institutions more representative'. In short, the big bank says, gender equality is 'smart economics'.[2]

Meanwhile, the Inter-Parliamentary Union (IPU) examined 110 national parliaments to see whether female representatives did anything different to male representatives. It found that:

> ... while not a homogenous group, women parliamentarians share certain general interests and concerns ... Women parliamentarians tend to emphasise social issues, such as childcare, equal pay, parental leave and pensions; physical concerns, including reproductive rights, physical safety and gender-based violence; and development, which includes human development, the alleviation of poverty and delivery of services.[3]

This is not a biological-essentialist argument; there is no claim that women are naturally more peaceful, generous or community minded. It's simply a reflection of the fact that people with different life experiences will have different perspectives and concerns. If a society expects women to be the main caretakers of children and the elderly, underpays women's work and under-reacts to violence committed against them, then it's unsurprising that women will be more likely to notice, raise and fight for resolution of those issues.

Which is not to say that women leaders only care about the issues that personally affect them. One study of women in local government in India found that female leadership 'positively affected the provision of public goods at the local level in ways that better reflected both women's and men's preferences'. Other studies from India and Nepal found that when women were given greater input into resource management, conservation outcomes 'improved significantly'.[4] And the UNDP reports that in the Indian states of West Bengal and Rajasthan 'the number of drinking water projects was 60% higher in female-led than male-led councils. In West Bengal, female-led councils undertook road-building projects at a higher rate than male-led councils … ' While in Bangladesh, 'people report a higher rate of satisfaction with the decisions made by local women representatives in terms of the distribution of public resources and allocation of projects'.[5]

It's easy to see how the Pacific Islands, which currently have among the lowest rates of women's political representation – around 2.5% if you exclude Australia and New Zealand – and the highest levels of sexual- and gender-based violence in the world, might benefit from an investment in women's leadership.[6]

It's easy to see too how those benefiting from gender-based injustice would see anything that helps combat it as a destructive force. But, as the following case studies of joint destroyers from around the world show, destruction for the corrupt or controlling elite is life-saving, world-improving progress for everyone else.

> Each village had one or more chilling story of a woman's murder or suicide … The stories were different, but the underlying theme was the same. Class, caste, religion and patriarchy all collude against women. We wanted to bring this issue into the open. We wanted people to discuss it.
>
> *Madhavi Kukreja, founder of Vanangana*[7]

In Banda district in India's most populous state, Uttar Pradesh, the Dalit ('untouchable') women are doubly discriminated against, shunned by the 'upper-caste' community and victim to gender-based violence perpetrated by both strangers and male family members. It was to help these women gain access to the most fundamental of resources – water – that Madhavi Kukreja began a non-profit organisation called Vanangana. As Dalit women were denied access to community water pumps due to their 'untouchable' status, Kukreja decided that the women should learn to build and maintain their own water delivery systems.

After much intensive lobbying, Vanangana succeeded in establishing a government-run, UNICEF-supported hand pump mechanics training course for 45 illiterate Dalit women. Those women were then employed by the local water board to supervise and repair 1000 water pumps. In undertaking the training and then the work, they challenged long-established ideas about the capabilities and appropriate roles of women. They also began to break down caste discrimination as higher-caste people needing pump repairs were directed to the 'untouchable' new recruits. That first set of women went on to train another 800 pump mechanics – many of them men – and Vanangana won support and funding from the World Bank in order to solve the water problems of the region.

Once well established and funded, Vanangana widened its scope, by setting out to tackle violence against women. In a stunning example of cross-cultural solidarity, 800 Dalit women marched against the death of an upper-caste victim of spousal abuse and then continued to publicly apply pressure on the authorities until they prosecuted the woman's husband.

Vanangana has since worked on large scale awareness campaigns about women's and children's rights, set up counselling and legal advice services for survivors of violence and begun strategising to bring about policy change in regards to violence against women.[8] So it is that an organisation that started out trying to fix some water pumps is now destroying the misogynist, classist, caste-riven joint in a seriously big way.

> Here in Afghanistan, people believe a woman belongs to her house or her grave. It's a common saying … Our purpose is to fight the belief that women do not belong to the outside world.
>
> *Noorjahan Akbar, co-founder Young Women for Change*[9]

In July 2012, 50 young Afghan women (and several supportive men) took to the streets of Kabul to protest the aggressive, sometimes violent, street harassment to which girls and women of the city have become accustomed. Insulting comments, groping and even being pushed to the ground are everyday events for women who dare to go out in public without male escorts. Sometimes the police help; sometimes the harassers are the police. Many parents try to protect their daughters by keeping them inside; some women withdraw from participation in the outside world because they can no longer stand the daily assaults.

The message of the protest was clearly communicated by the signs the women held: 'This street belongs to me too', 'I have the right to walk in my city safely', and 'I will not keep silent the next time you insult me'. By world standards the demonstration was small, but its impact was huge. Organised by Young Women for Change (YWC), a feminist organisation started in 2011 by two nineteen-year-old Afghan women, Anita Hadiary and Noorjahan Akbar, the march made headlines worldwide and prompted a wide-spread, passionate, nationwide discussion about the right of women and girls to exist in public spaces without harassment.

'Thursday, July 14, 2011 was the first day I felt like I belonged to the city I have lived in for most of my life,' Akbar told *The New York Times*.[10] Since then YWC has held monthly lectures on women's issues, conducted research on street harassment, produced a documentary called *This is My City Too* and opened Kabul's first women's internet café.

When Akbar and Hadiary were in the earliest stages of establishing YWC, the police stopped them from meeting at Kabul University because they 'did not want women making problems for them'. But the women aren't making problems – they're addressing them. The joint is rotten and the young women of Kabul are destroying it one defiant public-space-occupying woman at a time.

> If we are to seize this window of opportunity, we have to get women into positions of political and economic power. And not women who will just say 'yes' to the existing government structure, officials and laws, and not just quota-fillers, but women who will actually stand up for women.
>
> *Alaa Murabit, founder of the Voice of Libyan Women*[11]

With her brothers off fighting at the front of the revolutionary war against Gaddafi's regime and her doctor father coordinating medical treatment for the wounded, 22-year-old Alaa Murabit felt driven to make her own contribution to the revolution. Specifically, she wanted to ensure that the women of Libya were not forgotten or sidelined during the reconstruction process.

In August 2011, she started the Voice of Libyan Women (VLW), an organisation dedicated to eliminating violence against women and increasing female political participation and economic advancement. VLW has since played a vital role in the turbulent peace and democracy movements, holding an extensive series of roundtable discussions and conferences in which Libyan women of all backgrounds and political and religious stripes have been invited to voice their opinions on the nation's future. Local political leaders as well as members of the international media and representatives from various international NGOs were invited to the discussions in order to ensure the women's voices were being heard widely.

In partnership with several other Libyan NGOs, VLW also developed a Libyan Women's Charter designed to influence those drafting the new constitution, released its National Policies on Ensuring the Economic Empowerment of Women in Libya, and undertook extensive voter awareness and education initiatives in the lead-up to the historic National Congress elections in July 2012.[12]

The revolution may have destroyed Gaddafi's joint, but Murabit points out that 'women are no better off … We have to look at what the next step ought to be. What can we do to ensure the economic security for women and how can we secure them more influence?'[13]

> Women are very effective and fast communicators. Once they decide that an issue is of importance to them, they get on to it, get the word out and mobilise others to join.
>
> *Zeinab Blandia, Director of Ru'ya*[14]

The state of South Kordofan is the site of a long-running, brutal conflict between the South Sudanese, supported by the local Nuba Mountain people, and the Sudanese Government. The African Rights group calls what is happening to the people of the region state-sanctified 'genocide by attrition' and yet few outside of Sudan are even aware of it, meaning that the people receive very little international aid or peacekeeping assistance.[15]

In 2001, a group of women from the Nuba Mountains, tired of having their voices and experiences ignored by the leaders in their communities and country, established Ru'ya ('vision') to advocate for the rights of women and increase their participation in democratic and community organisations.

Its efforts were particularly important during the lead-up to the 2011 local government election. Ru'ya directly provided civic and voter education to 5000 people and trained 30 women from the region to go on and educate others. It also provided policy development and campaign training for ten women candidates from across five parties and facilitated agreement from women's representatives from all twelve political parties to a state-wide joint Women's Agenda prioritising, among other things, women's economic empowerment and citizenship rights and the rights of disabled women.[16] It is largely due to Ru'ya's efforts that, despite the restrictions that their traditional, rural society places on women's civic participation, and despite the fact that most women in the region are illiterate, a majority of the voters who turned out for the election were women.

Sadly, shortly after the election, the Sudanese military raided the Ru'ya offices and destroyed their records and files. The staff was forced to flee the state and, after ongoing threats and harassment, many have since fled the country. They have not, however, stopped working for the women of South Kordofan. Now refugees themselves, the women of Ru'ya are working to record the testimonies of those who survived the post-election violence and made it to refugee camps. They will not allow women's stories to go untold, their voices to be silenced. They will not allow the atrocities committed by those running the joint to be lost to history.[17]

> It is important that women are represented during the peace talks and are part of the peace process with the Burma Government ... Our role needs to be officially recognised and our voices heard.
>
> *K'nyaw Paw, Women's League of Burma*[18]

The people of Burma (Myanmar) have suffered under a century of occupation, civil war and violently repressive military rule. While recent moves towards liberalisation and democratisation provide some hope, there is much difficult, and potentially dangerous, work to be done before Burma can be said to be at peace and its people free.

Despite the fact that the most well-known and influential figure in the Burmese democracy movement is a woman – Nobel Peace Prize winner Aung San Suu Kyi – women tend to be politically, socially and economically marginalised due to the combination of traditional patriarchal power structures and harsh rule by a male-dominated military regime. Many women, particularly those of the ethnic minority groups, report being raped, abused and forced into servitude by soldiers. There is some evidence that such attacks are part of a concerted strategy to terrorise and silence political activists and insurgents.[19]

The Women's League of Burma (WLB) was formed in 1999 'with the aim of increasing the participation of women in the struggle for democracy and human rights, promoting women's participation in the national peace and reconciliation process, and enhancing the role of the women of Burma at the national and international level'.[20] All of the league's work is underpinned by an understanding that peace and freedom cannot exist without gender equality.

Among the activities organised by the WLB are workshops in negotiating ceasefires and building peace and monthly political forums to encourage grass-roots community activism. It also runs forums on how to stop cycles of violence, collects and publishes data on violence against women and provides crisis and long-term support services to survivors. Recognising that many Burmese – particularly those from ethnic minority groups – have been forced to flee their homelands, the WLB conducts its programs in refugee camps in Bangladesh, India and Thailand, as well as in Burma.

There's a long way to go, but the WLB is optimistic that the joint is steadily crumbling, reporting that

> … there is a notable shift in the traditional perceptions of gender roles and gender stereotypes in communities throughout Burma and on the Burma border … There is evidence that men and women are beginning to understand and acknowledge the importance of women in the peace process and recognise the necessity of their involvement in order to achieve lasting peace in Burma.[21]

These examples comprise a tiny, tiny proportion of the women-led joint destroying currently taking place around the world. With better support there could be even more.

'Fair dinkum, mate … $320 million to increase the number of Pacific women in leadership and decision-making roles, to increase women's access to financial services and markets, to improve the safety of women through better violence prevention.'

Yes, please. In Australia, in the Pacific, everywhere. More money, more women, more joint destroying. Bring it on.

Birth of a Movement

Destroy the Joint Administrators

When we heard on a Friday night in August 2012 that Alan Jones had declared that 'women are destroying the joint' we considered it a ludicrous statement worthy of ridicule. Coming from an 'old white man' with wealth and power, the phrase smacked of hypocrisy.

With those five words Alan Jones told us that no matter how hard we worked he would always consider us lesser beings, simply because we are women. In uttering those five words he stood shoulder to shoulder with other sexist and misogynist men we have encountered in our lives, who have discouraged our ideas, denied our voices and devalued our achievements. If women are destroying the joint why is violence against women a major problem in our society? Why does the Gender Gap exist? Why do women remain marginalised despite forming a majority?

Alan Jones's statement was ludicrous for many reasons and it plainly demonstrated a fear of change and fear of others. We know that marginalised groups are not given sufficient power to destroy the joint. We allow them enough power to destroy their own joint, but there are well-established methods to prevent them from destroying the joints of the powerful. Although Jones's statement referenced the marginalised group of 'women', his comments were not about sex, but about power. Who has it, who wants it, who takes it, who gives it and who fears losing it.

Months have passed since Alan Jones's five words.

We are proud to be administrators of the online Destroy the Joint (DtJ) movement, a movement that arose in response to those five words. We are ordinary Australians – a handful of tens of thousands. But with tens of thousands of Australians, we have been involved in an online movement whose existence is a tribute to ordinary Australians who are fed up with sexism and have agreed that enough is enough. Our reasons for becoming involved are diverse but we all agree that women are not destroying the joint.

Many have wanted to know who is behind the Destroy the Joint online movement. When Macquarie Radio Network faced a massive backlash over Alan Jones's 'died of shame' comments, they expressed bewilderment that they had not been able to get in contact with the leaders of the group. In traditional patriarchal style, they wanted to know who the leader was, so that they could attack them and tear them down. Still people ask: Who is behind the group? Why did you start it? What did you, the DtJ administrators, do?

We started the destroy the joint Twitter hashtag on 31 August. We started the Destroy the Joint Facebook page on 2 September. We recruited and organised over 40 volunteer moderators, realising that the sheer number of engaged individuals required significant effort to keep a semblance of order. Most of the DtJ administrators and moderators had never met or heard of each other – but the crowdsourcing approach worked. We contributed to the more than 110 000 signatures on an online petition to 2GB advertisers. We decided to listen to 2GB Breakfast Radio daily to create a list of its advertisers, asking people to call the advertisers and express their thoughts in a civil manner. We faced 2GB. We researched. We created a pledge. We created memes, montages and word clouds. We created posting guidelines and a list of hundreds of profanities for a blocked word list. We answered thousands of questions.

We could attribute specific actions to specific individuals, but that is not the point. While as individuals we appreciate recognition for the work we have done, it is the actions of the community that are pivotal to changing societal attitudes about sexism and misogyny. Together we have learned about trolls and cyberbullies. We have faced smears, threats of violence and online flaming attacks. We have learned techniques to make online spaces safer. The DtJ administrators have written posts and tweets that have been seen by hundreds of thousands of people – including a Facebook post after the death of Indian student Jyoti Singh Pandey that was so compelling it was shared with friends by well over half the people who viewed it. We have also written posts and tweets that may well have had people wondering if we've had an intern filling in for the day. The proposed posts are offered up to administrators and moderators for discussion and editing prior to posting. We like to think we can guess how others will respond to an idea or an issue, but we recognise that we are fallible and that we make mistakes. Sometimes we get it wrong. We feel we need to better address issues of intersectionality and inclusion. We wonder if perhaps the community's expectations of us are greater than that which a group of busy volunteers can deliver. But again, it is not our individual actions that create change – it is the actions of our community. Can a Facebook page or Twitter account change the world? No. But when thousands of people are talking and taking action online, at work, at home and in their communities, *that* can change the world.

How do the Destroy the Joint administrators roll? We're like the individuals who post on the Facebook page. We talk, we argue, we support, we joke, we share, we laugh and we rejoice. We disagree on many things. We disagreed about writing this. As we write this sentence, we know that another administrator may well suggest that it should be edited or deleted. But we also know that those who stood up against the phrase 'women are destroying the joint' will not judge this writing as that of a woman, or a group of women. They may say that we are destroying the joint, especially now that the meaning of that phrase has been transformed, but they will not attack us on the basis of gender. Their criticism will not dismiss or devalue us simply because we are women, and for that we are most grateful.

The thought structure of online groups is sometimes referred to as the hive mind, but we think it more akin to modern democracy than the social structure of bees. The DtJ administrators are a microcosm of the wider group: the conversations that we have with each other are no different from the agreements and disagreements that exist on the DtJ

Facebook page or from those that everyone has in their day-to-day lives. Each of us is an individual; we have differing skills, experiences, knowledge, resources and ideas. But we recognise that with teamwork we create something that far exceeds what any individual contribution can do. Our individual contributions are important and we appreciate recognition for what we have done but prefer to focus on what the community has done and has the potential to do. We love seeing what the community does with the tools, information and resources we have helped to build.

We don't have a CEO. As far as leadership structures go, ours doesn't fit into the usual patriarchal model. Ours is a collaborative approach. It is rare that the DtJ administrators have complete consensus on decisions. It is not unusual that one or more of us feels uneasy or uncomfortable – but this is reality, not utopia.

The phrase 'women are destroying the joint' invoked negative emotions for each of us when we heard it, but now the phrase 'destroy the joint' brings many positive emotions. For that we are grateful. Grateful that a group of diverse Australians united and have remained united. Grateful that they have continued to examine the existence and impact of sexism and misogyny in Australia and are acting for change.

Each woman whose writing is featured in this book has a story that deserves to be told. The individuals are important, but more important are the outcomes of the collective actions of individuals working to eliminate sexism and misogyny. The beauty of the collective was displayed in the montage images that became a vivid symbol of the face of DtJ. We asked Destroyers to opt-in their Facebook and Twitter profile images for a group picture. The messages flooded in by the hundreds and the resulting montage pictures comprised over 2400 individual images. These montages took an incredible effort to create, but they would not have been possible without the contributions of every individual. The image illustrates the importance and beauty of collective action. It's that collective action that will achieve change.

Although you are reading this article and may be wondering about us, the focus should not be on any single individual when it comes to Destroy the Joint. But when it comes to the impact of the online movement, it's not about the individual. It's about the collective. It's about education and re-education for those who don't understand. It's about giving the marginalised a voice. It's about creating a safe place to talk about important issues. A safe place to laugh, and to cry. It's not about naming specific individuals and who has done what.

That's not to say that we don't discuss and consider our individual actions as administrators, and the intended and unintended effects that our actions may have. We feel a responsibility to the community to behave in an ethical manner and to live up to high expectations. Having an online audience of tens of thousands is new to most of us. It's daunting and frightening for each of us to know that we might mess up in front of all those people, including all the other administrators and moderators. Each of us knows it's frightening because we have messed up, and then felt awful. Thankfully this is a tolerant and respectful group.

Are we feminists? Sure, we're happy to own that label. But it doesn't matter if individuals who engage with DtJ identify as a 'feminist' or not. What matters is that they are aware of sexism, aware of the widening gender pay gap, aware of the male privilege in our society. Translating this awareness into real-life conversations and actions is what will affect sexism in our society.

Can we also have a real world impact through our online targeting of organisations, businesses, individuals and advertisers who engage in sexist behaviour? Yes, but perhaps the major impact of such action is achieved through the empowerment of individuals. The DtJ community has shown that we will stand up against sexist behaviour. We have shown that standing up and expressing your opinion in a civil manner can have results. Occasionally we see that the courteously expressed opinions of hundreds of people does not result in a heartfelt apology or change in behaviour. And this is important too – because it is important not to be discouraged by this, or to take it personally. Not everyone responds appropriately to a civil request. But many do and we should feel able to speak up.

Does DtJ mentor individuals and teach them to speak up? Not in the traditional sense, but there is a mentoring element to the online community as online conversations allow women to engage with others and discuss their opinions and ideas. Many women have said that because of DtJ they have felt empowered to ask for a raise or express a particular opinion. Many have said that, as victims of sexual assault, the conversations have helped them not to feel so alone. It is not the action of one administrator that has led to this, it is the action of the collective.

As volunteers, we are not motivated by money. We each have our own political, spiritual and feminist beliefs, as is true for any group of people. We are not motivated by a desire for fame, which is why you haven't seen us shouting our names from rooftops. We are motivated by a desire to eliminate sexism and misogyny and a belief that the collective action of hundreds of thousands of Australians is the most effective and enduring way to achieve real change. The administrators differed in opinion about putting our names to this essay (see Contributors). If we put our names to this essay people could form inaccurate assumptions about our beliefs or about the nature of the DtJ movement. We could receive threats of violence against us and our families. We could encounter discrimination in our careers, workplaces and personal lives.

There are still people who don't understand that the thousands of Australians who are taking a stand against sexism and misogyny are doing so as a collective. Haters will hate.

Discrimination remains a major problem in Australia.

And you know what we say?

We say: it stops with us. Each of us.

Spanners and Mirages

Jennifer Mills

2012 was an intense year for women in public life. It seemed that everywhere we looked, women were being challenged, denigrated and insulted by men attempting to discredit, shame or frighten us into silence. Comment feeds filled with intimations of sexual violence or outright threats. Women were not silenced. Blog posts and articles proliferated about the phenomenon; social media campaigns like #mencallmethings exposed the trolls. Still, for many women in public life, defending their right to be there took up a huge proportion of their energy.

Fed up, I chose to make a strategic retreat from opinion pieces and journalism, not out of fear of bullies, but out of disgust with the tenor of public discourse. I did not want to work in a place of subliminal violence. I did not like the terms of the discussion; I did not want to keep flying at the sticky mess of misogynist backlash. I had other, less despair-inducing work to do.

But 2012 was also a watershed year for feminism, filled with potential turning points. Moments when it seemed that we were teetering on the edge of change.

Every so often the spectacle factory that passes for political media in this country has a major glitch. There's a horrible scream as the machinery grinds to a halt, the steam lifts, and for a few moments we get a glimpse of the belts and gears of manipulation: the illusion at work.

These moments operate in a similar way to financial crises. They come regularly, irrefutably, and in the midst of one they can be very cathartic and slightly terrifying – it can seem like the world is about to end. But the system always manages to pick itself up. These crises ultimately allow the machinery to reset itself, to carry on with new parameters, incorporating new narratives, appropriating new desires and colonising new markets. In the same way that the global financial crisis made way for the Occupy movement, these media glitches give us an opportunity to make the invisible machinery of power visible. Scales can fall from eyes. #destroythejoint was one such moment.

I read the hashtag twenty times before I heard Jones's comments. Like most of my news these days, it came filtered through Twitter, and I guessed what had happened, triangulating it from the various reactions of people and organisations to whom I choose to listen: expressions of humour, outrage, protest and defence. I actually think this is a pretty good way to get the news – more on that later. But the reaction to Jones far outweighed the import of his remarks. Let's say it was a feeling in need of a phrase, an idea whose time for expression had come.

Seeing other women struggle and speak has made it clear this problem is more than just a current of resentful men. It's a systemic problem with the way media is structured, the role it plays in our political culture.

Women *are* destroying the joint, insofar as that joint is patriarchy, and it was our intention all along. Those awful misogynist groans are the death throes of patriarchal media. That this misogyny also plays out in parliament – that it is inextricably linked not just to politicians' talk but to the agenda and outcomes of our political system – is a sign of the severe entanglement of politics and media in this country: not so much a marriage as a co-dependent relationship between parasites.

The media no longer bears the weight of holding politics accountable. The idea of the fourth estate is dead. If there was any doubt of this, 2012 has made it clear.

The Slipper 'scandal' was a textbook example of manufactured spectacle with no basis in fact. The prime minister was under constant questioning, the Opposition relying on the repetition of doubt to destabilise her credibility. 'Throw enough mud and some will stick' is a rule learned from newsrooms. While this mudfight grubbies our parliament, 30 people on Nauru are on hunger strike and the Doha round of climate talks fails to make the urgent changes needed for climate stability. Our political-media complex – and let's not kid ourselves that they are separate entities – is too busy attempting to manufacture an illusion to bother with the real.

Our political institutions have absorbed the tactics of the tabloids like a giant sanitary product. The domination of spin, with political image managers intricately connected with media personnel, sees our political discussion operate as a subset of the corporate media, and our politicians strategising in much the same way as the media does: asking how do we push and prod and suck up the desires and frustrations of the electorate, transforming them into something that articulates the will of the powerful. It manufactures not just consent, but dissent and outrage and doubt, in a ceaseless production line of images.

When the machinery jams, these interests become starkly visible. Jones's comments were one such moment, articulating the real fear of patriarchal institutions that feminism may be gaining ground. Julia Gillard's misogyny speech was another instance, cutting through the dominant mode of image manufacture and speaking almost authentically about a real phenomenon. It took a dreadful personal slur against her late father to make this happen. After two years of 'don't mention the misogyny', with our PM presumably advised not to appear like a whingeing feminist, her savage dressing-down of Abbott went viral in large part because of its cathartic quality. It mattered because it came after two years of frustrating spin.

This was Gillard's moment, and it is likely to be all she will be remembered for. But the mainstream media turned a wilfully blind eye to the story. The machinery went on grinding, her detractors in the press relentlessly focused on Peter Slipper's resignation as speaker. Many people were surprised to find that something we found so compelling, something we liked, linked to and shared, talked about with our coworkers and showed to our children, went so wilfully unmentioned in the newspapers. There was a gaping crack between the political reality we saw, and the story the media was constructing. That gap was as much of a political moment as the speech itself.

Perhaps reality is the wrong word to use. Politics as it is played in the institutions of Australian democracy is not about reality, but about a war of images and stories. Politicians vie for human sympathies in a popularity contest that is often a grab for the nastiest attack, since antipathies are so much easier to manufacture. In this context, women are always at a disadvantage; women in politics are shredded by a culture that finds their very presence in leadership roles abhorrent. As in the media, they are asked to justify that presence over and over again.

Our first female PM's appointment and subsequent election seemed to be the answer to a twofold promise made to feminists long ago. A promise that we could reach the top; and a promise that when we got there, things would change. Gillard's refusal to be drawn on gender for the first two years of her prime ministership had feminists holding our breath, but it was understandable. Any successful woman is challenged by questions about the source of her exceptional status.

Even after almost 70 years of women representatives in the Commonwealth Parliament, the participation of women is still exceptional, painted as a surprising new phenomenon to which the system has not yet adjusted (but 'we' are making room for 'them' – 'they' should be grateful). With a female PM and female speaker, there is ample opportunity for the discourse to change direction. Trouble is, there are other forces at work.

Just as more female CEOs will not suddenly bring about the end of capitalism, more women at the top doesn't shift the structure of our politics, nor of our political discourse, which is channelled through corporate interests.

Adding more women's voices in the media will not change the structure of our media, either. They go some way to changing the narrative, and they certainly give other women better access; in large part that increased access is what brings about the backlash. But the system is sicker than that. It is not enough just to get inside the machinery. We need more radical strategies to change its direction, and to dredge this cesspool politics in which so much vitriol thrives.

Fortunately, old, centralised media is dying an undignified death. If 2012 was a year of new feminisms, it was also the year that trust in media broke down completely. Between phone hacking, Wikileaks, huge corporate mergers and radical sackings, the interests of large media organisations became clear. The days of protected white men sitting in an office or a talkback station in Sydney or Melbourne and speaking to people from the centre out, are gone. The agenda-setting authority of the opinionated white male voice is still omnipresent, but its authority is slowly being chipped away and redistributed.

#destroythejoint clearly showed that feminists on social media can hold those old media voices accountable. We're the ones who break that authority down. Now it becomes our task not to replace it, not to climb into the vacated seat of power, but to harness the capacity of social media to do more: to redistribute narrative power, the power of the image, and institutional power too. What this means for responsible media and responsible citizenship is an enormous challenge, and we need to take it far beyond the limits of hashtag feminism.

I don't want to burst the #destroythejoint bubble. In the struggle for a truly intelligent media, one that can hold our leaders accountable, one that is independent of corporate rule, such moments of – for want of a more polite term – calling people on their shit are rare. When they happen, they are exciting to us because so often we let sexism go unchallenged. This is as true in our homes and workplaces as it is in Parliament House. It isn't always convenient, polite or safe to speak up. Nobody wants to be the only person complaining. But it is utterly necessary.

Hashtag activism – that Facebook or Twitter pounce – can be very effective, and in that sense social media goes some way to replacing the accountability role that the mainstream media once, if only ideally, held. The new accountability is emergent, decentralised, social. The fourth estate is dead – long live the fifth. But what is its ultimate end? If we go into battle as keyboard warriors, then we choose to go on feeding energy to the dominant culture's spectacle factory. Every time we take up these cycles of outrage, old media learns it can retain its position by posting sexist crap as revenue-generating clickbait. Our cycles of outrage, frustration and boredom become a repetition of the mainstream pattern – a propaganda of distraction in voluntary miniature.

Social media has its problems, and certainly its fair share of bullies, but it also has enormous potential to form a new media structure, a new democratic culture of broad engagement. Social media offers a unique opportunity to shift not just the content, but the structure of our political discourse. We offer ourselves that opportunity, because social media is us, in all our multiplicity of concerns, perspectives, agendas, obsessions and flaws.

I might not get accurate, fact-checked stories of great depth in 140 characters. But reading the news as multiple filtered streams of information is an honest approximation of the layered agendas at work. The contradictions and contrasts become visible, the agendas and perspectives clear. This multi-layered media consumption is becoming the norm.

For example, I watched the US presidential debates with six tabs open in my browser: a live video feed from CNN, my Twitter timeline and a #debate timeline, the Salon fact-checking live blog, ABC News 24 for back-up video feed/commentary, and an unrelated article open just in case I got bored. My computer overheated, but I got a story in which there was an interplay and argument between many different voices. Quips about Mitt Romney's tiny face jostled for attention with speculation on Obama's policy subtext. This is my media diet: a process that I couldn't imagine even five years ago.

It's much better than the sources of news I grew up with: one newspaper in the morning, one or two TV bulletins in the evening. If you combined those sources you would assume there was a fairly steady consensus in Australian politics, even when they disagreed.

The six-tab approach requires some energy and political savvy to decipher, but I don't think that's necessarily about my level of education. At any rate the critical thinking tools I had to learn as a young feminist – check the context, look for an agenda, don't believe everything that you read – are becoming second nature to kids growing up with social media's layered realities. Bullshit still thrives, and rumour is rife, but an early grounding in media literacy means a generation of people who will doubt first impressions, who will not settle for single-source news. This is a generation much, much harder to manipulate. A generation that expects it is being lied to. And eventually, a generation of feminists raised by feminists will find a way to hold our political system accountable for one of its greatest lies: the lie that we could expect full equality in our lifetimes.

Of course, some media needs to be quality controlled, fact-checked, and that is where paying for good longer form journalism and research-based stories comes into play. Increasingly I put my trust in crowd-, subscription-, or publicly funded entities that do not have a big business agenda. Entities like *New Matilda*, *Crikey*, *The Conversation*, and the ABC. Many other start-ups are joining them; many edited by fiercely intelligent women. These new media organisations are as likely to be run by activists as they are by old-school journalists. There are plenty of strong, intelligent feminist voices in the media if you know where to look. There is the will and the energy for more. But are we doing enough to change the structure of image manufacture that has infiltrated our democracy?

Pouncing on Jones, or Bolt, or any other professional shit-stirrer, is satisfying in the moment, but it does little to take their power away. There's a strong argument that it gives them more. Holding people and organisations accountable for defamatory statements goes some way to shifting a culture of attacks on women, sure, but it is not social change. When it helps, it mainly helps those in public life, predominantly white, well-educated women – the ones who know to expect better than we are getting. At worst, it adds fuel to the bigots' fire.

The media is the only way that most people engage with the business of Australian democracy. We might have meetings at our workplaces, confer with our voluntary organisations, participate in local council if we can bear the bureaucracy. But none of this filters up. At best we will march or write a letter or phone an MP when something extreme enrages us. Most of us rely almost entirely on the translation of our political process through media filters. We are dangerously dependent on mainstream media narratives and agendas.

I say it's time to cut out the middle man.

No amount of progressive opinion pieces will change the problematic structure of our media landscape. Feminism needs to move beyond the limits of adding to or interrogating public discourse. We now have the technological capacity and the intelligence to deconstruct *and rebuild* our media landscape in our own democratic, participatory image. We have shown we are able to exert influence on the political-media sphere, to hold power accountable, and even to set the agenda – but now we need to find better ways to make the decisions.

#destroythejoint and similar hashtag activism has enormous potential for feminists, if we are willing to defend more than middle-class white women, or our place in patriarchal institutions. If we are ready to take the battle out of the corridors of institutional power for the privileged few, and into the real world, of which social media is now a central part.

Direct democracy is not about strengthening consultation – who among us has ever been consulted about anything anyway? – but about returning agency to communities. Now that we have built online communities of identity, of interest, of inclination, we should be demanding more. Our politics is crippled by the fact that so many decisions are made by demographic guesswork, by the manipulation of media polls. This ignores something fundamental about society: it is made up of *people who talk to each other.* We are talking to each other at a greater rate than ever before. Instead of the hashtag producing the media producing the lobbying producing the decision, which is an eminently corruptible chain, why not imagine an online discussion around climate targets, or asylum seeker policy, or media regulation in which we made our own decisions? Because what social media offers, if we know what we are capable of, is the deliberative processes longed for in radical democratic theory for decades, theory that was and is the best offer feminism ever made. Now that we have the technology, isn't it time we started putting it to use?

We are only seeing the earliest intimations of the potential of discursive accountability for democratic engagement. What begins as a hashtag could become an experiment in reviving our democratic culture and offering some engagement beyond the polling booth and the evening news. Unfortunately, there is very little such experimentation going on (the new Institute for Democracy and Human Rights is a notable exception). But I think feminists, with our intergenerational wealth of autonomous organising experience, are the ones to make this happen.

I know it is possible that social media – particularly given its ownership and surveillance – is just another extension of corporate control. But even if that's its direction, I don't think we're there yet. More to the point, I don't want this generation of feminists to be remembered as another missed opportunity.

What feminism lost in the 1980s with its co-option into individualist capitalist ambition – its obsession with its own reflection in the glass ceiling – was a chance to dismantle the structures of power. Perhaps we lost our nerve; perhaps capitalism was stronger than us. Those images of success seemed real to us then, just as the 'have it all' promises seem real now, as they will continue to seem real next time, and the time after that. But they are capitalist mirages, generated by the spectacle factory that passes for politics. We are a generation of feminists raised by feminists. We know all about broken promises.

Fighting for access to corporate media or justice within its bounds is fighting for a cleaner prison cell. Public life can be much more than the production of scandalous images.

Next time that machinery grinds to a halt, next time the production line of image and outrage is jammed by a hashtag, maybe we'll have learned something new about its workings. Let's see if we can find a bigger spanner to throw. Aim at the machine and not the mirage. Maybe we'll surprise ourselves with what we're capable of.

Love Tweets

Yvette Vignando

Dear @Twitter – a big thankyou for existing & for connecting me with some of the world's most witty, generous and clever people.

It was 25 Sep 2008, I was sceptical about you at first, @Twitter – you seemed full of disconnected, incomplete phrases … like this one.

About to launch @happychild, I knew I needed to join your community, but I had no understanding of your potential.

At a glance, @Twitter, it looked hard to join your social whirl – a zippy line of conversations, statements & natural disaster warnings.

Where and how to jump in? I watched you, @Twitter, like a wallflower at a community dance.

I recall very early tweets with @KerriSackville,

@LanaHirschowitz, @SarahPietrzak & @kylie_ladd.

They were women who shared a similar sense of humour, didn't mind being interrupted & were also navigating the @Twitter waters – perfect.

I soon realised you were a valuable resource, @Twitter – especially when used for good and not evil, and you are also fun.

Forget all that nonsense about IRL – @Twitter, you ARE part of real life; you are conversation & that's precious.

And you're also the source of #destroythejoint and many other entertaining, life-saving and informative memes & #hashtags.

I explain @Twitter to my non-tweeting friends as 2 things: a child's dot-to-dot drawing & an endless dinner party with flexible table sizes.

When I first tweet someone on @Twitter, I know just one or two things about them – the first few numbers of their dot-to-dot drawing.

I join the dots, getting to know their sense of humour, values, blogs, politics, taste in food & I 'meet' their @Twitter followers.

Very occasionally, I decide I don't like the @Twitter drawing that's emerging, so I simply stop joining the dots.

But most dot-to-dot drawings emerge from @Twitter for me as brilliant, engaging and ever-evolving works of art.

And the @Twitter dinner party thing? Well it's a party where you can come & go, make one comment or more, bring food …

… bring drink, show family photos, interrupt, leave suddenly, engage in debate or just tweavesdrop – seems ideal to me.

I also love how @Twitter forces me to be concise, challenging me to be brief, articulate & to get my point across efficiently.

So thank you, @Twitter, you rock. You've educated & entertained me, & given me new friends & a voice – I deeply value it all. Yxxx

PS Although @2GB_AlanJones is an inactive @Twitter account (and that's probably a good thing for @2GB873) …

… I choose to imagine @2GB_AlanJones is going to read my tweets

Dear @2GB_AlanJones … 'Sticks and stones may break my bones but names will never hurt me.' As you know, that's not true –

Powerful words can #destroythejoint. @2GB_AlanJones, my pop fought in WWII – he used #destroythejoint as a joke – never to disempower women.

Pop believed in my innate abilities. Your #destroythejoint comments are not old-fashioned, @2GB_AlanJones, they are out of line.

Aust ratified the UN Convention on Elimination of All Forms of Discrimination Against Women in 1983

@2GB_AlanJones: 187+nations endorse it.

Your comments won't change the world @2GB_AlanJones …

But 1000s of tweets & RTs laughing at the inanity of singling out women as #destroyingthejoint remind misogynists they're a minority.

It's your right, @2GB_AlanJones, to state your opinion, but you're wrong to label #jointdestroyers bullies.

#destroythejoint & #destroyingthejoint trended on Twitter @2GB_AlanJones, because opinions opposing yours are very popular.

#destroythejoint wasn't 'cyberbullying' & calling advertisers wasn't 'cyberterrorism' @2GB_AlanJones – it's democracy.[1, 2]

@2GB_AlanJones, you've urged people to write to politicians, call radio stations & act on issues they feel strongly about. Good for you.

But shame on you, @2GB_AlanJones, for losing enthusiasm when people used @Twitter to hold your comments up for scrutiny.

@2GB_AlanJones, when I read your on-air #destroythejoint comments, I laughed. They were, frankly, idiotic.

I know you won't mind my using pejorative terms, @2GB_AlanJones, because you're fond of them too, aren't you?

@2GB_AlanJones, I laughed, and social media was laughing alongside me, about women #destroyingthejoint.

@2GB_AlanJones, you and I would disagree on whether women as a 'category' are less suitable leaders than men, but …

… I wonder, @2GB_AlanJones, if you would ever be prepared to substantiate such an idiotic suggestion?

Leaving politics aside, @2GB_AlanJones, why don't you take a look at a small sample of some of the great women building our country?

Try following @LizBroderick, Sex Discrimination Commissioner, and @JanOwenAM, CEO of the Foundation for Young Australians, @2GB_AlanJones.

Or, @2GB_AlanJones, check out @yassmin_a, founder of Youth Without Borders, or @SuzanneSaveCEO, head of Save the Children Australia.

I'm guessing you won't take up my suggestions, @2GB_AlanJones, and that's OK – but it's also OK for tweeps to challenge yours.

It was bad timing, @2GB_AlanJones, making your idiotic comment before your much more offensive one about @JuliaGillard's late father.

Because, @2GB_AlanJones, you made your destroy-the-joint bed and then had to lie in it.

To be fair, @2GB_AlanJones, you said those comments were 'unacceptable' and you 'got it wrong'. I'd have chosen other words.

And I was going to leave it at that, @2GB_AlanJones, but I can't quite...

Because in your admission of wrongdoing, you said if 'you are going to eat crow you should eat it while it's hot'.[3]

And @2GB_AlanJones, you said that sometimes you just have to 'man up'...

I don't like that 'man up' term either, because words are powerful. Women are equally capable of facing the music when they should.

The 'crow' is still hot, @2GB_AlanJones – the question is, will you really eat it?

Will you educate yourself about the equal worth of men and women in our society, @2GB_AlanJones?

Imagine if you tweeted me, @2GB_AlanJones?

Your third tweet since you joined @Twitter on 13/11/09 could be to @yvettevignando, LOL.[4]

I wouldn't ask you to 'man up', @2GB_AlanJones, I'd just ask you to read & reflect on #destroythejoint & perhaps join the conversation –

It's a bit like talkback, @2GB_AlanJones – but we all get to talk.

I realise those last few tweets are a little over-optimistic, @2GB_AlanJones, so...

I'm thankful @2GB_AlanJones that few of your audience are

the younger generation simply because you can't destroy their joint with your words

I'm grateful to you, @2GB_AlanJones, & the #jointdestroyers for the opportunity to be creative & use #destroythejoint for charity.

In the spirit of humour, @2GB_AlanJones, I set up http://www.cafepress.com/destroythejoint. So far, over $850 has been raised for charity.

Please excuse me, @2GB-AlanJones, while I tweet with the future drivers of this country.

Dear Young Aussies, I love your energy and I love how you have embraced social media. I believe in your power to drive social change.

More of you are on Facebook than Twitter, but I'm sure many of you will join @Twitter as you enter your mid-twenties.

Young Aussies, you're steadily increasing your consumption of social media & using the internet more as your source of entertainment & news [5]

But you need to be discerning media consumers. You aren't listening to @2GB_AlanJones but you might listen to @kyle_sandilands.

One of Australia's strengths is that freedom of speech is valued; I hope you Young Aussies treasure & protect that human right.

For example, IMO, many of the comments made daily by @kyle_sandilands and @2GB_AlanJones are distasteful and offensive.

But those broadcasters remain free to be provocative, as long as they don't break laws or infringe on other people's rights.

At the same time, Young Aussies, you have to be vigilant about participating in public conversation about rights and your community.

Social media is in your hands. #destroythejoint showed you how individuals can publish opinions & how they gather momentum.

#destroythejoint was a great example of how we can never be disenfranchised, if we use social media wisely.

Because we can use humour & creativity; we can use social media for social change & ensure that Young Aussies participate.

@Twitter is just one of many ways Young Aussies can make their voices heard – please never underestimate the potential of this platform. Y x

PS Speaking of humour, I think you might want to follow @janecaro. She's pretty funny sometimes.

Dear @janecaro, I love how #destroythejoint fell out of your phone and into the Twitterverse one night.

@janecaro When you asked for 'new ways of "destroying the joint" being a woman & all' you'd no intention of being the catalyst for activism.

One funny suggestion from you, @janecaro, & women & men were off. I loved the hilarity of using that nonsensical phrase from @2GB_AlanJones.

Thanks, @janecaro, for humour and your quick wit. And it was simply a lot of fun, @janecaro, until it became more serious …

… because @2GB_AlanJones's comments that disrespected the PM's grief were the metaphorical last straw.

Thanks, @janecaro, for showing that public profiles can be used for good & that social media belongs in a 21stC democracy.

I deeply respect your use of humour, @janecaro, to disarm & to make a point as pointed as it can get. #destroythejoint did that so well.

So thank you, @janecaro, and all the @jointdestroyer tweeps for reminding people that social media is now part of IRL.

We are all capable of looking after and building this 'joint' we call Australia.

Best wishes to all, @yvettevignando.

The Writing on the Walls

Jenna Price

It's 1979. My record is clean and I plan to keep it that way. A good Jewish girl doesn't want too much trouble.

My boyfriend is driving the getaway car, a brown Morris 1100. He is dressed in tan cords and his shoes have pink laces. I'm in what I remember as overalls. We have the spray cans in the back.

We're in Sydney's central business district. Time and time again over two hours, he pulls up and I hop out. He keeps the engine running.

Equality is a myth. Women are better.

Huge red letters, dripping. The aerosol technique left a lot to be desired yet the politics were heartfelt.

We don't know it, but we are destroying the joint. My mother would have been horrified.

More than three decades after that foolish graffiti was sprayed across as many of Sydney's office buildings as two not-quite-teen not-quite-bandits could possibly cover, the first half of that sentence is still true. And if women are better (and I'd happily settle for equal), you would be hard-pressed to discover that in public conversation. Or even in mainstream media.

We women are the exception. We are the single mothers, the mothers-of-three, we are barren and we are sluts. We ask for it. We accuse falsely. We are so hot. Or not. We are menopausal bints. We want to work part time while our husbands, partners, toil in the fields. And we want to work part time and have power.

Oh. My. God. Is there no end to our infamy?

We are the examples.

At the end of 1981, Vic Carroll, the then editor-in-chief of the *Sydney Morning Herald*, and Alan Peterson, the then news editor, interviewed me for one of a dozen cadetships at the *Sydney Morning Herald*. Mr Carroll asked me why I wanted to be a journalist. I said I enjoyed being nosy. Where did I see myself in ten years' time? To Vic Carroll I said, I want your job. I was so ambitious, I could barely sit.

But I was also a secret feminist, wearing heels and lipstick so no one would find out on this particular occasion. I would not mention that I'd volunteered at an abortion referral clinic in Brisbane in the 1970s. I would definitely not mention the graffiti. And if they asked whether I wanted children, I would lie.

What I didn't say to these two men about to make a decision on my future was this: your newspaper needs to run stories about what women are actually doing now. Your newspaper needs to start writing stories about family life because that is what we all do when we are not closing very important business deals. Your newspaper needs to stop calling single girls 'Miss', because it makes unmarried women sound as though they've missed out on something. And your newspaper needs to describe women in the way it describes men. Or the other way around.

Geez, I could just about have that conversation now.

And yeah, maybe I should have been transparent. But all those other feminists I was dying to work with, I bet they'd never confessed feminism to anyone either, just on the cusp of being offered the best job in the world. *In the world.* If I wanted to change the world – or as I think of it now, destroy the joint – I'd better do it in the dark and not let anyone know what I was thinking.

Making women more central to the discussion was a job almost every woman journalist seized: sainted Yvonne Preston, Margo Kingston, Adele Horin, Pamela Bone, Gay Alcorn, Anne Summers, Wendy Bacon. It wasn't all that easy. Men still controlled news rooms and news lists, still do today, and those women who make it to the job of editor in mainstream news don't last long.

Looking back now, it seems foolish to have got quite so worked up about the case for 'Ms'. But we argued even more passionately the case for reporting on 'women's issues', welfare and equal pay and equal opportunity and childcare and health and education and reproductive rights. Childbirth! Breastfeeding! For every page one story, there were a thousand others that never made it anywhere. I remember one occasion when it became apparent that the fees for long day childcare were about to go up 25%. I wrote the story on the Monday and then carefully shepherded it through the week until a sympathetic page one editor – with a feminist wife and two small children – splashed it on page one.

In 1985, the year the first of our three children was born, the newspaper where I worked started a features page focused on those same women's issues. The editor at the time was Eric Beecher. He was no secret feminist, he just assumed that the Agenda page would run stories about family life and that readers would be fascinated. They were. Photos of caesarean childbirth on page one of the *SMH*. Photos of families, straight and gay. Stories about schools and health and relationships. Not treated as if they were 'women's issues' but as if the stories would grip everyone. Some of it was what we now call campaigning journalism: the right for parents to understand fully what all those HSC scores meant; the right for gay families to have access to health insurance in the same cost structure as traditional families; the right of access to reproductive health technologies; the right of women to leave abusive husbands, to get help – sure we had no-fault divorce, but the personal freedom to understand that you could protect yourself, that was a different thing.

And stories which said it was OK to be the kind of woman you wanted to be. The right to understand that there really was no man shortage. Be very bloody picky and don't let some manipulated numbers make you think you are on the shelf. Stories about women who didn't want kids. Not that they couldn't have them: they actually didn't want to exercise their, ahem, god-given roles as women.

Over eight years, the Agenda team of editors and reporters put those stories on page one and inside, time and time again. My god, it felt so good.

These days, of course, there is not the same shortage of women on the front page, no shortage of women used as sources for stories. Those line tamers, the people who look at row after row of data, who do detailed audience analyses, have the figures on what stories get good hits. Sex. Celebrity. Kittens. Celebrity sex kittens are very clickable.

It's kind of sweet – and sour – that 30-odd years after starting in the Best Job In The World, I still count women's bylines, still check how many of those bylines made it to page one, still consider whether the woman who is the talent in the story is eye candy or IQ candy. Australian research shows that women get just 30% of newspaper bylines on page one; and it's the same percentage if you look at main focus of news stories. About blokes, by blokes.

And then, I sit there and wonder why it is that when we announce Australia Day honours, the percentage of women who win them is low and the stories are mostly about the male winners.

I'm still counting and circling, with a blue pen, every honours day.

Yet those women who are in those stories, who are writing those stories, are not as safe as men were when they marked out their front page territories. Those women are not as … maybe the word is *venerated*.

Maybe it is the shift from the inert media of the 1980s, where you could just talk to the audience and they would consume but be silent. Now we media workers interact with our audiences minutely. Now the boundaries between subject and audience are blurred. Those boundaries brought distance and respect. And they are gone. I don't miss the boundaries, the safety nets, but they did protect me.

The women in those stories and the women who write

those stories, they must fend off the trolls and the baiters by themselves. When some media organisations say they use moderators to look at comments before they are posted, I wonder what it is they moderate. And I wonder if the editors who employ those moderators have a thought for us. Would they do it differently if their daughters were subject to the hate email? Women are the bait. We gather their audience, we make their market.

There is an excellent book, *What Money Can't Buy*, by the professor of government at Harvard University, Michael Sandel, and there's a bit where he says: 'Markets leave their mark.' It's a book I want to force editors to read, those who run the newsrooms of the moment, where it's rush, rush and a flood of comments. In the marketplace you make, with your moderators who barely moderate, the mark we leave on women reporters and journalists, on any woman who dares to write or speak an unpopular view, is that they are ugly and old; criminals, sluts and whores.

Did you know, editors, that women now say to ourselves and to our women friends, 'Never read the comments'?

Of course, reporters in the past had the odd strange hatemail, silly phone calls, the occasional heavy breather. I fondly remember the lunatic who would ring me at home every single time I wrote a story about abortion. Two o'clock in the morning, there he'd be, a senile Labrador. It amused me to imagine I could hear his spittle dripping through the holes of his handset.

Now, the nut jobs are out there en masse, attacking the subjects of stories: those women out there on page one, on the homepage, on television, and on radio.

In some respects that explosion of fruitloops and worse, the crazy ones who have no limits, who taunt women to the edge of suicide, have done us all a favour. That seething hatred of mothers, lesbians, girls in dresses short and long, equal pay activists, the barren, women who want to work even though they have children, mobilised us, mobilises us still.

It's hard to recall this clearly now but in the days just before Alan Jones made his comments about women destroying the joint, the prime minister gave a long press conference, about 70 minutes all up. Prime Minister Gillard had had enough of a public smear campaign against her, partly generated by underemployed cartoonist Larry Pickering. She was mad as hell. And she said to gathered reporters: 'I'm answering your questions now. If you've got questions, put 'em.'[1]

Bang. Gillard took aim at what she called the misogynists and nut jobs out there on the internet posting about her conduct seventeen years ago while working as an industrial lawyer.

Bang. The prime minister said claims in the national newspaper *The Australian* about her involvement in setting up a questionable trust fund had been fuelled by internet rumours.

Bang. The claims were 'false and highly defamatory', but they came from a 'sexist smear campaign' that started on the internet, and that should have been ignored by the mainstream media.

This is what resonated with women. No matter your politics, she was pointing out, if you interact on the internet as a woman, you are putting yourself out there to be scorned, humiliated, belittled, harassed.

There were claims and counterclaims around her conduct and PM Gillard made this quite clear: there was a new kind of news cycle – the recycling of material found on the internet, which feeds, unchecked and unverified, into the mainstream media and back again on an endless loop. And not even unverified: stuff just made up.

I remember watching, transfixed, the prime minister's press conference. A quote popped into my head: 'You always remember the first time someone calls you ugly on the internet. I imagine – although it hasn't happened to me – you always remember the first time someone threatens to rape you, or kill you, or urinate on you.'[2]

When I looked it up, later, just to check who'd said it, it turned out to be Helen Lewis, deputy editor of *New Statesman*. It stuck in my head without an author because it could have been any of us saying it. A contemporary proverb.

And Prime Minister Gillard continued. She said that there was no end in sight to this kind of behaviour.

'In terms of people who continue to circulate these claims, will the misogynists and the nut jobs on the internet continue to circulate them? Yes, they will.'

Can we do anything about it?

Misha Ketchell, managing editor of *The Conversation*, an online publication where academics write in plain English for a broad audience, rang me just a couple of hours after that press conference. He asked me to write about the prime minister's proposition of nut jobs and misogynists. I wanted to oblige, in his unreasonably short time frame, to see if I could unravel some of the problem, at least in my own mind.

That meant chasing Martha Nussbaum, Ernst Freund Distinguished Professor of Law and Ethics at the University of Chicago, who had spent a lot of time examining the boundaries of morality and decency and written *The Offensive Internet*. She had little time, we could correspond by email or not at all. I explained the misogynist/nut job scenario and I'd barely pressed send before the return email came.

In Nussbaum's view, the prime minister was accurate about those who post on the internet: '[Your prime minister] is entirely correct.'

She wasn't familiar with the word nut job. Most Chicagoans aren't. But she did send me a horrifying story of what happened on one particular website: '[It] existed only to defame named female law students by writing pornographic stories about them, and [while it] caused serious employment problems for them, [it] was protected from all liability. Only the posters were liable, and they were anonymous.'

That wouldn't happen here. Would it?

Australians have different legal protections from US citizens. After all, courts here have used mechanisms to make internet hosts cough up the IP addresses of those who post. But professor of journalism and social media at Griffith University and author of *Blogging and Tweeting without Getting Sued*, Mark Pearson, says it's rare: 'Thousands of messages are unactioned [i.e. people don't take legal action] every day.' And embedded in those thousands – thousands – of messages is unadorned hatred of women.

Tory Maguire, editor of *The Punch*, remembers the night of the Rudd spill. Maguire, a meticulous comment moderator, was up late into the night, sifting through the river of posts that were coming in. 'The comments coming in, the torrents of misogyny, were quite shocking to me,' she says.

For me, this kind of misogyny is not new. As I said earlier, reporters and columnists have always had hate mail, the kind where the authors are so keen to preserve anonymity they've cut out individual letters and then pasted them on to sheets of paper. I've had those, threatening to kill me. Or: 'I know where you live.' But the effort of putting together anonymous origami hate mail is great, it takes time and so there was never much of it.

These days though, the comments flood my email inbox, my Facebook messages, my Twitter feed. It can be just as anonymous and takes far less effort.

A column I wrote about the obscene funding of Olympic athletes on the ABC's commentary website, *The Drum*, had this response in my Facebook inbox from someone called James 'Bolo' Gurr: 'All you achieved in your article is making yourself come across an angry, bitter and ignorant woman who either had no dreams, or never came close to achieving them … for people as ignorant as yourself, here is your cut: a middle finger from, I can almost guarantee, every athlete who dared to be great. Throw in a laugh at [your] profile picture, I can see why you are angry at the world.'

What I didn't realise was how much worse it was going to get for me. While I was researching my nut jobs article, as I affectionately called it, I rang Greg Jericho, the blogger and author, who documented internet misogyny in his book *The*

Rise of the Fifth Estate. Jericho has a word for what happens when women put themselves out there and the dark forces of the internet descend. For example, when Mia Freedman couldn't gear herself up to thoroughly endorse Cadel Evans's victory in the Tour de France, she was the victim of what Jericho calls a 'pile-on'. Freedman said she was 'called every name you can think of – bitch, dog, skank, mole [sic], idiot, loser, cow, slut'.

The comment explosion might, Jericho says, just be a response to what he describes as political correctness – what men can no longer say in public, they say anonymously on the internet. Jericho, of course, is not endorsing it, just observing it. When you interact with him on Twitter, he is one of the most courteous correspondents you could find. He had no solutions to the pile-on and neither did women who've been nutting out the sexism problem for decades, such as Eva Cox and Ann Curthoys. Cox, a feminist writer and social analyst, said it's not internet misogyny, it's just misogyny. Curthoys, ARC Professorial Fellow at the University of Sydney, agreed. Her view was that the anonymity of the internet just allows misogyny to be expressed more freely. That mid-August press conference of the prime minister's? It articulated what women thought and felt – but it did something else. It set the scene for what was to come. We women were pissed off. We wanted payback. We were sick to death of the hatred.

In the chronology, it's the prime ministerial press conference and then the Alan Jones 'women are destroying the joint' comments. Then comes the 2012 AFL Grand Final.

As often as I can, I settle down to watch the footy. Watching football – any kind – is a cure for everything, really, and I'm multicultural in my sporting passion. League, rugby, what used to be called soccer. I watched it all with my dad and with my brother; now with husband and, occasionally, my son, although he thinks I get too excited. But my favourite is probably the Australian football league. If the Swans are playing.

So it was on that Saturday, late afternoon, 29 September.

Cheer, cheer, the red and the white.

The 2012 AFL Grand Final is memorable to me for two reasons: Swans were slammed in the third quarter but blew the Hawks away in the final term (I was leaping around my living room like a lunatic). And that day, a story was published that would push already furious Australian feminists into overdrive.

At 7.42pm that Grand Final day, when I was still transfixed by anything Swans-related on the telly, a tiny little tweet made its way from the fingers of a man I didn't know. The first response to that tweet said #boom. I can't remember who sent that tweet now, but #boom? Well, that turned out to be an understatement.

The tweeter's name was Brenden Wood. He works as a news producer for Southern Cross Austereo, does podcasts for James Manning's *MediaWeek*. And he's a first grade NRL referee. Every Saturday night, he buys an early edition of the *Sunday Telegraph* and tweets out the front page. Depending on what it says, he might put the #auspol hashtag on it. That's where everyone who likes to tweet about politics congregates. It's also the place you go if you are in the mood to make a bit of trouble: *Lesbian finance minister makes baby with wife. #auspol*

That night Wood pulled up at his local servo, filled up, looked at page one and tweeted a photo of it.

For decades, what makes news has been decided by those in news conferences. These people have senior positions in news organisations. They are usually men and have not had a good track record in being sensitive to – or even interested in – women's issues. Of course, it was a bloke, Neil Breen, who advertised the Jones story on page one of the *Sunday Telegraph*. And a woman, Claire Harvey, who thought her publication should cover the young branches of each political party in the first place.

By the time Brenden Wood tweeted the *Sunday Telegraph* front page, which pointed to a story about Alan Jones on page five, there were already thousands of us in a different kind of news conference. One in which we believed that women's issues were more than the cost of boob jobs. And more than discovering whether pink is the new black. And – even more – discovering where you could plug the man shortage.

That news conference was called facebook.com/destroythejoint.

That particular Facebook page was set up on 2 September – immediately after the Alan Jones 'destroy the joint' comments and a week or so after the prime minister's press conference – by Sally McManus, the secretary of the Australian Services Union in New South Wales and the Australian Capital Territory. There's one I created too, somewhere in the Facebook archives, which implored everyone *in the universe* to storm 2GB. They were both set up within a day or so of Alan Jones's initial impossibly sexist comments naming Prime Minister Julia Gillard, Sydney Lord Mayor Clover Moore and Christine Nixon, former chief commissioner of Victoria Police, as leading destroyers of the joint.

The main aim of these Facebook pages was to highlight incidents of sexism although, yes, I confess, the prospect of storming 2GB did make me feel kind of Wonder Womanly. Sally's idea made a ton more sense. When she sent out invitations to join her page, I joined quick-smart. I'd met her just once at a feminist conference two years earlier.

In the intervening weeks between Mr Jones's foolish remarks and his cruel comments at a young Liberal function in Sydney that the prime minister's father had died of shame – as reported in the *Sunday Telegraph* – the Destroyers aggregated a community that had had enough. Not just of Alan Jones, but of the entire tone of the national conversation around women.

In six weeks, the page gained 20 000 followers, a reach on some days of nearly 300 000 and had a broader network (what Facebook calls Friends of Fans) of more than three million people. These days, that broader network is four million and growing. Advertisers pay to get that kind of influence. On social media it is free.

On the Sunday morning after the AFL Grand Final, when Mr Jones was hauled back from his Southern Highlands hobby farm in order to apologise for his calculated remarks, there were thousands of Australians who'd had enough. One senior 2GB staffer said he knew that after the first five minutes of Mr Jones's press conference, the station had a disaster on its hands. Twitter thought so too. It tossed up between hashtagging Jones's Sunday morning press conference #alanjonesapology or #alanjonesnonapology. Users chose the latter.

But there were already hundreds of us using a hashtag devised a month before, #destroythejoint, created by fellow Destroyer Jill Tomlinson. As we all sat glued to the telly, we watched a man who couldn't say sorry. And who kept on not saying sorry until the very end when a reporter asked him if he thought advertisers would stay with the program.

Mr Jones replied: 'You don't see them queuing up to leave.'

The folks at Sack Alan Jones, which ran the change.org petition calling for the removal of the broadcaster, put pressure on advertisers. At Destroy the Joint we listened to every broadcast, kept lists, encouraged members to contact advertisers, kept members up to date. Every day, Destroyers listened in and found contact details. Even when the ads were taken off the program, then off the digital stream, we at DtJ published the latest list every morning. El Gibbs and Amanda McNulty were the joint chief wranglers of a big team. Kept the pressure on. And were utterly methodical in making sure the voices of 20 000 Destroyers were heard. We were and are quite, quite separate from Sack Alan Jones. Personally, I don't think people should lose their jobs unless they really resist training and education; and more education and training.

Our efforts were belittled by almost everyone in mainstream media. *It won't work. It won't last more than a week. It won't have any serious impact.* But the same media outlets were putting women on the homepage of every major Australian news site. Those women on those homepages were not dressed in bikinis. These were stories about feminists taking action. You could have knocked me over with a feather. When I was still that secret feminist, in the early 1980s, this was what I hoped would happen. The fact that we had help from someone who would never want to help a feminist, someone who thinks women destroy the joint, made it even more pleasurable.

A month later, long after the first advertisers withdrew their sponsorship because of social media pressure (and emails, texts and phone calls are definitely part of social media), long after a furious Mr Jones railed against car manufacturer Mercedes for backing right away from him at the speed of an SLK, Tim Burrowes of media news site *Mumbrella* admitted he'd underestimated the impact of the campaign: 'Reputationally, definitely, it will have a long-term effect. The commercial impact may not be that great but people will remember what went on.' But Burrowes did say that he thought the Sack Alan Jones campaign had a bigger impact than Destroy the Joint, which he claimed was limited to social media.

Months later, Sack Alan Jones is barely active. Destroy the Joint has thousands of members and growing, has posts every day, and runs regular successful campaigns.

Every day, Destroyers post. What comes up under the DtJ avatar is a collaborative decision – calls to action, reminders of events, successes we've had, an unending stream of information on the rights of girls and women. Now fewer and fewer people are saying we won't last. It's been months already and, in February 2013, we tried one more strategy in dealing with sexism and misogyny. A few weeks before, in the DtJ Facebook private messages, a woman wrote to us begging for help. She had escaped from years of domestic violence and now had an apprehended violence order against her former partner. She had asked Telstra for a silent number (that means neither listed nor available on caller ID) but a call centre operator had told her that there would be a charge. Maybe $36 doesn't seem like much to you – but at that point, for our Destroyer, that seemed like an unsurmountable sum.

We wrote to Telstra's CEO on her behalf – but made the point that we wanted those rules to change for all victims of domestic violence with apprehended violence orders. It took weeks. There were certainly days when I lost my patience and I know that other admins felt the same way. But on a Thursday in February, Valentine's Day, Telstra agreed it would fix the issue for the woman who had come to us. Now management has also agreed to fix it for everyone.

The aim of Destroy the Joint is to call out sexism and misogyny, although we didn't distinguish between mainstream and social media. And I'd estimate that the 40 or so women and men who administer or moderate the Destroy the Joint Facebook page as a social service are united in trying to make Australia and Australians less sexist (we aren't united about much else because our politics vary widely and wildly).

Is there someone in charge of Destroy the Joint? At this moment, there are eight of us who administer the page and our story is featured in 'Birth of a Movement' elsewhere in this book: eight of us, 34 other moderators, over 25 000 members and rising.

Are there members of any political parties in this group? I find it best to employ the Don't Ask, Don't Tell strategy. It doesn't bother me either way. The cause is bigger than any party – much, much bigger. Where people work, what union they belong to or even if they don't belong to one, whether they belong to a party: it amazes me that some people think those elements might somehow discredit what Destroy the Joint does. If one more person asks if I am aligned to the ALP, I may tow them out to sea in a chaff bag – but like the good feminist I am, I would also provide a safety vest and swimming lessons.

When Destroy the Joint was successful in urging advertisers to boycott the Alan Jones program because of his utterly appalling comments, for one reason or another, I ended up speaking on behalf of the thousands of women and men who make up Destroy the Joint, traipsing from one interview to another, sixteen separate interviews on the first day that no advertising ran on 2GB. When 2GB radio announcer Chris Smith's producer rang me to do a phoner with him, something my University of Technology Sydney work colleague Eurydice Aroney had said months before stuck in my head: 'Never do phoners. Go in to the studio and do the interview.' It took Smith's producer an hour to get back to me to accept my kind offer of an in-person conversation. Fortunately, a Destroyer, Emily Mayo, came with me, otherwise I would have been vomiting solo. She also lent me lip gloss when I found, to my horror, that 2GB had invited all the television networks to film the interview. Lip gloss that I used on both my lips and my hair.

Here's something I've never told anyone. On the second day of the period when there was no advertising on Alan Jones, I received a phone call from Macquarie Radio Network's managing director, Robert Loewenthal (MRN owns 2GB). He said that the boycott was hurting small business. Honestly, my little heart went out to those small businesses, so I told Mr Loewenthal that if he could get me a transcript of everything his presenters had said about me and my fellow Destroyers, then we would be really happy to meet them. I never heard back.

Didn't ever contact me or Destroy the Joint again.

Of course, we knew there would be payback. I discovered some things about myself that day, and in the days to come. When I get stressed, very stressed, small things bug me. Who knew I could be so offended at the use of the word 'Mrs' before my name. Perhaps I had to focus on the small things so what seemed like the big things didn't make me go out of my mind.

I could cope when my Facebook profile was hacked and when my photo was stolen and appended with tags from *bitch* to *cunt* to *whore*. In some ways, this brought me closer to my adult children who were on the lookout: *Lock this down, Mum. Don't answer that, Mum. Mum, DO NOT READ YOUR EMAILS today.* I'm good in cyberterritory but they are millennials; they are better.

It was unnerving that the university where I work received letters calling for me to be sacked, and I hated the thought that the kind women who make up the admin team at University of Technology Sydney had to deal with the crazies. The violent emails and the deranged mail, complete with loopy handwriting, ended up as part of a police investigation. Police were busy with us – Sally McManus also had death threats and hate mail. That's what happens when you get those on hate radio spraying bile, using your names over and over again.

It's not my nature to praise crazily but the Destroyers were there with me. They are not family, and not really friends either, but sisters-in-arms. None of what we are all trying to do, none of this would be doable without sisters-in-arms.

And of course, it was utterly ridiculous to be called a dyke, a lesbian and a menopausal old bint. As if any of those labels is an insult. And very misleading, as even a cursory examination of my life would reveal that my beloved spouse is a man. Also, FYI, I'm postmenopausal.

All of this was water off an old chook's back.

What killed me? What nearly killed me was the voice message left on my work phone, early on in the piece:

'I'm going to find your daughters and rape them.'

I rang the boy in the tan cords and pink shoelaces to tell him about the voice message. He was, as ever, calm, and ready to drive the getaway car.

Now it's misogynists who won't get away anymore. We are on to you. Everyone is on to you. Even, finally, the commercial media.

In 2011, between 31 August and 4 November, Factiva, a database of news articles, features and websites, found 125 mentions of sexism in all the Australian media it cites. A year later, from the day that Mr Jones said women were destroying the joint, through the time when it was reported that he said the PM's father had died of shame, to 4 November 2012 – same length of time – that number measured well over a thousand.

All those stories in all those papers, on all those websites, on radio, on television, they frighten the blokes. Now, when men utter the phrase 'not sexist but' I rejoice. I know what they are about to say is inevitably stupid and demeaning to women but that phrase just makes me smile. They've had to account for themselves, had to think about what it might mean to constantly degrade and belittle women they know and women they don't know. They have had to position themselves.

As we Destroyers have positioned ourselves.

I love that Destroy the Joint put feminism on the front page – all the news outlets, all the sites, all the channels, all the stations – but even better than the front page, I love that Destroy the Joint puts feminism, puts women, on the front foot.

Now we are reconstructing the joint.

Parts of this contribution have appeared in my Canberra Times *columns,* The Drum, The Conversation, *the* Walkley Magazine *and my own rants to husband, family, friends, Destroyers. They are all very patient.*

We Appointed a Woman Executive Once ... It Didn't Work Out

Catherine Fox

While Alan Jones's radio program may not be regular listening for business executives, the publicity from his Destroy the Joint comments had an eerie familiarity for many women in the corporate world.

It's the sentiment they recognised – the unstated but potent belief that femaleness and failure go hand in hand when it comes to senior jobs. The message from countless performance reviews and interviews, meetings and tea-room chat. The media reports that attribute any mistake by a woman in business leadership to her gender, and crucifies her for everything from clothes to hair colour. The stark lack of women who have braved the parapet.

And like women from all around Australia, they had the same gut reaction: anger and exasperation built up from years of being insulted, bullied, fobbed off or told to calm down.

Not too long ago it was unremarkable to hear senior management explain away the lack of women in their ranks in exactly these terms: as a failure of female nerve, talent and ambition, borne out by the sad failures littering the pathway to the top. Of course, we have tried women in these jobs, they would tell me, but it wasn't a success. Not too far below the surface of these fatuous comments – how many women, for example, did they actually appoint or even encourage? – was the unspoken but bedrock belief that women can't really manage or lead, particularly if they have a family. They don't want the roles, and if they happen to get them, disaster soon follows.

Destroying the joint? The very cogs of international commerce – and those smoothly run consensual board meetings – were at threat, many of the great and the good in the executive suite seemed to think. The sheer irony that one gender was overwhelmingly running the joint as the global financial crisis unfolded has been commented on but is rarely held up as proof of male inadequacy. Women are tarred with the same brush when it comes to leadership failure but not men, it seems.

It's all a question of perspective. But absurd negative generalisations about gender in the business world tend to apply to one sex more than the other. Would a man have been subjected to the same kind of vitriol faced by former Pacific Brands CEO Sue Morphett after she closed down several clothing factories in 2009? How could a woman do this, asked one media report. Stories about Gail Kelly often focus on her steely demeanour and her superwoman status to explain her lone role as head of a large listed company. But most examples occur behind closed doors, a combination of biased attitudes and systems that are then used to bolster a story about the fate that awaits those women who get too big for their boots. This idea is still so pervasive in business circles when gender is discussed that the name for the syndrome – the deficit model – is just another part of corporate-speak these days.

Where to start with the illogical thinking and the lack of evidence for these claims?

Certainly, women in business leadership roles are still so rare you'd be struggling to get a quorum. The gender composition of upper ranks has barely shifted in decades despite agitation. There are only twelve women CEOs and just 9.2% of executives in the ASX500 are women.[1] The glass ceiling may sound passé these days but it doesn't mean it's disappeared. Most business sectors have similar profiles when it comes to a gender breakdown: even where women outnumber men, the senior ranks are male dominated and the picture has barely changed at the top end for a decade or so.

In practice, this ridiculously small number of women business leaders means they have novelty value and are often scrutinised through a gender lense – not for what they do but the way they do it. Even if you accept women have a set of unique qualities that they alone bring to the table there is still no accepted norm for women as leaders. The result is a reliance on stereotypes, which means women executives are more likely to be held up to higher, 'caring' standards of behaviour than their male peers, for example. It's not as though men in leadership are entirely free from stereotypes either – research from the USA and Australia shows tall, good-looking men are far more likely to succeed in business than their plainer, shorter peers no matter what their talent quotient.

But why let pesky facts, such as the binders of research showing intelligence levels are not linked to physical appearance or gender, get in the way of some well-established and convenient scapegoating? Thus the business world has resisted changing the political – moribund traditional business structures and processes – and gone for the personal when it comes to a rationale for the male-dominated C suite.

Women, it is routinely asserted by business management, are the problem, and just need more confidence, backbone, rigour and ambition. They lack networking skills, emotional control and even, amazingly, problem-solving ability, according to an Australian study by Bain and Chief Executive Women in 2012. The research found men in senior jobs thought men were twice as good as women executives in this fairly essential skill, which came as a surprise to many CEW members. Women, we often hear, also basically hate each other and go out of their way to stab female colleagues in the back. And so on.

As a psychological package, this list of inadequacies (or just a failure to match up to a male stereotype, when you think about it) makes it a wonder the whole lot of us haven't been committed to a joint rather than just accused of destroying it.

This deficit of innate skills that gives women their destructive power is largely anecdotal and highly subjective. Even those 'female only' behavioural patterns that stand up to some scrutiny through research (less likely to ask for a pay rise or speak first in meetings, for example) probably simply reflect the dynamics of a minority group dealing with a more powerful cohort. In her excellent book *The Loudest Duck*, American feminist Laura Liswood explains why many qualities deemed particularly female – better empathy and listening skills, more collaborative – are classic behaviour for an 'out of power' group. So-called female intuition may be more about survival tactics in the face of dominant groups than an inherent gender trait. In fact, minority racial or subservient groups historically exhibited similar patterns, she points out.[2]

Australian psychologist Cordelia Fine, in her book *Delusions of Gender*, clinically dissects and debunks the idea that women's brains and thinking are vastly different and usually inferior to men's.[3] There is simply very little evidence of any major differences at all and certainly none showing significant female weaknesses. Women are just as capable of learning maths and science, although tell them often enough they are lousy at these areas and they start to perform poorly – it's called stereotype threat.

The focus on women's supposed failures as a rationale for their minuscule numbers at the top – and their joint-destroying tendencies if they get there – often comes at the expense of more rigour around the actual mechanics of who does the recruiting and promoting in business. Time and time again research shows that people with this role are much more likely to select candidates who look and sound like them. This was recently corroborated by a study in US law and consulting firms by Lauren Rivera, from Northwestern University's school of management, in a paper published in the *American Sociological Review*.

She found, after three years of laborious research, that 'similarity was the most common mechanism employers used to assess applicants at the job interview stage' and that 'hirers at these elite firms favour people like themselves'. One law firm partner told her that the company was 'looking for cultural compatibility, someone who will fit in'. More than half of the 120 people she interviewed rated the candidates' ability to fit in culturally above analytical thinking and communication skills.[4]

It's becoming clear from studies such as these that even those who believe women are joint destroyers may find it a struggle to continue blaming women, and women alone, for not getting up the ranks. Men are clearly still in charge and making most of the decisions about who gets ahead, gets the pay rise or who looks like they will fit in. Similarly it will be more and more difficult to rely on the old excuse that there are not enough qualified or experienced women for senior jobs. The evidence is simply irrefutable.

Women are in the workforce in ever increasing numbers with their participation increasing to 65.3% in 2011 from 60.3% in 2001.[5] More are staying in their paid jobs even when their children are small (under five years of age), with the number of women in this category increased from 61% to 66% between 2001 and 2009.[6] And they are pouring out of universities, with women awarded more than 60% of undergraduate degrees in Australia. About 66% of law school graduates are now women.[7]

But as Alan Jones's comments show, it will take more than the facts to change minds. Even the most optimistic advocates for better gender balance in workplaces have been surprised by how tenacious the old excuses are. Biased and blinkered, but with a strong incentive to see the business world remain in their 'safe' hands, this is a group that is clinging on to power with all their might.

Women in business aren't wrecking the joint, but they are increasingly holding it together while being paid and rewarded less than their male colleagues – the current average gender pay gap is 17.3%, the same as 25 years ago.[8] Even at this bargain price they are also expected to behave well and keep the team happy while bearing the brunt of the household and caring chores too. Their failure to climb the ladder isn't due to some mysterious female deficiency that opens the hobs of hell, but plain old-fashioned and lazy discrimination, which relies on familiar models of authority and equates difference with risk.

Alan Jones, of course, ticks all the boxes of this outdated pale, male and stale model. He, like many of the men running our corporates, is deeply uncomfortable with and affronted by the notion of women in charge. Even a scarce few at the top are to be feared for the inherent female ineptness they bring to the decision-making table. What an excellent reason for not letting them get anywhere near the pinnacle in the first place. Business as usual – no matter what.

Destroying the Joint in Twelve Easy Lessons

Catherine Deveny

LESSON NUMBER ONE

Beware of anyone using the words 'respect', 'traditional', 'family values', 'honour', 'unacceptable', 'morality', 'uncalled for', 'inappropriate', 'unnecessary' or 'offensive'.

Particularly beware of the word offensive.

It's code for 'Pipe down princess, back in your box'.

Offence is taken not given and more harm is created by taking offence than giving it.

Offence is subjective.

Just because you are offended does not mean you are right.

You're offended? Block, unfriend, change the channel, switch stations, turn the page, talk to someone else or call the wahmbulance. No one has the right not to be offended.

Offence is used as a mode of social control. Do not be oppressed by feeling you're supposed to lie down in some chalk outline drawn for you by a society that once upon a time would have burned you at the stake for such unladylike behaviour. Now all they can do is accuse you of transgressing some social norm constructed by the patriarchy to put you in your place. And the reason you have to be put or kept in your place is in order to fortify *their* place. And their place would be the one with disproportionate access to power, control, decisions, leisure, money and the ability to control women's bodies.

Watch language. Language is a friend to joint destroyers. Men have opinions, women are opinionated; men speak, women are outspoken; men are passionate, women rant; men have mouths, women are mouthy; and when was the last time you heard a man called feisty, bitter, sassy or shrill?

As Laurel Thatcher Ulrich said, *Well-behaved women seldom make history.*

LESSON NUMBER TWO

You are not imagining it. You are not overreacting. Women are not being listened to, and when they are heard they are told they are dominating. Not only are they discouraged from speaking, when a woman does speak and is not enabling the patriarchy, she is used as a human piñata to set an example for others and keep them in their place.

Twenty years ago I came across a cartoon, which I have kept in front of my desk ever since. And it is as true now as it was then.

The scene is a boardroom table. Five balding men in suits. One woman. The caption? 'That's an excellent suggestion, Miss Triggs. Perhaps one of the men here would like to make it.'

I've always said I wished there was a scientific way to prove that women who colour outside the lines cop a thousand times more vitriol and it's a thousand times more vicious. There is.

I appeared on *Q&A* in 2012 with Anglican archbishop,

Peter Jensen, and copped a bucket load. Academic, historian and writer Chrys Stevenson undertook a detailed study into that particular episode.

'According to comments on the *#qanda* Twitter stream, Deveny is: an ugly, extremist, stupid, unintelligent, idiotic, thoughtless, self-righteous, self-centred, self-absorbed, nasty, confused, frustrated, bitter, twisted, humourless, unfunny, unreasonable, unrespectable, disrespectful, sarcastic, mocking, catty, hateful, boorish, blustering, bullying bitch.

'What's more, she is: combative, vicious, shouty, loud-mouthed, arrogant, aggressive, angry, abrasive, childish, silly, garbled, inarticulate, intolerant, hypocritical, pathetic, disgraceful, disgusting, rude, condescending, bigoted, preachy, patronising, dogmatic, offensive, immoral, discriminatory and "up herself".'

According to the mob, which included everything from private messages to national broadsheet newspaper editorials, I 'rudely talked over fellow panellists, shouted, yelled and dominated the conversation'.

Stevenson not only found Peter Jensen spoke twice the amount of words as I did (his 36% to my 17%) but we both interjected/interrupted four times each, host Tony Jones only asked me to speak four times and asked Jensen eight, and I was asked twice to 'keep it brief'.

Stevenson consulted an audio engineer, who found my voice was at the same consistent level as the other panellists and the host. And she ascertained my contributions were argued eloquently, politely, passionately and tolerantly.

So what was my crime? Until recently, the Powers that Be, the Masters of the Universe, the Captains of Industry and The

Gatekeepers of Information have been able to control who says what, how and where. And it seems us Joint Destroyers are really taking the jam out of their donuts. Keep in mind they are *still the ones with the donuts.*

LESSON NUMBER THREE

Collect statistics. Keep statistics. Use statistics. Spread statistics.

The following week on *Q&A*, Liberal MP Christopher Pyne interrupted the host and other panellists a total of 34 times. And no one, apart from Chrys Stevenson, mentioned it, which is the only reason I know how many times the mincing poodle ejaculated into the show.

Dale Spender coined the 'one third rule' in her book *Man-Made Language.* As soon as women are: more than one third of the speakers at a conference; more than one third of the members of the house; more than a third of the authors on the review pages of the papers; or one-third the contribution to the conversations the impression is – for both genders – that women are taking over.[1]

In late 2012, Chrys Stevenson completed research into how women are represented in Australian newspapers and found, by her comprehensive byline count and content analysis, the percentage of stories written by women with women as the subject, quoting women or using women as an expert or in the photo is between 20% and 30%, similar to findings from separate investigations all over the world.[2]

LESSON NUMBER FOUR

It is about numbers. Be aware of the Gender Adjusted Representation Scale.

Here's part of a piece I wrote for International Women's Day for *The Age* newspaper in 2009:

> This newspaper itself reflects the ingrained gender imbalance in media. It's not uncommon for the opinion page to feature a middle-aged, middle-class white man in a suit, followed by another middle-aged, middle-class white man in a suit, followed by another middle-aged, middle-class white man in a suit, followed by Peter Costello. Of the last 69 opinion pieces published by *The Age* newspaper, only thirteen have been written by women. Four from *The New York Times*' Maureen Dowd and of the nine left, only three had opinions. The other six were just 'sharing experiences'. And why, with the ratio of 56 men's voices to every thirteen women's on the page, is it not called 'A Men's Page'. Because if you inverted the numbers and it was thirteen men's voices and 56 women's I can guarantee it would be called 'A Women's Page'.
>
> Time and time again when a typical television show, opinion page, radio station, court bench, ballot paper, board table, conference or church altar has a line-up of 80%, 90%, sometimes 100% middle-aged middle-class rich white straight (or acting), god-fearing (or pretending) men I ask people to subvert the gender balance to the same ratio of women. It then becomes clear that if this really were the case it would be considered a women's show, newspaper, radio station, political party, company board or religion. Why are people so blind and/or accepting and consequently enabling of such discrimination?

> If aliens came down they would take one look around and have no other choice but to make the assumption rich old white men were the smartest people on the planet.
>
> Panel shows are perfect microcosms of the accepted gender bias. The ratio is about one woman to every four men. The one female gives an illusion of equality, which shows how accustomed we are to the token nod. One woman, it seems, is equal to four men, if you're lucky. I call it the Gender Adjusted Representation Scale.

You call it when you see it, Destroyers.

LESSON NUMBER FIVE

Don't just look at numbers look at the culture.

The all-women morning show *The Circle* regularly gets mentioned when gender representation and women's voices come up. People hold it up like proof there is equality. Again, beware the Gender Adjusted Representation Scale.

OK, *The Circle.* One show. From the hundreds on air every week. On at nine in the morning. The female presenters were expected to be bubbly, pleasant and not at all controversial. The show was promoted as a little bit opinionated on a few inconsequential topics. But it was mostly, 'Later in the show we'll be talking to Marina Prior about her workout tips and after the break we will be cooking cupcakes for our audience of pregnant mummies!'

The Circle was promoted as smart and relevant, the Australian version of *The View.* Which it most certainly was not. But it was most certainly smarter and more relevant than any 'women's show' in Australian television history and its foreseeable future. *The Circle* was a good house in a bad street.

The show's marketing spin told us the women were smart, opinionated and funky. The reality is they are far, far more fabulous off screen. If the presenters were allowed to be themselves on screen the show would have been called 'provocative, controversial and offensive' and, let's face it, wouldn't have made it to air. The choice of women and the limited versions of themselves they were permitted to show is a perfect example of the Smurfette Principle and goes part of the way to illustrate how women are less likely to support each other professionally because of the perception there are only a few spots for a female and only certain kinds of women need apply.

If there is only one 'women's show' on television (which, if one show is described as a 'women's show' the rest are, therefore by default, 'men's shows'), why these women? And why this show? And even more curious, why when there is only one 'women's show' on Australian television, when one presenter goes on maternity leave (Gorgi Coghlan) they have a guy (Colin Lane) fill in?

So *The Circle* was axed late 2012 because, despite its popularity, Network Ten had to cut costs and it was cheaper axing the whole show than getting out of a six-figure contract with unpopular breakfast host Paul Henry. An amount they never would have agreed to pay a woman.

Having *The Circle* was fine. We just need as much variety and diversity of women's shows and women on television as men and 'men's' shows.

But don't just count the women, look at how they are expected to be, look, act and respond. How integral are they? I recently did a presentation on Women in Australian Television. The title was 'Garnish'. That's what women in Australian television are. Not the meal, the garnish.

LESSON NUMBER SIX

What all women should be encouraged to achieve is FOS: Fuck Off Status.

When I was nineteen, I met a woman called Patricia O'Donnell, who I am still buddies with today. O'Donnell is a successful restaurateur, businesswoman and all-round brilliant. When I was nineteen, she didn't know me. But I was sitting at the bar of her establishment, The Queenscliff, waiting for some of my mates, her staff. She said to me, apropos of nothing, 'You know what you need, young lady? You need Fuck Off Status. You need to have your house, and your business and be able to tell anyone you don't want to deal with to fuck off.'

Best advice I have ever been given. We need to encourage all women and girls to aim for Fuck Off Status – not to dream of just marrying a footballer – and encourage all men and boys to enable and support it.

Women are 50% of the population, do two thirds of the work, earn 10% of the money and own 1% of the land. What do we want? Fuck Off Status! When do we want it? Yesterday!

And while we are on tips, I am often asked what tip I would give women wanting to be successful, so here they are:

1. Stand for something.
2. Never have any more children or any larger mortgage than you could manage on your own.
3. Use public schools, public healthcare and support public housing and affordable, accessible, high-quality childcare and the rights of carers and the disabled. All these things enable number 4.
4. Aim for Fuck Off Status. I got mine in December 2012, aged 44, when I finally had a mortgage and a house title in my name alone.

LESSON NUMBER SEVEN

Don't buy the argument that women have less because we live in a meritocracy.

We don't. It's sexism.

I can't walk out my door without tripping over a woman who has something to say. And could – brilliantly, passionately, articulately and repetitively in print, on telly, or on the radio. No problem. Given the chance. Or lead in government, corporations, the law or religion. Given the chance. So why aren't they given the chance? Because they're women.

It's not a meritocracy. It's sexism.

LESSON NUMBER EIGHT

Don't placate strangers.

Women out alone attract a huge amount of unwanted attention. If there is a drunk, nutter, pissed bogan or sleaze, they will hassle the woman on her own. They will walk past the group of tradies, the bunch of old women, the couple on the bench, the young man in a suit, and pester or inflict themselves in ways that always appear to be random and spontaneous outbursts.

You don't have to feel sorry for any drunk, nutter, pissed bogan or sleaze, or be kind to them or nice to them or excuse them as pissed, old or deranged. You do not have to give directions to, have a conversation with, tell the time to anyone, if you don't want to. You do not have to be kind or nice if you don't want to. Why do we so often override our own unease only to find ourselves in a vulnerable position?

If a stranger walks up to you and wants the time, directions, spare change or a chat and you don't want to interact, don't.

You *never* have to engage with strangers. It's another form of harassment.

Here's how to avoid finding yourself involved in unwanted conversations, even those that begin harmlessly enough: always have a line up your sleeve to nip unwanted intrusions in the bud. Don't let them escalate into annoyances or into huge liberties taken by a stranger – or worse.

Here's mine: 'Sorry brother, I'm in a hurry.'

And just keep walking.

If they persist I just tell them in a deep and low voice to fuck off.

I know we shouldn't have to need to do this but how many times have we been nice and kind – our default setting – and finding ourselves in an unpleasant, annoying or unsafe place *with a total fucking stranger.*

I am very friendly. I see men as brothers not predators, I routinely give directions, spare change, a loan of my phone and even the odd dink to guys I don't know. But I use my instinct, which, like a muscle that gets flexed, is very strong.

Don't feel sorry for them if you don't want to. Let someone else. If these random guys really are losers, drunks or nutters, why are they always so able to contain their unwanted attention until when they come across a woman on her own?

Fuck that.

LESSON NUMBER NINE

Do not assume a woman in a powerful position is automatically a feminist.

And do not assume a male in a powerful position is necessarily a misogynist.

I have had as many males as females support me in my life and career and as many females as males be obstructive.

Where did the assumption come from that patriarchy advantages all men and disadvantages all women? Plenty of women – many of whom present themselves as champions of women, see editors of women's magazines for further examples – are actually utter chauvinists and sexist creeps bursting with internalised misogyny and being rewarded for it. These women have joined what they consider the only game in town in an attempt to get power, position and privilege.

According to Germaine Greer: 'The present condition of men is nothing to aspire to.' Greer also asserts feminism is the last great revolution and reckons the women's liberation movement hasn't even begun.

Patriarchy damages us all and the axis of evil – patriarchy, religion and the state – is being dismantled, dissolved and detonated at an unprecedented rate by the holy trinity of atheism, feminism and the internet. But the axis of evil is still putting up quite a fight. It was never going to be easy.

The truth is, there is not one feminism, but many feminisms. And just because you are pro women does not mean you are anti men. In fact, I think one of the main reasons I am a feminist is because I love boys and men so much and I have hated the way society has expected them to live, love and be. Feminism is not anti men. It's anti arseholes, misogynists, pricks, creeps, thugs and bigots.

LESSON NUMBER TEN

Clothes don't turn women and girls into sluts. We do.

The most dangerous place for a woman is in her own home and she is most likely to be injured, abused, raped or killed by a man she is related or married to.

Babies get raped; old ladies get raped; boys get raped; men get raped.

Clothes have nothing to do with it.

There is only one cause of rape. And that's rapists.

If anyone tells you not to walk the streets alone or take care or to be scared or to get a man to walk you to your car, you say, 'Don't tell me not to walk my streets. Tell people not to rape me.'

What is a slut? I'd like to get a series of pictures of a female from birth to old age: a baby, toddler, school girl, teenager, young adult, pregnant, with her children, mature, aging, each wearing the normal transition of clothing, and ask people to point to pictures in which she looks like a slut.

What is a slut? A woman who likes sex? Wants sex? Has had a lot of sex? Who dresses in short skirts, high heels and low-cut tops? What is the definition of *a lot*, *short*, *high* and *low*?

So what if we could all agree on the universal definition of the word slut and we could accurately identify a slut? So what? Women should be able to do what they want and expect not to be judged, shamed or punished for it. And if they are, they need to speak out.

Women have the right to wear what they want, enjoy sex and have sex with as many people as they like.

There is nothing wrong with being a slut. Whatever that is.

Clothes are not safe or unsafe. People are.

When I asked my boyfriend if he was coming to Slutwalk with me, he said, 'Sure. 'Cause you're not allowed to rape sluts either.' Couldn't have said it better myself.

BONUS LESSON

Listen to the gospel according to Gloria.

> The truth will set you free. But first, it will piss you off.
>
> *Gloria Steinem*

> Any woman who chooses to behave like a full human being should be warned that the armies of the status quo will treat her as something of a dirty joke. That's their natural and first weapon. She will need her sisterhood.
>
> *Gloria Steinem*

> I've yet to be on a campus where most women aren't worrying about some aspect of combining marriage, children and a career. I've yet to find one where many men were worrying about the same thing.
>
> *Gloria Steinem*

LESSON NUMBER ELEVEN

Loving your body exactly the way it is is an act of civil disobedience. Do it.

Sometimes I think people are most offended by my confidence in who I am and how I look. The fact I am not just happy but thrilled with who I am. The absence of self-deprecation and apology for not fitting into their idea of who I should be. And how I should feel about it.

Someone out there would kill to have your body. Seriously, they would. And the owner of the body that you would kill to have is probably as dissatisfied with their body as you are with yours. Same goes with level of health, amount of money, value of assets you own, troubles you have.

Let's stage a coup on dissatisfaction. The constant portrayal of the skinny, teenage, heterosexual, white and able body as the 'only' desirable body is *unfair and untrue*. I'm furious with people who manipulate the world to make women feel not good enough. And even more furious with women for being sucked in to it.

It's a choice between fear and love. A choice. You choose.

I watch people look at old photos of themselves and exclaim, 'I looked so slim, so young and so gorgeous! No wonder the fellas were gagging for me back then! I had no idea at the time how beautiful I was. I wished I'd known and just enjoyed it. I hated my ankles and thought my skin was too blotchy and my body too fat.'

Women seem to go through life always thinking they are not good enough. There will be a moment in our lives when we will be the prettiest, the thinnest and the happiest we'll ever be, but we will never know when it is.

I was in a supermarket once and I saw this skinny, withered old woman, maybe 75, flicking through a magazine called *Slimmers*, and I wanted to tap her on the shoulder and say, 'When are you going to stop worrying? You are good enough.'

I have only been thin twice in my life, when I had cancer and when I was suffering severe depression. It was awful. I would have paid a million bucks to be twenty kilos bigger and happier.

Stop buying those women's magazines – they are self-loathing manuals. Buy clothes you love, that you look and feel great in and surround yourself with images of diverse body shapes.

Loving your body is about feeling well and healthy.

LESSON NUMBER TWELVE

Who we should remember and how we should try to be remembered.

Hi Catherine,

I don't know if you remember the end of an International Women's Day lunch you did at Monash University a couple of years ago, where a young lady at the end asked a question about 'what was going to happen to me?' etc., etc. I was that chick. At the time I was working part time, trying to finish my thesis, and looking after a baby (and in a shit relationship) – the works. I actually wasn't even attending the lunch – technically I was working, handing out sandwiches.

You answered my question so well, quoting Winston Churchill ('when you find yourself in hell, just keep going'). And you gave me the flowers that were presented to you after giving your talk.

I thought I'd drop you a line to let you know I've just finished my PhD thesis – the bound copies are on my desk now. After I submit them to the Chair of Examiners I'll be well and truly done with it.

Thank you for those words that day. I did keep going and things did get better. Hope everything in your work and life is truly good.

I can't say how much that unexpected little interaction turned things around for me – I felt very brave that afternoon. I'm so happy I've had this opportunity to thank you.

Warmest wishes,

Jane.

I have written many of these letters myself and also received a few. When I met Patricia O'Donnell again for the first time twenty years after meeting her when I was nineteen, I opened my greeting with 'you probably don't remember me but you told me to aim for Fuck Off Status'.

She didn't remember me. But her words made such a huge impact on my life.

We have to support each other, brothers and sisters. Start where you are, do what you can, with what you have. When you don't know what to do, do anything.

Don't ask for your rights. That suggests someone else has the power to grant them.

Demand your rights.

Women Talk Back

Wendy Harmer

It was in Charlotte, North Carolina, in 2000 at an NRA convention that the late Charlton Heston held a rifle aloft and declared: 'From my cold, dead hands!'

We can well imagine, years later, in Sydney, New South Wales, Alan Jones hoisting a gilded microphone and uttering more from that infamous speech: 'When loss of liberty is looming, as it is now, the siren sounds first in freedom's vanguard!' (Cue Sting/traffic and weather, together/ads for security doors/ life insurance/superannuation/excavation equipment.)

Jones is one of those infamous old, white men who, as Heston did, fancies himself patrolling a beleaguered outpost of decency that must be defended with all his might and main. His steadfast morality is the last bulwark in an ideological war against a seething horde of infidels, single mothers, welfare cheats, dole bludgers, feminists, asylum seekers, greenies, loose women, deadbeat dads, communists, homosexuals, druggies and atheists all out to destroy the Australian Way of Life.

His mentality is in a permanent state of siege.

In his own epic imagination, he's an upstanding, heroic figure – like Heston's Moses, Ben Hur or El Cid. His destiny is to lead his persecuted tribe from the daily travails of Struggle Street to the Promised Land.

There's a corporate box full of such men from an older generation who have an iron grip on Australia's commercial AM radio airwaves and they have no intention, whatsoever, of letting go. They imagine and broadcast a mythical Australia built in their own image. It's an Australia from a bygone era that listeners recall with misty-eyed nostalgia. In that rear-vision mirror, women do not attain the office of prime minister, governor-general or lord mayor.

That's why Alan Jones was so apoplectic that women were destroying 'the joint'. He was incredulous and affronted to find that his joint – a rickety construction he and his cohorts have painstakingly assembled and constantly repaired for many, many years now – was being rocked by the enemy.

And this time they weren't the usual suspects – they were powerful women.

'I'm just waiting for them to die off,' said Susan Mitchell, author and former radio host on Sydney's 2GB and 2UE. Whether about Jones, or his audience, it's an oft-repeated sentiment. Is this style of radio – what former PM Paul Keating described back in 1994 as 'middle of the road fascism' – on its last legs?

Writing in *The Conversation* recently, Jennifer Rayner, doctoral candidate in Australian Politics at the Australian National University, argued that it is.

The high-water mark of influence for Jones was during the Howard years, she said, when, as prime minister, John Howard frequently availed himself of the gilt-edged welcome mat. Now that Prime Minister Gillard pointedly will not take Jones's calls after his appalling comment that her father must have 'died of shame', the jig is up.

'I think the prime minister and the government have decided Jones just doesn't matter that much anymore, and as a consequence, they're no longer prepared to slavishly cultivate him in the way that all sides of politics have done for the past fifteen years,' Rayner wrote.[1]

Of course, radio is all about ratings, and in crunching the numbers Rayner came up with this: 'In 2006, Jones commanded an average daily listenership of 185 000 people in the Sydney catchment area alone. Six years later in 2012 this number is down to 151 000. His is still the number one-rated show, but that's because there are fewer listening overall … '[2]

Jones knows his audience well. He's 71 and the overwhelming majority of his audience is made up of retirees over the age of 65.

However, even if Jones does hang up his headphones and his audience shuffles off, there are many more men who will take his place for a new generation, all keen to emulate the magic 'us v them' formula of faux outrage perfected by Jones and John Laws – the one that brought them unparalleled power and great riches.

Look at any commercial AM radio line-up across the nation and you see that it's an exclusive gathering of white, anglo males over 40. It's the proverbial Old Boys' Club, which decides who can join and makes all the rules. One where women are only admitted as auxiliary members.

I've been a radio broadcaster in Australia for some twenty years now and have heard every excuse under the sun from these gatekeepers as to why women are not fit to command a microphone on an AM talkback program – no matter that they do so on the ABC with aplomb and garner big ratings. Women don't like to hear other women's voices on the air. Women don't have enough opinions and they're not tough enough. When women argue, their voices sound strident and shrill. And when men get older they lose the upper range in their hearing and women's and children's voices become indistinct. (How convenient.)

As for the idea of two female co-hosts? A radio executive told me: 'You have to think of the male listener. I mean, you've been nagged all weekend by your wife and then you turn on the radio and you get nagged by *two* women.'

The excuses are risible, but, as evidenced by the above comments, the management of these radio stations don't need any excuses for not hiring female broadcasters. These airwaves are not 'public', although freely available to listeners. They are owned by private business interests that have negotiated their own set of operational guidelines as administered by the Australian Communications and Media Authority. And nowhere in those guidelines is there any exhortation to make the voices on commercial radio reflective of the diversity of modern Australian society. If you could call representing half the population a win for 'diversity'.

The market rules and as long as these broadcasters can find a sizeable audience, even in a dwindling market, they will have a job. Of course, the market rules until, shockingly, one day it doesn't, as many a media empire has found out to its cost.

In fact, even when the old formula of wall-to-wall conservative, opinionated men doesn't work, as it didn't with the ill-fated Melbourne Talk Radio (MTR) station last year, there is still a refusal to contemplate a change. After racking up a speculated $15 million in losses, broadcaster Steve Price said at MTR's closure that the venture had been 'very successful'.

Still the Old Boys' Club doesn't heed the siren sounding three-quarter time.

Last year there were excited whispers in radio circles that Sydney's floundering 2UE might challenge the paradigm and put women on air and so it was that, as a successful broadcaster, I was summoned and found myself sitting in front of the desk of a man in his 80s. He was pleased to hear that I was married and that my two children had been confirmed as Catholics.

'It's time we got women on the air,' he said. 'We just have to find you a co-host. A right-winger who can balance out your opinions.'

A few other women were considered – Prue MacSween and Tracey Spicer looked to be in the running for an afternoon shift – but look at the line-up now and it's Jason, Stuart, Paul, John, Tim, Mike, Andrew, George, Murray, Luke … you get the picture.

Sharina hosts a program called 'Psychic Encounters', offering her mystical insight, tarot and numerology abilities. The only other women on air are Tracey Spicer, as a 'guest co-host' and Sarah Morice, who co-costs the breakfast program with Ian 'Dicko' Dickson.

'They throw this line at you that women are not interested in listening to women, which is absolute crap. I still get emails from women who loved listening to me,' a disillusioned Prue MacSween said of a high-rating stint she had filling in for the late Stan Zemanek on 2UE some years ago. 'It's just an excuse they use to validate the fact they don't feel comfortable with opinionated women on radio.'

My on-air partner, Angela Catterns, with whom I broadcast on ABC 702 breakfast occasionally as the 'Early Girlies', was controversially sacked from talk station 2SM some years ago.

'I was told I was too intelligent for our audience and that women don't like listening to other women on radio,' she later said. Catterns subsequently went to ABC radio where she beat Jones in the ratings on the breakfast shift.

One of the most high-profile women in the land, with a legion of admirers, former *Women's Weekly* editor Deborah Thomas had a disappointing experience working at Sydney's 2GB. She tweeted: 'According to radio execs "women don't work on radio". Maybe because they don't give them a go or support. Unfounded nonsense.'

The 2013 Australian of the Year, Ita Buttrose, was similarly tried and rejected and, despite being one of the most influential women in the nation, cannot find a home for her considerable talents.

It's all too, too familiar. Most women in radio have a similar tale to tell.

Last year, the very popular Amanda Blair resigned from 5AA – at the time she was the only woman in any Australian city to have her own daytime show on an AM radio station, a list that includes 3AW, SEN, 4BC and 6PR.

Blair's assessment of her time at 5AA was frank: 'I have normal life where things are regulated and where people say decent things to each other and people are rewarded for being intelligent. And then I flip into radio world where sometimes you feel like you've got to play the role of Frances Farmer post-lobotomy to survive.'

She recalls asking a 5AA executive what he thought of her program.

'And he said, "Yeah, it's OK, but sometimes it's a bit girly." At that point my eyes actually rolled back into my head. And I said, "I'm just wondering if you tell the men that their shows are OK but sometimes they're a bit blokey? Considering I'm the only female, is that a bad thing?"

'I said, "Why do you think it's a bit girly?" And he said, "'Cause you talk about cooking sometimes." And I said, "What do you mean?" And he said, "Well, you were talking about MasterChef today." And I said, "Yeah, that's 'cause it's the highest-rating television show of all time."'

Although privately, younger male AM broadcasters will tell you they think women are eminently capable and should be on air, fact is, the few high-profile talk shifts available are jealously guarded. The men too are on notice in a brutal industry that demands instant success – there is no time to grow a new idea or an appreciative audience.

And so the medium remains caught in a time warp.

There is simply no way of knowing the size of the audience available if AM radio changed its tune. However, I'll wager that there's a tribe of female nomads who graduate from FM radio, don't care for the ABC, and would consider tuning in to AM if they could hear more about their lives and interests presented by feisty females.

In the world of FM radio, it's not a lot better.

There are more women on air, certainly – ARN's Mix stations in Sydney and Melbourne now have two female duos – Chrissie Swan and Jane Hall; Yumi Stynes and Sami Lukis – in what's been called 'a quiet revolution' by those in the industry. This is a welcome change, but those in management are few. And where it matters most in program and content direction? At time of writing there are only two in the nation, both in Adelaide – Irene Hulme at Nova 91.9 and Donna Puechmarin at SAFM 101.7. I find it absolutely baffling that women are not equally represented in managing the medium of FM radio. How can it be more suited to the talents of men?

Writing in *The Hoopla* last year, media consultant Scott Muller addressed this glaring inequity: 'With two dozen commercial FM stations across the five biggest markets, by now you'd think roughly half those stations might have Content/Program Directors who are women,' he wrote.

'There are no signs of progress being made in addressing the gender imbalance in the most significant on-air and off-air roles.

'To be clear: in roles that have the greatest impact on the audience – whether on-air or off-air, on AM or FM – it's not a slight imbalance, it's not even a major imbalance … there's just no semblance of balance.'[3]

Muller recalls a programming conference where the attendees were asked why this bias towards men persisted. 'One serious response was "but their [women's] brains work different". My jaw hit the ground and started dragging right alongside that person's knuckles,' he wrote.[4]

I don't intend to examine here the serial outrages and gaffes that have made Sydney's 2DAY FM presenters the subject of national and international headlines; however, the station has no women in its management structure and some conclusions may be drawn from that.

But I can give you one example of where a senior woman with influence at a radio station can make a difference.

During my time on air at 2DAYFM with the 'Morning Crew' – we won 84 out of 88 surveys in that eleven-year stint – we were asked by management to do some very silly stuff. One suggestion was that we give away a breast augmentation as a prize to a lucky listener. I said no. Although, given the consistent ratings garnered by Kyle Sandilands and Jackie O on 2DAY for just such demeaning stunts and pranks, maybe I was wrong.

More women in the radio industry does not mean the joint will be destroyed. It doesn't even mean it will lean to the left – the political views of females are just as diverse as those of males. Nor does it mean the joint will be suddenly transformed into a perfumed, worthy new home where everyone minds their manners.

But when women are consistently excluded from the joint, no one should be surprised that one day it just falls over in a splintering heap as female listeners look for alternatives.

For commercial AM radio certainly, that may come sooner than we think, as women take a jackhammer to its very foundations.

Speaking Truth to Power: Sexism, Outrage and the Public Consciousness

Paula McDonald and Abby Cathcart

> Because I am a woman, I must make unusual efforts to succeed. If I fail, no one will say, 'She doesn't have what it takes.' They will say, 'Women don't have what it takes.'
>
> *Clare Boothe Luce*

Alan Jones's now infamous comment that 'women are destroying the joint' sparked a flurry of observations and interpretations in the national and international media and in the blogosphere about the motivations and meanings of such a statement. The overriding tone of this commentary was outrage – how dare an influential figure like Jones state with such blatant and provocative hostility that women are at best unsuitable for leadership and at worst, damaging our public and private institutions? The answers, as we have seen, are likely to be complex, but an alternative question could also be posed. Why the outrage? Public male figures have, throughout history, made derogatory, demeaning and sexist remarks about women, and the material effects of gender inequality continue to be felt – consider the gender pay gap and glass ceiling phenomenon for starters. So why did this particular comment ignite such widespread indignation and anger?

The answer, we believe, is that the sexism in Jones's comment was entirely unconcealed. It crossed the proverbial line in the sand where a reinterpretation or alternative explanation could not be posed. Rarely is the deliberate, unashamed demeaning of women – *all* women, no less – heard in public parlance. Nor is it tolerated very well. Numerous social, cultural and economic shifts have influenced this trend towards fewer outward attacks on women, including the proscription of sex discrimination in law, public and organisational policies that promote gender equality, the increasing visibility of women in leadership positions, and an increasing intolerance by women, and some men, of demeaning gender-based put-downs in everyday conversation. The shift towards political correctness – or, to put a positive spin on the term, appropriate, respectful language that seeks to minimise social and institutional offence – has almost unquestionably modified blatantly sexist statements in public rhetoric.

However, the shift from deliberate to subtle sexist remarks has also allowed for those who use them to reinterpret their original meanings when it suits their purposes. Tony Abbott, for example, in his recent response to the decision to scale back the baby bonus payment after the first child, stated that the decision revealed a lack of experience within the government of raising children. The meaning of Abbott's comment was patently clear, but its oblique nature allowed him to later deny suggestions he was referring to the prime minister's lack of children.

Most would agree that an increasing intolerance of overtly sexist language is a step in the right direction. However, there remains a significant lack of understanding of covert sexism, or its behavioural counterpart, covert sex discrimination. Take workplace sexual harassment for instance, which has been the subject of a recent three-year study (see www.sexualharassmentinaustralia.org) by Paula McDonald from the Queensland University of Technology and Sara Charlesworth at the University of South Australia. A typical sexual harassment scenario is usually imagined as an individualised problem characterised by inappropriate, usually salacious workplace conduct, by a male boss towards a female subordinate.[1] This characterisation of sexual harassment as individualised and blatant (a 'bad apple'), minimises the link between sexual harassment and many of the hidden and sometimes normalised structures and practices in many organisational contexts. These structures and practices include sex segregation, particularly in male-dominated workplaces, and sexualised put-downs, such as 'stupid bitch', as well as non-sexual forms of harassment and discrimination.

The reality is that such structures and practices often underpin sexual harassment, sanctioning intimidating and unwanted sexualised conduct in a wide range of Australian workplaces. For the most part, however, sexual harassment itself and the gendered organisational structures and practices that allow it to flourish are divorced from one another. This constrains the development of shared community understandings of sexual harassment as varied, complex and dynamic. As we have suggested, when jokes, comments or other sexualised conduct that fall under the definition of sexual harassment are enacted in subtle ways, they also leave open the possibility that they were unintended, misconstrued, or meant to tease or entertain, but not offend. Such reinterpretation is highly effective in shutting down objections because it portrays the affronted person as overly sensitive or a whinger, as up-tight and without a sense of humour, or worse still, as a feminist – with all the extremism and marginwalisation that the term now implies. The ease with which subtle sexual and sex-based conduct can be reinterpreted by harassers as 'just a joke' or unintended is one of the primary reasons why sexual harassment is seriously underreported. Indeed, cases of sexual harassment read about in the media – recent examples include the David Jones and Peter Slipper cases – reflect a very small tip of a much larger iceberg of both overt and covert sexual harassment experienced in Australian workplaces that goes unacknowledged and unpunished. Ultimately, concealed sexism and sex discrimination powerfully constrains women's opportunities to achieve economic independence, opportunities for satisfying and meaningful work, and physical and psychological safety, in equal measure to men.

There is ample evidence to show that overt forms of sexism, sexual harassment, sex discrimination, and sexual and gender-based violence and assault continues to be experienced in Australian workplaces as well as in private spheres. The existence of covert sexism is also evident in empirical research but also more anecdotally where views held privately by individuals sometimes 'leak out' into social conversations.

Often exacerbated by alcohol, the weekend barbecue is a classic site for such revelations of sexist attitudes. In our own social circles we have heard all too often both men and women who work as managers in large companies and small businesses alike discussing the 'potential problem' of dealing with parental leave and turnover when deciding whether to recruit a woman of childbearing age. Yet these same individuals would never ask a woman (at least not any more) her fertility intentions in a job interview. Likewise, we have heard rationalisations from both women and men about the emotional suitability of mothers for childrearing; the attribution of few women in leadership positions to a lack of ambition; and how it was not surprising that a daughter was not good at maths because 'girls generally aren't'. Of course, these same individuals would also espouse general support for increasing the proportion of women on company boards, acknowledge the need for more opportunities for women to participate in male-dominated professions such as engineering and science, and oppose intimate and partner violence, without considering that the formerly mentioned stereotypes are closely connected to these forms of persistent gender inequality.

As we have argued, in the public realm at least, there has been a shift towards more subverted sexist attitudes and behaviours. This raises another important question that goes beyond why Jones *did* make the remark and that is why he thought he *could* make it? Clearly he believed that a large segment of his audience would agree with him – and this may well be true – but sexist and stereotypical views about women, much like racist or homophobic attitudes, are usually confined to the private realm and rarely voiced quite so openly, especially by such a public figure. We suggest that one of the key reasons that Jones chose to so openly attack women was because he believed that in doing so, he was not being overtly sexist, but rather was simply speaking truth to power. This phrase was first used in the title of an anti-fascist pamphlet published by the Quaker-affiliated Society of Friends in 1955.[2] The term has become increasingly seen as a way to describe challenges to powerful people and institutions. In a case that parallels the attack by Tony Abbott on Julia Gillard for being childless, in 2007 Barbara Boxer attacked Secretary of State Condoleezza Rice by drawing attention to the fact that Rice did not have children. Later, trying to defend her words, she claimed that she was simply 'speaking truth to power'. In effect, the argument is that people in power are fair game, and that the power*less*, or underdogs, can and should use any weapon in their armoury to challenge this power, including personal and sexist insults. The irony here, of course, is that Jones is himself powerful, wealthy and influential but that, despite all the evidence to the contrary, he sees women as holding all the cards and hence needed to speak truth to power. This may seem paradoxical but it may also be cause for optimism in the sense that if Jones, and others like him, feel threatened enough to spit openly hostile comments such as a suggestion that the prime minister be thrown out to sea in a chaff bag, then perhaps we are starting to see genuine change in the gender landscape.

In retrospect, it was hardly surprising that Jones's comment about women destroying the joint provoked widespread outrage, even among individuals who probably don't consider all that often how sexism plays out in their everyday lives. In that sense, Jones's comment, and many others that preceded it, may well have contributed to raising the public consciousness of the gender-based hostility that continues to bubble under the surface of so-called political correctness and which, if Jones's comment is anything to go by, may even be trending upward with women's increased visibility at the highest political levels. Importantly, however, Jones was not speaking truth to power, but rather revealing his blatant hatred of women who threaten historically entrenched notions of patriarchal control. The good news is that if men like Jones are feeling threatened to the extent that they feel the need to 'up the ante' from covert sexism to blatant hostility, this may reflect a real hope that Australian women have effected substantial and permanent change. However, for real change to continue and be sustained, there is also a dire need for widespread outrage about the subtle yet powerful forms of sexism that continue to permeate Australian workplaces and other institutions and which constrain women's and some men's opportunities and outcomes.

Sexist attitudes may hide under a shiny surface of professionalism, politeness or risk-aversion most of the time, but they are widespread, deeply held, sometimes even unconscious, and their effects are significant. It is only when we see widespread indignation about and intolerance of sexism in nuanced as well as unconcealed forms, will gender equality goals finally be realised.

There's Nothing Funny About Misogyny

Clementine Ford

Sometime towards the end of last year, a small comedy club in Richmond, Victoria, found itself at the centre of an online frenzy after a promotional poster for one of its events went viral on the internet.

The poster was designed to reflect a 1940s movie sensibility, and featured an animated man and woman locked in a physical battle. Underneath this image of domestic brutality was the event's title: 'There's Nothing Funny about Rape'. And beneath that were printed the names of the people engaged to deliver this so called comedy 'debate'. There were six of them, and they were all men.

It didn't take long for the internet to react. Images of the poster were quickly doing the rounds on Facebook and Twitter, the internet's most accessible meeting rooms for outrage and vigorous debate. The event's venue, Station 59, came under justifiable attack from people astonished that the concept had even been floated let alone given a green light. Members of newly minted online activist group Destroy the Joint were vehement in their belief that the event itself needed to be shut down. 'Destroyers', as they call themselves, were given the telephone number of the pub and encouraged to register their disapproval and protest. Later, it would emerge that some people (whether official Destroyers or not) had tracked down the venue's manager's home phone number, and continued to register their protest there.

It's always disappointing when places and communities that we'd assumed to be allies reveal themselves to be just as rife with sexism and misogyny. But when we talk about 'the joint', we have to remember that it's very, very big. And sometimes, we have to look inward as well as outward when it comes to destroying it. I was among those who saw that poster and felt sick over its implications. That the event itself seemed swamped in ignorance and privilege was one thing. That they had chosen to promote it using the kind of flippant language that can only stem from a culture that normalises rape is another. But their additional choice to employ imagery that diminished both the severity of the act and its impact on its victims reached an altogether baffling level of idiocy. Who were these men who thought it was their place to debate such issues and try to parse them through a comedic framework? And what kind of deeply entrenched privilege must one have that it wouldn't occur to them to book even one woman to redress that balance – particularly given the marginalisation women already experience in the comedy industry?

The responsibility for the event fell at the feet of one man: Kieran Butler, a comedian who runs the weekly Open Mic night at Station 59. In the days following the uproar, Butler went out of his way to address his critics. Oh, not in the way you might imagine. There was no contrition, no apology. He demonstrated very little in the way of trying to understand why it might have been hurtful for people to see the topic of rape humour bandied about with so little empathy, particularly as it came only a few months after the highly publicised rape and murder of Jill Meagher (a tragedy that led to 30 000 people marching down Sydney Road, Brunswick, in a peace march) and also on the back of endless gobsmacking commentary regarding rape and 'legitimacy' courtesy of the US Republican Party. No, after Station 59 decided to cancel the event, Butler responded by planning another debate for the following week while grumbling about 'censorship' and 'freedom of speech'. The debate this time would concern itself with *why* it wasn't inappropriate to host a rape debate in the first place – as if the potential offence caused to rape victims had been far outweighed by the grievous *actual* harm being done to freedom of speech. This was for democracy. It was for every comic who'd ever sat in his room and dreamed of one day telling a story on stage about sexual assault to raucous laughter, without having to deal with the panty-waisted politically correct brigade trying to stop him from walking all over the edge, *man*.

Trying to cover all his fox holes, Butler made sure to invite a woman to speak: twenty-year-old Genevieve Stewart. Stewart had been one of the most vocal opponents of the initial event, a fact Butler made sure to reiterate in his justification for prolonging what was fast becoming the most cringeworthy event in Melbourne comedy's history – a curious repetition, given that Butler also seemed manifestly interested in protecting the illusion of free speech. Later it emerged that he'd also been insistent that another opponent, Aleksia Barron, come down and 'defend [her] point of view'. She declined. It was as if Butler *hoped* to suddenly appear welcoming and inclusive, yet was too consumed by the childish feelings of censure to properly conceal the fact that what he really wanted was for Gen Stewart to justify her opposition and vindicate him as the edgy, dangerous comedian he fancied himself to be. Instead, what happened was this:

> Gen took the stage and announced that she was trying to explain why rape jokes normalise rape and harm rape survivors. She set out to talk about the topic of rape jokes generally then describe her own experience, but she was interrupted and heckled so many times during her general discussion she decided to go straight to the story of her own rape at age fifteen. Again, she was repeatedly interrupted. When she expressed her anger and hurt that comedians could listen to such stories and still heckle, she was heckled further.
>
> *Eyewitness account, from an article by Helen Smart in* Hoyden About Town[1]

A further account published in Melbourne's *The Age* revealed that Butler had grabbed the microphone from Stewart while she was in the middle of recounting her story. Prior to this, an audience member had yelled at her, 'Where's the joke?!' while another called her a 'faggot' on the way out.

So much for freedom of speech.

And yet despite the testimonies of women and men who felt it wildly inappropriate for comedians – and fledgling ones at that; Butler later defended his Open Mic nights as a place for comedians to 'fall and test out their material ... and see whether it will work'[2] – to use the ruse of a comedy debate to belittle and ignore the experiences of women like Stewart, Butler still seemed fixated on the idea that he was suffering from some kind of gross oppression. It almost beggars belief, but he revisited the issue *again* when he insisted on being given right of reply after Melbourne comedian Courtney Hocking wrote a critique of the entire affair in online newspaper *Crikey*. In it, he asserted himself as the kind of freewheeling comedy booker who provided a safe space for 'fledgling' comedians to perform with 'absolute freedom of speech, including a licence to offend, to play in dangerous territory'. He claimed the room was celebrated as a supportive and friendly space for comedians to try out new material and, amazingly, that it had 'stood for freedom to speak long before "Destroy the Joint" started boosting the ratings of Alan Jones'.[3]

In his defence, Butler focuses primarily on the rights of comedians to have access to safe spaces in which they can perform untested material. There is a notable level of irony in his refusal to see how the safety he values here is conceptual and theoretical – that it comes at the expense of actual safe spaces for women (and men) threatened by sexual assault and rape.

It's interesting, too, to note how quick Butler was to distance himself from the poster and its creator, Rob Caruana. Unlike Butler, Caruana took no time in issuing an apology on Station 59's Facebook page once he realised the distress that had been caused. And unlike Butler, Caruana was also quick to take sole responsibility for what can only be described as a massive conceptual fuck-up, despite the fact it was the former who was the organiser and therefore ultimately responsible.

But such scapegoating seems in keeping with Butler's conduct throughout the entire SNAFU. Butler defends what he calls 'the values of the room', but he dismisses the values of an empathetic culture in which rape victims are already too often the butt of people's suspicion let alone their jokes; he does not recognise that the comedic value of rape is so tenuous that only the most experienced of practitioners should be allowed near it. He declares the discussion 'topical' and one that 'comedians needed to have', without considering *how* those comedians may be having it and whether or not it might just be slightly hyperbolic to suggest it's the conversational equivalent of Stonewall. And crucially, he does all of this without once acknowledging that the weight of his defence is reserved for an industry populated by mostly men, maintaining their 'right' to make jokes about a horrific abuse inflicted against mostly women.

It's easy to imagine comedy as an area that values women, particularly if you frequent the kinds of rooms that feature Proudly Left Wing Comedians. But good comedy doesn't just make people laugh – it also exposes the foibles of society, poking fun at the least offensive of our idiosyncrasies and outright lampooning deeply held prejudices that diminish us as a people. It's for these reasons that I believe jokes about racism, sexism, war, death, poverty and yes, even rape, are not necessarily verboten in the world of comedy. Because well-constructed jokes about these topics can succeed by exposing the privilege of those who don't have to deal with them. They can also succeed by being cleverly explored by the people most likely to experience them. Effectively used, they can help 'destroy the joint' as we know it.

When black people tell jokes that ostensibly use racist ideology to make a punchline out of white privilege and racism, this is funny. When Sarah Silverman tells a joke about the confusion felt by a Jewish woman who's been raped by a doctor, this is funny. Because in both of these cases, the punchline is never the victimisation of one person at the hands of another. But when Daniel Tosh – a privileged white male comic who made a name for himself talking about other people's YouTube videos on a cable TV show – makes a joke about rape and then heckles someone upset by it by asking, 'Wouldn't it be funny if that girl got raped by like, five guys right now ... like right now?' that isn't funny. And I don't think we need to be holding ersatz 'debates' to explore the difference, when it's clear that their only reason for existing is so that subpar comedians can continue to confuse being lazy with being dangerous. To quote the late journalist Molly Ivins, 'Satire is traditionally the weapon of the powerless against the powerful ... When satire is aimed at the powerless, it is not only cruel – it is vulgar.'

Unfortunately, this kind of insidious sexism is all too common in industries and groups that would appear – on the surface at least – to be allies. It's experienced by women like Rebecca Watson, the founder of *Skepchick*, who are active in the atheist and sceptic community, who find themselves struggling to come to terms with the abhorrent sexism and misogyny they experience at the hands of fellow atheists and sceptics – people for whom the concept of rejecting religious and social oppression is core to their beliefs. It's experienced also by filmmakers like Anita Sarkeesian who, for the crime of pointing out the rampant sexism on display in the gaming world – a community ostensibly and stereotypically made up of people who don't adhere to society's expectations – was rewarded with rape threats, violent memes depicting her being beaten and/or raped, and ongoing anonymous harassment. And it's experienced by women within the socialist movement, who are told that their rapes and sexual assaults at the hands of leading members are not worthy of police investigation, and will not be properly addressed by the party.

It's worth remembering that our allies can sometimes also be our foes. The oppression that some men may experience in those arenas will never be quite the same as the oppression experienced by women, but they will imagine that it is and respond to any criticism accordingly. In Kieran Butler's *Crikey* defence, he criticised Destroy the Joint's methods of protest, comparing them unfavourably with his (according to him) more effective stance against Eddie McGuire and the Collingwood Football Club. Unlike DtJ, McGuire didn't try to 'silence any future criticism of the Collingwood board by people like us on the grounds he supported freedom of speech'. He goes on to cite further examples of his anarchist streak, such as his public satirisation of MICF director Susan Provan and an incident in which he 'ruffled feathers' at *The Scotsman*.

That Butler imagined his stand against the Collingwood Football Club's board to be at all similar to the stand taken by people against his rape debate is telling. To conflate evidence of that stand – plus his skit about Provan and some discord at a newspaper – with a protest against using rape as the basis of a comedic 'debate', and then using them as evidence that 'kicking up' is like, *his thing*, is an even bigger indicator of just how little he understood the issues at play in November 2012. As a writer, I've always suspected a good rule of thumb might be that if you don't understand the issues, you should be very wary about fighting to the death over your opinion of them.

Yet fight to the death these people do. It's a particular problem within left-wing politics, because the dominant misconception among its members is that their I-care-about-everyone-therefore-I-can't-be-oppressive credentials should give them greater leeway when it comes to individually fucking up. You see it with the Butlers of the world for whom the biggest issue facing them is whether or not their audiences will tolerate jokes about rape; the socially oppressed gamers who don't like being exposed as misogynist oppressors themselves; the atheists who speak loudly and loftily about truth and freedom and then tell their female colleagues that they 'just don't get it' or that they 'can't handle it'; the socialists who hail the rights of the workers and cover up a rape in their own ranks. If there's one thing common across all of these areas, it's that the oppression of women is always seen as secondary, not as important, not felt as deeply, a problematic distraction from the real issues. And the real issues, we're told, are what happens when the petty concerns of minorities trample over the rights of men to express themselves without being made to feel bad.

So yes, the joint is very, very big. And we must be vigilant about covering all sides of it. Sometimes our biggest enemies are the ones who think that, just because they loiter occasionally on the outside of the status quo, they lack the ability to oppress those who are forced to live there.

A Letter to Feminists from a Man Who Knows Better

Corinne Grant

Feminism is an embarrassment. What a lot of moaning over nothing! Haven't you got cakes to cook or clothes to mend? Haven't you got menfolk to look after? And where are all your babies? In childcare, I'll bet, learning how to snort heroin and be gay.

Feminism is the work of idle minds. If you found more constructive ways of filling your days (like putting on some make-up and doing your hair) then you wouldn't be sitting around getting your panties in a twist over stupid little things that don't concern you.

Oh boo hoo, men objectify women. Of course we do! It's fun! You're just jealous. If you didn't spend so much time complaining and instead concentrated on Jazzercise and learning to hula hoop, maybe we'd ogle you too.

Feminism is exactly the kind of first-world problem crap that annoys men like me. Things could be heaps worse for you women, therefore you have no right to complain about anything. Think of all those poor ladies in Afghanistan who wear blankets over their heads and never, ever get the chance to look pretty for their menfolk. How would you like that? We give you the chance to be pretty every day and what do you do? You throw it all away by refusing to look like Miranda Kerr.

And as much as you are damaging and upsetting men, you're doing yourselves a far worse injury. Women were happier before feminism. That is a fact. How do I know that to be true? Because before feminism, you never heard a lady complain about anything.

However, all is not lost. Even if you are one of those bra-burning, hairy feminazis, it's not too late to return to the happiness of a bygone era. You just have to knock out a few of those irritating misconceptions about the world and about lady rights – or whatever you call them – and you'll be all tickety-boo again.

Here's a checklist of criticisms you need to sort out so that men like me will like you.

FEMINISTS AREN'T LADYLIKE

Ugh. Women speaking their minds. Who asked you for your opinion in the first place? No one! You just open up your mouths and start yapping like you have a right to it. Half the time you don't even make any sense. Who the hell ever heard of going to university and getting some sort of PhD thingo just so you could talk about politics or the economy or something? I don't have any degrees, I don't even read the papers, but I know what I know and I know it's right because I know it. You bring in all your shitty facts and big words and honestly, it just turns me off. Shut your mouth and stare at me wide-eyed and impressed.

YOU COMPLAIN THAT YOU SHOULD GET PAID THE SAME AS MEN

Why? You're lucky we pay you at all! You turn up to work and blather on with a whole lot of crap about 'ethics in the workplace' and 'inclusive managerial styles' and 'providing a safe and nurturing workplace'. God on a stick, woman, whatever happened to the days when you were the secretary who made the rest of us cups of tea and bought our children birthday presents on our behalves, and we spent all day trying to see up your skirt?

You know why we don't pay you as well as we pay ourselves? Because you wreck everything. You've taken all the fun out of the workplace. I can't talk about women how I want to anymore, I can't treat women how I want and worst of all, I'm expected to show respect. I just want to get drunk at lunch and slap someone on the arse. If you're earning less than the blokes I employ, you've only got yourself to blame. You take away 20% of my freedom, I'll take away 20% of your wage.

STOP THINKING YOU CAN RUN STUFF

Women aren't made to lead anyone, unless it's up the garden path. Everybody knows that. There's never been a woman who has run anything, ever.

OK, there's never been a woman who has run anything successfully, ever.

OK, there's never been a woman I've wanted to root that has ever run anything successfully, ever.

Leadership is all about perception. You say Julia Gillard is leading the country, I say she's not. Who wins the argument? I do, because I'm a man. If I say she's useless, then she's useless. End of story. You can't argue with that because as soon as you do, I'll bring forth a million more men like me that will drown out your so-called 'voices of reason' with a lot of nonsensical yelling.

You can't win. And you know why? Because I have more power than you and I get to define reality. Ha ha ha! You can blather on all you like, you can get gaggles of other women and supporters of these women's 'rights' to back you up, you can start email and Facebook and Twitter campaigns, you can take over the online world but I'll still have the radio and the television and the newspapers. Ha ha ha! And the radio and the television and the newspapers will never die! Ha ha ha! Oh wait ...

YOU ARE TOO HAIRY

Shave your armpits, for god's sake. What are you, an animal? God gave women hair in order to take it off. It gives you something to do in between all the wet t-shirt competitions. And what is it with those women who shave their heads and not their underarms? Are you some kind of horrible reverso Barbie doll? I pull at your pits and it shortens on your head? It's against god and nature, it hurts my eyes and it frightens the shit out of me. If you don't want to look attractive for me, what do you want me for at all? Probably nothing. That is unnerving. Fix yourself up and stop giving me the heebie-jeebies.

FEMINISTS MAKE MEN FEEL BAD

I remember this hilarious time that I got on Facebook and told some whiny chick to pull her head in. I called her a dumb bitch and all my mates high-fived me for being hilarious. That was a good day! Until some other bloody woman told me I was being mean. What the hell? Don't try and make me feel bad when I'm having fun! No one likes to feel bad. I should be allowed to say and do whatever I like without anyone ever telling me not to. If that attitude was good enough for me when I was six, it's good enough now I'm a grown man. Boooooo, ladies! Booooo!

WOMEN JUST AREN'T THAT MUCH GOOD

I don't like watermelon, I look terrible in yellow, and I think women are evil and must be destroyed. Why is it all right to have an opinion on watermelon but not on chicks? It makes no sense! Lift your game, ladies, and stop taking it personally. Watermelon has pips in it and has a funny texture; women have vaginas and think they're people. If you can't see how that is exactly the same argument, then you are clearly stupid. And probably a woman.

WHICH BRINGS US TO YOUR OBSESSION WITH THE WORD *MISOGYNY*

Don't try and tell me that the definition of misogyny is 'nuanced' and has 'changed over time'. Pfft. As if words have ever changed their meaning. Misogyny means hatred of women pure and simple and for all you hysterical, vagina-riddled harridans out there, here's some news for you: hatred of women does not exist.

I mean, I don't like women all that much, I think they're idiots, but that's not the same thing as hating them. Women are inferior to men in every way except dinner cooking and miniskirt wearing. I don't think they deserve a place in society and I will do everything I can to keep them out, from paying them less, to harassing them in the workplace, to ridiculing and bullying them and yelling at them until they cry. That's not misogyny, it's just sensible. I'm keeping women out of the world because they don't belong there. That's for their own good as much as it is mine.

If you call me a misogynist just for thinking like that, then you are a man hater. You are trying to censor me and ruin me and take the world away from me. See? I told you women needed to be stopped.

FEMINISM IS ABOUT PITTING MEN AGAINST WOMEN AND STARTING A GENDER WAR

If women just kept their mouths shut, there'd be no need to fight with them. What's wrong with just sitting there looking pretty? No one fights with pretty. It's when you open your mouths and say something stupid like, 'Of course I understand percentages. I have a degree in mathematics,' that you irritate me. Who gave you that degree? Another woman? That sounds about bloody right, doesn't it. See how you annoy us? Just shut up!

Have you ever thought about the emotional toll all of this talking has on men? No wonder we suffer from more heart attacks than women. All those loud-mouthed ladies deliberately riling us up with their crap about equality and being respected. It's enough to make a gentleman's heart burst its poo-foo valve.

Men die because women are mean to them. Fact. If women weren't so bloody antagonistic, men would be immortal and then we wouldn't need women to re-populate the earth because we'd have it all to ourselves. Women force men into their graves so there is a biological need to keep their lady parts around to re-populate. We see through your cunning plan, ladies, we see it all!

FEMINISTS HAVE NO SENSE OF HUMOUR

When men make jokes at women's expense and women don't laugh, this means they're uptight. And probably frigid. The correct response to a manly man's joke about women being stupid, ugly, fat, dumb and so forth, is to giggle girlishly and then stare wistfully at his penis. You are not, I repeat not, supposed to roll your eyes or look at him disapprovingly. The joke wasn't *for* you, it was *about* you – you weren't a part of the conversation so stop trying to join in.

And don't, whatever you do, think you can do comedy yourself. What is it with women thinking they're funny? Men are funny. Women are sarcastic and bitchy. Why not stick to being adorable and leave the yuck-yucks up to us guys? Funny is when you girls do something sweet, like getting Panama and Pomeranian mixed up. Or when you laugh at our jokes. It's not when you make jokes about blokes like Alan Jones who are just trying to earn an honest living through speaking their minds.

Look, I know this is all a lot to take in, but it's for your own good.

Ladies, you are not destroying the joint, you are destroying yourselves. Every time you ridicule good men who just want ladies to be ladies, every time you bang on about women's rights, every time you demand respect, every time you argue back and insist that your opinions are valid, men like me think less and less of you.

Is that really what you want?

Think about it: a world where men like me don't find you attractive. A world where we refuse to marry you or put babies in your tummy or give you money to buy nice things with lace on them.

You're thinking about it right now, aren't you? You're thinking about what the world would be like if there were less of me and more of you crazy, worked-up femmos banging on about yourselves.

Can you see it? Of course you can. There's a good girl.

How lovely. Nothing is as satisfying as watching a woman finally see the light.

Outside Manners

Susan Johnson

Mrs June Robertson, for it was she, had lived for many long years beneath the wrath of her husband. Twenty or more years ago she had watched the late Australian media magnate Kerry Packer on television and she could have sworn it was her husband's secret twin. Mr Colin Robertson, her husband, more commonly known as Robbo, did not look like Kerry Packer – that is, platypus-lipped, swollen, a few too many slices of fatty bacon down the cakehole – but he spoke exactly like him. Kerry and Robbo conversed in a kind of antiquated, shouted-out Australiana, where going to the toilet was 'I'm on the bloody toot, June! For Christ's sake! Shut up!' and men got 'snaky' rather than cross and 'crook' rather than sick and where women, of course, were still referred to – no irony intended – as 'sheilas'. Robbo was a businessman, in clothing, not the fashion kind but the manufacturing kind and business was going down the bloody tubes. Business was going down the tubes because of China and bloody sheilas like Julia Gillard and that bloody sheila who was the union rep, who kept holding meetings on the floor of the factory, getting all the other mad bloody sheilas steamed up. In truth, Mrs June Robertson knew, as her husband did not, that he was too old and too snaky to be still working. Men who were 71 next birthday were not supposed to be going into the office shouting at young women and making them cry but when you owned the company you could do anything you bloody well wanted.

Mrs June Robertson knew you were supposed to like your husband. She could not have said at what exact point her wild, outsized passionate love for young, sinewy, good-looking Colin Robertson had changed into something else.

'June!' he shouted now. 'Jesus Christ! How's a bloke s'posed to find his bloody shirt in a joint like this?'

How had this happened to her? How had she – lovely, beautiful even, any-man-should-be-proud – how had she ended up with such a grumpy husband?

Her husband drank too much. He'd given up smoking long ago but she had not. She sat out on the back deck, smoking her fucking lungs out, drawing in the poisons, suck, suck.

'What?' she said, coming into the house.

'Where is that bloody blue shirt?'

'Which bloody blue shirt?' She kept walking, through to the en-suite bathroom, past the photographs of all the overseas trips they had taken, all those first-class flights, all those airline lounges keeping out the bloody riff-raff wearing thongs. It was a pity budget travel meant everybody travelled these days, she thought, the mighty unwashed as her husband called them, the mighty unwashed en route. Once, only rich people went to Paris and London.

'The blue shirt, June. It was here five minutes ago. Where'd you bloody put it?'

'This one?' she said, walking straight to it in the centre of a row of freshly laundered and ironed shirts. 'Have a mummy look next time.'

'Hmph,' he said. You had to know Colin Robertson to know that this was his version of thanks.

Sometimes, secretly, June Robertson had the horrible thought that she had traded in her soul for a life of airline lounges, first-class travel, beautiful shoes and a big house in Sydney worth squillions, a house with many bedrooms, many with en-suites.

She marvelled at the English. Once she went to London to visit an old school friend, a girl who sailed from Australia at a tender age to see the world, a nurse. In those days, 1960 to be precise, a girl who had a dream of going to London, taking six long weeks at sea to get there, no riff-raff. Her friend had won the jackpot and later bagged a doctor. June Bates, as she was then, had never been quite brave enough to board that ship of dreams. She had not bagged a doctor either but skinny, handsome Colin Robertson, who told her she was the most beautiful thing he had ever seen in his life.

Her old school friend, the nurse who had bagged a doctor, turned out to have bagged not just any old doctor but an anaesthetist. For some reason the word 'anaesthetist' made

June laugh and if she found the thought of being married to one funny, she did not tell her friend. Her friend lived in a grand house overlooking Regent's Park. It was the summer of 1976, which later went down in the records as one of the country's hottest summers, so that even now she has trouble remembering London as anything but a golden, heated dream. That bright summer they walked through Regent's Park and up to the very top of a hill that overlooked London. 'It took me a long time to get used to the formality of the English,' said her friend, as they admired the view.

June noticed that her friend always called her husband 'darling', as in a movie, and that the anaesthetist treated his wife as if she was someone he had only recently met; that is, he used his outside manners inside, at all times. 'Darling, I'll see you tonight,' he said, as he went out the door the afternoon of June's visit. 'Thank you so much for the marvellous lunch.' After he had left, June's friend confided that her husband was still the most courteous man she had ever met, almost twenty years into their marriage. 'He is unfailingly charming,' she said.

June, who was about to head back to the hotel in Bayswater to meet her own husband, thought of him waiting there, impatient, cross, a man who did not bow to outside manners or inside manners. Her husband was the same unleashed, bad-tempered, shouting person outside and inside and never noticed the effect he had on any man, woman or child. All three of their children stayed away from him, the youngest son, a drop-out, still craving his approval. The only person in the world Colin Robertson wholeheartedly approved of was Colin Robertson. Never in his whole life was her husband going to say, 'Thank you so much for the marvellous lunch, darling.'

June Robertson, for it was she, felt a rancour wash across her heart. Thereafter she thought of her friend married to the polite anaesthetist with not exactly malice but with something very like it; an angry, sour, twisted feeling. She did not think it fair that everybody else had a polite husband except her.

Now Colin had his blue shirt on, with an expensive silk tie she had bought him while they were stuck last month in one of the seven circles of hell that was otherwise known as Changi airport. His neck hung over the collar of his shirt, or rather his jowls did. He looked strangled.

'Are you coming to this shindig or not?' he said, on his way out the door. 'That idiot from the Shenzhen office is coming and bringing his wife. They're taking us to some Chinese joint to eat bloody octopus balls or something. Damien and his little feminist missus are coming too.'

June thought of all the evenings she had spent trying to make conversation with the wives of her husband's business partners, women who could barely speak English or else women who attracted the ire of her husband because he found out they were feminists who did not intend to have children. He was currently having trouble with his sales manager, Damien, a young bloke he thought was clever but who had the misfortune to be lumped with a bloody smart-aleck childless academic for a wife. The bloody smart-aleck academic, Claudia, lectured in 'women's studies'. 'You have to study sheilas now, do you?' he asked her. 'Which bit do you study?' The young woman had mistakenly attempted to answer him. By the end of the night tears were glistening in her eyes and June was doing her usual job of trying to make out that her husband was only joking. *Oh, Colin, don't be so terrible to Claudia! Stop pulling her leg!*

One of their children, their only daughter and eldest child, lived 10 000 miles away, on the other side of the world. She was an academic too, in English literature, at Amherst in the USA. Sarah rarely visited and when she did, she and her father fought like cat and dog. Once she refused to visit them for an entire year, after Colin had a bit too much to drink and asked whether she was a lezzo. She was 38 years old, unmarried, and never told her mother anything. The night her father asked if she was a lezzo was exceptional, in that after Colin staggered off to bed, Sarah did not flounce out of the room like she usually did. 'It's verbal abuse, Mum,' she said. 'You don't have to put up with it.' June looked at her daughter: a long, cold, withering appraisal. 'How dare you,' she said. When Sarah was 21, she shouted at her mother that the only thing in life she wanted was not to end up like her.

June Robertson, for it was she, loved shoes. Her middle son, her favourite, the one who did not live 10 000 miles away and the one who was not a drop-out, lived in the next suburb. He gently poked fun at her and called her Imelda Marcos. This son, James, did not make her feel like a failure, like her husband did, like her daughter did, like her youngest son did, his life ruined and lying all over the road for everyone to see. Some people thought she was a success! Some people in her family were still living in two-bedroom shacks out in the far reaches of Wentworthville! A shoe is a shoe is a shoe but sometimes a shoe is also a triumph.

Here is June Robertson walking into her dressing room. Here she is trying to make herself pretty again, the once pretty girl who once worked in a florist shop, who left school at fourteen. When she got married, in those far-off days when girls wore petticoats and girdles, she had a trousseau.

Here is her husband tightening his tie before they leave for the restaurant. Here he is in his usual foul temper, this time something about some stupid girl at work stuffing up some order. June is already dressed and ready but while she waits she goes out again onto the back deck to smoke.

'What do you have to do to get a feed in this joint?' her husband says to the waiter after he calls him over. The Chinese couple smile and nod their heads. June wishes she spoke Chinese.

The other guests are the sales manager, Damien, and Claudia, his smart-aleck wife. June notices a certain frostiness in Claudia's face that wasn't there before. Her eyes are guarded.

It is true that they have been waiting for menus perhaps five minutes too long. They let the Chinese couple order, a protracted negotiation that takes longer than expected. 'Blimey bloody Charlie,' says her husband, 'we're not ordering for an army! Just order any bloody thing except bull's semen soup.' Damien laughs, June does too, but Claudia does not even smile. 'I kid you not,' her husband continues. 'I had to eat the stuff at a dinner in Shanghai.'

When the ordering is done, Colin turns his attention to Claudia. 'I hear our Mr Jones has got you girls in a tizz,' he says. 'I knew we shouldn't have starting educating you.' He gives a big theatrical wink. Claudia's husband laughs but Claudia shoots Damien a look that can only be described as menacing.

'So Old Big Bum reckons society's only any good when you girls are politically involved, eh? What do you say to that, darl?'

'I say she's right,' says Claudia.

'Gone to the dogs since you girlies got the vote,' he replies. 'All this anti-male crap, these silly women banging on as if there was something shameful about being a bloke. Look at the newspapers! Full of lifestyle bullshit and celebrity crap – women's magazine crap has taken over! Talking about your bloody feelings and blaming us blokes for not showing ours. Listen, missy, who stayed on the *Titanic* when the ship went down? Who got slaughtered in their thousands upon thousands saving the necks of girls like you? It's all very well to bag us blokes until you want saving.'

Claudia's lips form a grim line. 'Which part of that rant do you want me to refute?' Damien laughs but it sounds nervous and forced. The Chinese couple keep smiling.

'Are you going to go out and fight when we're invaded, darl?'

'Who's going to invade Australia?' she says.

'I don't bloody know! That's not the point. The point is that you sheilas are great at banging on about the failures of men until someone climbs in the bedroom window. Then it's "Oh, help me, brave and strong man!" Who rescues you when your house burns down? A fireman built like a brick dunny, that's who!'

June laughs. You have to hand it to him, she thinks, at least he's a funny bugger. 'Come on, Claudia,' she says. 'He doesn't mean it.'

She is quite sure he doesn't.

Here is June, the corporate wife, outside the restaurant, on the pavement, smoking. She looks at the stars and thinks about the funeral notice of the husband of one of her friends that she saw in the paper yesterday. This husband had once felt her up under the table at a dinner party and she was so mortified about making a public scene that she let him leave his hand on her leg. She recalls how heavy his hand felt, and how after a while her leg – which she was too terrified to move – began to feel as if it were not her own. She was a married woman, the mother of teenagers, and she was only then beginning to see the years piling up ahead.

On the pavement, June Robertson, for it is she, draws in the smoke. She has been married all her adult life, cared for, protected. She thinks of her friend with the husband with wandering hands and of that polite husband, far off in London. She thinks of her own husband inside, shouting, destroying the joint. She thinks there is something she does not yet understand, hovering just outside the edge of her awareness.

She is thinking of lives changing, whole lives exactly like hers. There is a black man in the White House and a woman in The Lodge and she is an unremarkable woman smoking on a pavement in Sydney in 2013, wearing shoes more beautiful than Cinderella's.

Joint Destroyer, Born and Raised

Steph Bowe

Perhaps it should be said that I'm not very good at writing essays.

See, if you were a misogynist, you might interpret that to mean that all women are bad at writing essays. There are in fact a number of influential male writers who believe women can't write at all. (I assume they are all just drinking too much, as I like to think the best of people.) If you are a normal and rational person, you'll probably decide for yourself whether or not I'm good at writing essays, and you won't make grandiose statements about an entire gender based on the skills of one person.

That's one of the perils of being female in modern-day Australia: sometimes people think your actions represent three billion people on the planet. You get judged a lot.

Still, if I had a time-and-space machine, and got to choose when and where I would be an eighteen-year-old girl – imagining an egalitarian, utopic future is not an option, of course – I'd still choose right here, right now.

I wanted to open this essay with an anecdote, with a first-hand example of the sexism still prevalent in Australian culture, with a story from my youth, but I had none. I'm eighteen, so there isn't much youth to speak of. I've had what I wish every girl could have, and what many women before me have worked towards: an upbringing free of exclusion, harassment or discouragement on the basis of my gender. I have always been made to feel that I can become whatever I choose. I have many wonderful female role models. On a general basis, I'm exposed to some very sexist media, but on a personal, specific level, there's never been any sexism directed towards me.

I have never been pressured to conform to traditional ideals (sadly for my mother, I never really showed much interest in football), and I've no doubt that had I been born a boy my brilliant, matriarchal family would've raised me in much the same way: to be a kind, thoughtful and conscientious individual. Someone with faith in myself and my abilities, capable of contributing to the world.

I'm lucky. Generations of women have gone before me to fight for a lot of the rights women take for granted today. Fifty years ago, the world was a dramatically different place. There's been a lot of progress in a short period of time. As a result, there's this idea a lot of people seem to have that we are living in a post-feminist world, where absolute equality has been achieved. I think you'll find this is not the case. Representations of women are still distorted and unfair in society in general, giving girls and young women mixed (and often harmful) messages about what it means to be a woman and a feminist.

I think when girls do not have support and good female role models among their family, teachers and local community, they look to wider society. I think even when one does come from a supportive family, it's still easy to be affected by popular culture and the media. It's easy to be fooled into thinking a woman's worth hinges on how young and conventionally attractive she is when all you see on television and read in magazines is judgement of a woman's appearance. It's easy to be discouraged from going into male-dominated professions when you see how much flak women like Julia Gillard and Christine Nixon receive.

Young women need to be reminded that they are so much more than their appearance, that their worth doesn't decline with age. They don't need to be told that they are soft or incapable just because they're female. They don't need to be told that men are just biologically better at maths or science or politics, because that's blatantly untrue. They do not need to be told they are less than, or that they have to put down other women or denigrate men in order to become successful.

If you listen to some teenagers, you might be tricked into thinking that a feminist is one of the worst possible things to be. There is an incredible degree of anti-feminism among young women and men, as feminists are perceived to be militant and aggressive and anti men. I'm not sure where this attitude comes from. I guess there are a lot of people who don't care for women who don't behave as they think women should, and I guess everyone just remembers the extremists. The desire to be 'one of the boys' in order to be liked by said boys is also a powerful imperative among teenage girls.

The way the media covers feminist issues probably doesn't help with this image problem feminism has. There's that news story popping up every few months that says feminism ruined everything, and we're all so miserable these days because really we're *supposed* to conform to gender roles, *it's the natural way.* I highly doubt affording women the same basic rights men have is responsible for all human suffering, but that story gets coverage all the same.

Feminism is not about being better than men. It's not about turning us all into one big homogenous group. It's not about renouncing make-up and heels and bras, if you like those things. It's about people being afforded the same opportunities. It's about not being judged on the basis of your gender. It's about a lot of other things, but mostly it's about equality. Now forgive me if I sound a little too socialist here, but wouldn't equality be such a nice thing for us all to have?

Irrespective of your political beliefs, Julia Gillard is a brilliant example of a highly intelligent, highly motivated and very mentally tough individual. She's important: Generation Z will grow up to view a female prime minister as an ordinary thing, inspiring girls to go into politics and not see their gender as a barrier or disadvantage. The fact that more coverage is given to Gillard's manner of dress or her childlessness or her voice (how offensive that all women do not speak in dulcet tones!) rather than her policies is irritating. I fail to see how she is 'destroying the joint' but my judgement may be clouded by the fact that I don't believe women to be inherently inept or inferior to men, that they don't deserve to have power, unlike a certain radio broadcaster.

Though instances of overt sexism such as Alan Jones's comments are generally less socially acceptable and as a result rarer than they were in the past, it doesn't mean sexism is eliminated entirely. Far from it. If anything, these comments draw attention to the fact that misogyny is very much ingrained in Australian culture. The very phrase 'destroying the joint' denies the reality of our world: that everything is in constant flux. Progress is inevitable.

I think analysing and breaking down the belief system is more important than attacking the man. Jones alone is an extremist, a 'shock jock', but much more insidious is the idea that this belief system still exists. Of course, Jones would enjoy the comfort of a world with strictly enforced gender roles, as it is a world that's served him well.

That institutions, systems and the world at large are shifting and growing, that women are 'destroying the joint' is a wonderful and unavoidable thing. If institutions always remain the same, and wholly controlled by wealthy, middle-aged white men, that's a lot more worrisome. Changing the culture and changing the belief system of the masses is not something that happens overnight. But think how much has changed in the last 50 years. I have far more options available to me than my grandmother or even my mother did. So why do people say 'that's just how it is'? Sexism doesn't have to be a permanent fixture in our culture.

Think how much could change in the next 50 years.

Beyond Jeering: An Unapologetic Love Letter to Teen Girls

Dannielle Miller

Nine times out of ten when I am introduced as a guest on radio or television, the host makes a comment to the effect that I must be somewhat unhinged to have devoted my career to working with teen girls (insert knowing smirk at just how awful they can be) or looks at me with genuine bewilderment, almost unable to comprehend why anyone would enjoy working with a group that's 50 shades of trouble. I can see them thinking: 'Is she perhaps just naïve about what girls are really like?' At best, they may say I'm brave.

I don't see myself as crazy or brave. What I do see are the unhelpful common perceptions of teen girls in our culture.

How are our daughters labelled when they hit adolescence? They have been reduced to a series of caricatures. There's Little Miss Cynical, the eye-rolling teen dismissing everything with a 'whatever'; Little Miss Surly, the angry, no-one-understands-me bitch; Little Miss Stupid, the kind of girl TV executives love to portray on reality TV shows, helping to really ingrain the 'clueless' stereotype in our psyches; Little Miss Slut, she of the short skirts, provocative pouts and insatiable sexting; Little Miss Diva, too spoiled to work, clean her room or contribute to society; and Little Miss Queen Bee, who spends all her time creating burn books or *Gossip Girl*-esque sites where she can play the compare-and-despair game of ranking and rating her peers.

The media and entertainment industries are hypercritical of girls and take an almost salacious pleasure in exposing girls-gone-bad type stories. Every week I appear on a panel on Channel 9's *Mornings* show to talk about issues affecting girls and women. When they asked me to discuss a physical fight between two young women on the show *The Shire*, within weeks the clip of that discussion had attracted some 135 000 views – in comparison to the few hundred views most of my clips attract. It's hard to imagine a story about a fight between two young men on a dramality show garnering that level of attention from the media or viewers.

Even those who should have teen girls' best interests at heart, the people who write parenting books, often describe teen girls in terms that are less than kind or generous of spirit. Walk down the parenting aisle of any bookstore and you'll find plenty of covers depicting adolescent girls as sluttish or surly. As one girl said to me after a seminar, 'If I came home and found my mum reading a book that presented girls in the way some of these books do, I'd be so hurt. We don't read books entitled *Parents are Pains in the Arses*, do we?'

I am not naïve, either. I do not view girls through rose-coloured glasses. I began my career as a high school teacher and worked in schools for ten years, predominantly with students at risk, who always give it to you real and raw. Since I founded my own business in 2003, my company has worked with tens of thousands of girls from all kinds of backgrounds, and I have a teen daughter. Yes, I know girls can be challenging. But I wonder at times if they slip into this mode because they feel it is expected of them. There are times when my daughter can become almost a caricature of the difficult teen girl – a fully fledged Ja'mie from Chris Lilley's satirical *Summer Heights High* – and, in fact, the best way to snap her out of it is to casually call her Ja'mie and say that her behaviour is 'so random'.

Binge drinking, body image anxiety, friendship fallouts, self-harming, navigating the ever-changing online world: these issues are all impacting our girls, and we should care. But the answer lies in education – not moral panic, or policing and patronising. We must give girls the skills they need to make informed choices and encourage them to turn their critical gaze on their culture, not themselves and each other.

And truly, being a pain is not typical of only the teen-girl experience – look around you! Just as many adults are struggling with alcohol, poor self-esteem, toxic relationships and stress.

I think it is far too easy to lose sight of the fact that girls are not one-dimensional stereotypes. Girlworld is made up of a multitude of identities, personalities, talents, skills and ideas. It is this diversity and the vast complexity of girls that delights me and that I think our culture often refuses to acknowledge. Of course, girls might have their Little Miss moments of acting cynical or surly or spoilt, but they are so much more than that.

Bullying and bitchiness get a lot of press, but I am often astonished by the intensity of the affection teen girls have for each other. To see a group of teen girlfriends together is a beautiful thing. They hug each other and snuggle together, styling each other's hair, with giggled whispers and knowing looks. I wonder sometimes if we envy them their unbridled enthusiasm for each other and the intimacy of their relationships with their BFFs.

And this warmth, generosity and caring doesn't just stop at their circle of friends.

Teen girls *are* destroying the joint – but not through dysfunction, apathy and nastiness, as we are led to believe. Make no mistake, for every media report of a girl in crisis, there are stories aplenty in the real world of remarkable young women doing extraordinary things. Some sail off to explore the world, Jessica Watson style. But there are plenty more everyday girl heroes. I am full of optimism and pride in the way our girls are taking on, and making over, their world.

The teen girls at a school I worked at in early 2012 in Sydney were so inspired by Real Girl Power, our workshop on the history of the women's movement, that, at lunchtime, a group of them waltzed up to a particularly sexist boy in their year group. Samantha, the group's nominated spokeswoman, told him, 'You always like to say, "Go make me a sandwich," whenever we say something you don't agree with in class. Guess what? There will be no sandwiches for you. And you don't have to like what we say, but you do need to listen. If you try to dismiss us again, we are all going to start clapping loudly every time you speak. It's going to really shine the spotlight on you, and we're not sure you're going to like that.'

There were no more orders for sandwiches, Samantha emailed to tell me. *And we realised that collectively, we were strong. You could see the fear in all the boys' eyes after that … LOL.* I loved that this made her laugh – there is indeed a joy in claiming one's power.

A teen girl in Western Australia, named Daffodil, shared with me her own story of activism: 'This year, my school, St Brigid's College, has given me the opportunity to complete a personal project and … I have been inspired to raise awareness of self-esteem issues in teenage girls in our society. I have also started to create a beauty campaign for the school community, which includes posters and affirmation cards promoting true beauty.' Daffodil posted images in the school toilets and on classroom doors that reminded her classmates that they are more than just their bodies, they are somebodies.

A group of teen girls in Victoria decided they didn't know much about feminism and why it mattered, so they chose to do a research assignment on it as part of an interest project at school. They interviewed me and a number of other women. Then they presented their work to their classmates and invited them to join the Young Feminist group they were starting at school. They had a 70% take-up.

I am inspired by the fifteen-year-old who had a baby, as a result of being raped, and turned up at the school carnival the next week to join in sporting events and cheer on her classmates. And by the fourteen-year-old who sends me poems she has written on what being beautiful really means and tells me how she will survive being bullied and emerge a shinier girl.

I am impressed by Tess Corkish, who at age eighteen was outraged when a popular retailer began selling products she thought were sexist. She transformed her outrage into something positive by starting an online petition. Amassing thousands of signatures and drawing media attention, the campaign resulted in the products being withdrawn from store shelves.

Then there's Jemma Ryan, seventeen. After seeing me speak at a girls' education conference in Melbourne in 2009, Jemma successfully lobbied to have me present at Clonard College, where she was school captain. Jemma and I have stayed in touch ever since. She flew to Sydney earlier this year to stay with me and my family to help me in my office before she commenced her uni studies in journalism. *Anything you need I will do, no job too small!* she emailed me beforehand. *My goodness, it's an opportunity, a privilege I am so, so, so lucky to have!!* How is that for a go-get-'em, no-divas-here attitude?

Jemma also writes for her local paper; she has been doing that since she was fourteen. When I asked her how she had fitted in studying, her role as a student leader, her part-time job at Bakers Delight and writing for the paper, she explained, 'Well, I just have to be time conscious, I guess. My current boyfriend and I, for example – well, we decided just to be friends until I completed Year 12. There was no time for distractions. When we first met, I was in my final year of high school and was really committed to my studies . . . some would say school was my first love. My first love and I had been together for thirteen years, and I wasn't about to stop spending time with it for a boy! So when I did meet someone (a boy that is, not another school), I had to find a balance that worked for all three of us (yes, me, boy and studies). I know how it sounds, this girl was all about the parent pleasing, but that wasn't it at all, it was about values and priorities. I only had a few months of hard study to go, and I knew anyone that really liked me for me would respect my school lovin' ways!'

And what does Jemma plan to do with all her smarts and determination? Join the revolution, of course, and work on empowering the next generation of young girls. She says, 'I can't think of anything that would be more fulfilling!'

Me either, Jem.

The choices made by girls like these aren't often shared in popular culture – but they do deserve our recognition.

We must try not to let the slammed doors, angry silences or sarcastic asides of adolescence blind us to girls' essential *loveableness.* And we must also not be distracted by the toxic culture our girls are immersed in and that they do sometimes struggle with, for there is a risk that it can blind us to an even more important reality: not only the loveableness, but also the strength and resilience, of girls.

Leaky Ladies and Their Worrisome Wombs

Nina Funnell

The announcement came on a Monday morning during full-school assembly. As the students sat quietly in the school gym, the deputy principal took to the stage and with her usual unimpressed air, declared that the tampon and pad vending machines located in the girls' bathrooms had been deemed 'inappropriate'.

'These machines,' she announced, 'give an *unladylike* impression to our school's guests, particularly male visitors who, on occasion, have cause to occupy the female facilities. They will be removed immediately.'

I bristled uncomfortably. What exactly did she mean by 'unladylike'? How could there possibly be anything unladylike about products that – by definition – only ladies had cause to use?

The year was 2001, and I was a senior student at an all-girls high school located in Sydney's inner west. Contrary to what the Howard Government had announced the previous year, tampons and pads were not 'luxury items'.[1] To us, they were necessities. We were teen girls. We bled. We spotted. We leaked.

As a Year 12 student, I had already passed through the awkward first years of puberty, but the memory of my first period – and the embarrassment and uncertainty I had felt – was still raw. Looking at the younger girls seated in front of me, I sensed their body-angst, and I immediately recognised the message that this action would send them: our bleeding bodies were dirty and vulgar. Menstruation was a shameful secret that had to be concealed from view. We were just one big bloody mess.

This wasn't the first time I'd encountered the stigma surrounding menstruation. In Year 9 our religious education teacher had informed us that in biblical days, it was considered dirty for a man to sit on any chair that a menstruating woman had previously sat on. Boys joked about not trusting 'any animal that bled for five days and didn't die'. Even *Girlfriend* magazine – our own hallowed bible – often reinforced the view that menstruation was somehow shameful. Every month the magazine contained a section titled 'How Embarrassment'. It routinely featured 'true life' horror stories about girls who had been 'outed' as women who bled ('OMG! The tampon just rolled straight out of my purse, right in front of my crush! I almost DIED!').

But there was something else that troubled me about the deputy principal's announcement. Her specific reference to male visitors hadn't escaped me. It was clear that we weren't simply being body shamed. We were also being told to prioritise men's delicate sensibilities above our own hygienic needs. The idea that a man or teen boy might feel put off was apparently so appallingly unthinkable that it was preferable for us to be denied sanitary protection, rather than risk any male unease. Better our discomfort than theirs.

But what was so off-putting about the sight of a tampon machine anyway? Why did our natural processes have to be censored from view? And what image of us were these machines destroying for men, exactly?

Perhaps it was the thought of us bleeding (and the fertility this signified) that troubled them. Or maybe it was the idea of how tampons were *used* that caused the upset. The thought of young girls inserting things into their supposedly 'chaste' vaginas has always ruffled some feathers, after all.

At the time I knew all too well that the issue of teen pregnancy troubled many adults and that our emerging sexualities provided a constant source of anxiety. As is no different for teen girls today, our nubile, hormone-filled bodies were simultaneously fetishised and policed, and we were often made to pay the price for other people's sexual frustrations: 'Lower your hems girls and do up your top buttons! The male gardeners are feeling uncomfortable!' Now, once again it seemed, we were being punished for men's inability to deal.

At recess I took the issue up with my friends. We talked about the stigma surrounding menstruation and the ridiculous tampon and pad ads on television: Why do they always use that stupid blue dye? What do they think we are, Smurfs or something? And why do the women always dance around like getting their period is the Best Thing Ever? It's sooo patronising. Why can't they ever just portray the subject realistically?

We talked about the decision to remove the tampon machines and the significance of it being a woman who had passed down the order – what does *she* use when she's got her period? Doesn't she remember what it is like to be caught without a pad or a tampon? Besides, if you can't acknowledge female menstruation in a woman's bathroom, then where on earth can you acknowledge it? – and together we agreed that something had to be done. Someone had to take action.

The following day I met with the other members of our Student Representative Council. I raised the issue and there was universal agreement that the tampon and pad machines should stay. Later that week I met with our principal, a kind and liberal man who immediately recognised the ridiculousness of the situation; he overturned the decision and we got to keep our machines. It was a small victory but it gave me a taste of something bigger. Girls could rewrite the rules.

PAINFUL PERIODS IN HISTORY AND RELIGION

Throughout history, men from all different cultures and disciplines have claimed that menstrual blood is a pollutant of both the body and the world around it. In eighteenth-century Saigon, no women were employed in the opium industry because it was believed that if a menstruating woman were near, the opium would be ruined and become bitter. A century later, in 1878, the British Medical Journal claimed that a menstruating woman would cause bacon to putrefy. In the 1920s, a Viennese scientist, Béla Schick, coined the term 'menotoxins' to describe what he believed were plant-destroying substances that escaped through the skin of a menstruating woman. Schick further claimed that 'menotoxins' prevented dough from rising and beer from fermenting. No beer, bacon or opium? No wonder the men were worried.

But these superstitions are not confined to the past. While writing this chapter, my 26-year-old French housemate told me that growing up, her grandmother taught her that mayonnaise wouldn't emulsify if made by a woman who had her period. Another 25-year-old friend who was raised in Australia in a Muslim family wrote me the following:

> I still feel guilty if I ever use a tampon – as a girl it was drilled into me that tampons could take away your virginity and 'steal your innocence'. As a grown-up I know this is bogus but the residual guilt is hard to shake off.

Of course, it's not just women in the West who are made to feel shame over their menstrual cycles and indeed, it's vital that we acknowledge the experiences of women who live in other countries, particularly developing countries.

Today in certain areas of Nepal, menstruating women are not permitted to look at the sun, drink dairy products or interact with males or cattle. It is believed that if they touch fruit trees, the fruits will fall before they ripen; if they fetch water, the well will dry up; if they feed or milk the cattle, then blood will come out of the cows' teats instead of milk.[2]

Indeed, in Nepal, menstrual blood is considered so contaminating that women must be sent away from their homes for the duration of their period so that they don't 'pollute' their households. Instead they stay in small, confined huts or unused cowsheds referred to as chhaupadi huts (in the local language *chhau* refers to menstruation and *padi* to women).

Unsurprisingly, conditions in the chhaupadi huts are terrible, often dirty, dark and lacking in fresh food and water. They are also unsafe. Every year newspapers report stories of women who are raped or attacked by wild animals during their stays. Others die from exposure to the cold or snakebites.

In 2005, the Supreme Court of Nepal outlawed the chhaupadi system, but in practice, customs take time to die out. In 2010, the story of Gagan BK made headlines because he allowed his wife to stay home during her period. As punishment, both husband and wife were ostracised from the community, banned from attending all social gatherings and celebrations. It was reported that Gagan's own parents also admonished the couple, refusing to eat food prepared by his wife. The following year, newspapers reported the story of a nineteen-year-old girl who was beaten with nettles by other women from her town because she stepped outside of a chhaupadi cowshed a few hours after giving birth there. In Nepal, women who have recently given birth are also considered 'untouchable' and must remain in the chhaupadi hut with their newborns for eleven days after giving birth.

In other developing countries, the stigma surrounding menstruation also contributes to the social and political exclusion of women. In Rwanda, for example, many families cannot afford sanitary pads so women and girls make do with what few articles they can find including rags, bark and mud. These makeshift pads are highly ineffective so many girls are bound to stay at home during their period to avoid the humiliation and shame of being seen in public in soiled clothing. The result is that every year, teen girls miss an average 50 days of school – or work – because they simply cannot afford effective sanitary pads, the cheapest of which sell at about US$1.10 for a packet of ten, well outside the budget of most impoverished families. Over the course of their life, these women will miss out on the equivalent of five years of education or employment as a result.

Given that the stigma surrounding menstruation is literally killing some girls and creating a barrier to education for others, it's worth thinking critically about the cultural apparatuses that have both contributed to, and maintained, the menstrual taboo. While medical authorities have long played a role in pathologising the female body and stigmatising its natural processes, religion has also played an equally, if not more, significant role in the demonisation of menstruation. With the notable exception of Sikhism, virtually every major religion has, at some point, treated menstruation with contempt.[3]

In Christianity, the Old Testament states that not only are menstruating women unclean, but 'whoever touches [a menstruating woman] shall be unclean until the evening. And everything on which she lies during her menstrual impurity shall be unclean. Everything also on which she sits shall be unclean.' The book of Leviticus also states that women are to atone for their menstrual impurity by offering two turtle doves (or pigeons) to a priest at the end of every cycle as a sin offering. Sex is also strictly forbidden, and couples who copulate during a woman's period should expect to be exiled from their community.

The no-sex clause is also found in Judaism, Islam, Buddhism and Hinduism. Interestingly, the ancient Romans were also opposed to sex during a woman's menses and they attributed the deformity of the god Vulcan to the menstrual intercourse between his parents Juno and Jupiter.

It doesn't end there. In Islam, a woman may not enter any shrine or mosque during her period and she is not allowed to offer prayer, touch the Quranic codex, recite its contents, or perform other religious activities such as fasting. In Hinduism, the dominant religion in Nepal, women are prohibited from participating in normal life while menstruating and contact with menstruating women is also forbidden, with the exception of small children. Women cannot comb their hair or bathe, are not allowed to cook and cannot enter a temple. They are also forbidden to mount a horse, ox, or elephant, and they are not permitted to drive a vehicle. Buddhism also views menstruation as pollution, and in Judaism, the 'laws of family purity' expressly forbid any physical contact between males and females during the days of menstruation and for a week thereafter.

While not all modern followers of these religions will strictly adhere to these impractical and outrageous rules today, many have still internalised the view that menstruation is a 'curse' linked to impurity or sinfulness, as opposed to a natural, life-giving force. More to the point, these laws are significant because historically they have been used to justify the exclusion of women from positions of authority within religious hierarchies and this exclusion continues today.

This doesn't mean, however, that religions are solely responsible for the menstrual stigma and the role of other patriarchal institutions should also be examined. The medical fraternity, for example, has long pathologised women's uteruses and other bodily processes associated with reproduction. The ancient Greeks believed that a woman's womb could literally travel around her body – 'wandering womb' syndrome – producing any number of infirmities. Hippocrates also believed that menstruation functioned to 'purge women of bad humors'.

In the nineteenth century, dominant medical theories linked 'madness' and 'hysteria' in women to their wombs and sadly, it was not uncommon to treat 'madness' by surgically removing the sexual and reproductive organs of a woman.[4] Of course, women could be diagnosed as 'mad' for any number of reasons. Those who exhibited non-conformist or socially transgressive behaviours were often labelled 'insane' and sequestered to mental asylums. While this was clearly a form of social control, few people could point out that 'madness' was as much a political construct as a medical one, without being deemed mad themselves.

At other times, women who suffered menstrual cramps were sent to psychiatrists because menstrual cramps were seen as a rejection of one's femininity. Freud and other psychoanalysts have also read menstruation as evidence of 'penis envy' – women bleed as a reminder of their bloody loss of a penis. Ahem.

What all these theories have in common (aside from being totally bogus) is that by reframing women's natural bodily processes as diseased or disorderly, men were able to use medical theories to justify women's physical, political and social subjugation: just as religion has sought to control women by linking their cycles to sin, medical authorities have sought to control women by linking their wombs to disease.

IF MEN HAD PERIODS

Many moons ago, Gloria Steinem posed an interesting question: 'What would happen if suddenly, magically, men could menstruate and women could not?' In a brilliant essay that followed, Steinem suggested that things would be markedly different.

Menstruation would no longer be stigmatised, it would be revered and celebrated. Men would brag about their periods, boasting how long and how much. Religious and political leaders would assert that menstruation was a blessing, not a curse, that God had seen fit to bestow solely upon men (being the superior sex, and all). And governments around the world would immediately remove all taxes on sanitary items and instead, invest millions of dollars into funding research into alleviating menstrual cramps.

I imagine other things would change too. Religions would make it a sin to kill or eat a menstruating animal. Sports commentators would endlessly speculate about where in a cycle a male athlete was at: 'We believe he's in his third week, that should give him the extra lift he needs. Apparently Coach Stevens has all the male athletes living together so they can sychronise cycles before the big game.'

Leaking through one's pants would be considered a sign of virility. Porn would eroticise male bleeding. And since menstruation would be intrinsically equated with masculine strength and virility, it would probably be used to sell beer: 'A great long bleed requires a big cold beer, and the best cold beer is Vic.'

In short, if men bled, women would know *all* about it.

The real story, of course, is very different and menstruation remains a taboo subject in almost every culture; the word *taboo* itself derives from the Polynesian word *tapua* which means *menstruation*. In the West we may not exile women to menstrual huts or deny them access to education while on their periods, but this doesn't mean that we have a healthy or adjusted view of it.

Popular culture shies away from the issue or treats it with disgust – just check out the movie *Superbad.* Even pad and tampon ads refuse to discuss the subject openly. In 2012, a Carefree advertisement was censored by three networks in the USA for using that offensive, vulgar word: *vagina.* When the ad was reshot using the second-grade euphemism, 'down there', the ad was once again deemed too inappropriate for two of the networks.

In an article published on the subject, advertising analyst Kate Hunter suggested that while the ad would have been rigorously researched and tested by Carefree, the use of the word *vagina* was controversial and sure to divide public opinion:

> People are certainly talking. And they are splitting into two camps – the outraged and the, 'about timers'. The outraged, predictably, are worried about two things – how we can explain it to the kidlets who may or may not be ready for the 'Becoming a Woman' talk and the 'Slippery Slope Towards Debauchery' – if we are saying the word 'vagina', surely it's only a matter of time before we SHOW AN ACTUAL VAGINA (cue vulva police) in a feminine hygiene commercial! And then where will society be? Actually, there is a third camp, the fellas who cannot hear the word 'vagina' without going a bit pale and finding something else to do – at least 3km away. They are OK with the 'c' word and a 'p' word but 'v' has them running. Too anatomical, too medical.[5]

In other words, certain individuals are fine with words like 'pussy' and 'cunt', i.e. the words you find in porn, but any words that might be found in a medical handbook, or – gasp! – a gynaecologist's office, are strictly icky. It's an interesting point to consider because it suggests that the instant a vagina is presented in a non-sexual, non-erotic context, i.e. the moment we are actually talking about a woman's *health*, as opposed to her sexual function for men, certain people are going to lose their shit. This is not just men, by the way. There are plenty of women who cringe at the word *vagina*.

Breasts receive a similar type of treatment. When presented in a sexual light on billboards, magazines, in strip clubs, etc. very few blokes complain, but the moment breasts are presented in a non-sexual context, think breastfeeding in public, all sorts of men – and some women – start squirming with discomfort.

In fact it's remarkable how hostile Australian society still is towards public breastfeeding. Just ask Kirstie Marshall, a Labor MP who was escorted out of the Victorian parliament by the sergeant-at-arms, for breastfeeding her eleven-day-old daughter in 2003. In 2007, New South Wales created the nation's first breastfeeding-friendly state parliament by allowing mothers to nurse in both the upper and lower parliamentary chambers. It's a positive move, but clearly there is still a lot more work to be done.

In 2006, breastfeeding groups in the USA expressed outrage when a young, breastfeeding mother was asked to leave a store change room, and move to a nearby toilet to feed her hungry child. It didn't help things that the store in question was a Victoria's Secret – a lingerie company whose entire business model revolves around women's breasts. Apparently the shop assistant on the floor didn't grasp the irony of rejecting a woman for breastfeeding from a shop that *trades off* women's breasts and which *uses* women's breasts in almost all their advertising campaigns.

Examples like this serve as a reminder of the conditional ways in which women are permitted to display their breasts and bodies in public. They also reveal our culture's deeply ingrained mother/whore complex, where women are still expected to publicly conform to the role of either lascivious sexpot or virtuous mother, but never both at the same time – these roles are considered mutually exclusive. Indeed, the reason breastfeeding is seen as so troubling for some is because it takes an often eroticised part of the female anatomy and recontextualises it in a maternal context, thus blurring the distinction between roles.

Enter the 'yummy mummy' and the 'MILF'. In recent years these figures have gained increasing attention and on a superficial level, they appear to disrupt the entrenched mother/whore dichotomy. But both the yummy mummy and the MILF figures are fetishised precisely because they represent deviant aberrations to the 'normal' sexual order. What's more, both figures are relentlessly mocked within popular culture: they appear as caricatures of female sexuality, as opposed to being seen as legitimate sexual agents in their own right.

But the anxieties around breastfeeding go a lot deeper. According to academic Robyn Longhurst, Western society is simultaneously fascinated and horrified by the emission and transmission of bodily fluids – look no further than our culture's obsession with vampire texts.

In her book *Bodies: Exploring Fluid Boundaries*, Longhurst suggests that breast milk and other female fluids associated with reproduction – menstrual blood, morning sickness, breaking waters, etc. – cause a cultural upset because they reveal the 'leaky' nature of the female body. In workplaces in particular, bodies are expected to remain contained or 'sealed', thus crying, sweating or even sneezing can be met with revulsion or be seen as unprofessional.

> 'Professional' workplaces, especially in CBDs, are constructed as spaces in which bodies must not transgress their boundaries. Liminal zones where the insides and outsides of bodies sometimes become indeterminable – noses, vaginas, penises, eyes, sores – must be carefully monitored and kept under control at all times in workplaces. It can require enormous vigilance to construct the proper, professional and respectable body – to present a 'public face' – at work. This is one of the functions of the business suit. The firm straight lines of the business suit give the appearance of a body that is impervious to outside penetration. They also give the appearance of a body that is impervious to the dangers of matter that is inside the body making its way to the outside. The suit closets the body in respectability. However, although the suit helps to create an illusion of a hard, or at least a firm and respectable body that is automonous and in control, bodily boundaries can never continually remain intact ... Given that women function as the 'marked category' and that their bodies are socially constructed as 'modes of seepage', business

> attire takes on an added significance and importance for women.[6]

While women's bodies aren't the only bodies that 'seep' (men sneeze, spit, cough, ejaculate, sweat, cry, etc.), there is a double standard around men's emissions: not only is male ejaculation not seen as sinful or dirty, it is often valourised and celebrated, particularly within the context of pornography, where the 'cum shot' is considered of pivotal importance. By contrast, Longhurst suggests that a pregnant body produces more anxiety than any other body because it is constantly threatening to erupt (morning sickness, breaking waters, etc.). Likewise, the lactating body and the menstruating body also produce cultural discomfort because they are socially marked as 'leaky' bodies.

So what does it mean then, for pregnant, lactating or menstruating women, if a precondition of entry into the workplace, or indeed, the public sphere, is bodily containment? And how might our cultural aversion to bodily fluids contribute to the discrimination faced by breastfeeding mothers and other 'leaky' women?

After all, women aren't just people, we are *embodied* people. When we walk into our offices, boardrooms, courtrooms and universities we do not leave our wombs or breasts at home. When we agitate for equal pay, social equality and an end to violence against women, we do so while leaking. And as long as women's leaky bodies remain stigmatised, our voices in these arenas will not be heard or valued equally with men's.

LIFTING THE CURSE

> If you think you are emancipated, you might consider the idea of tasting your menstrual blood – if it makes you sick, you've a long way to go, baby.
>
> *Germaine Greer*

The year I got my first period was the same year that the movie *How to Make an American Quilt* came out. I remember this, because before seeing the film I had felt anxious and deeply ashamed about the changes that were occurring in my body. In the opening scene of the film, Winona Ryder's character introduces the woman she idolises: '[Marianna] had lived in Paris, which made her very mysterious to me when I was a kid. She taught me French, made café au laits and the year I got my period, she gave me a glass of red wine.'

This may not sound particularly remarkable. But as a thirteen-year-old girl, it had a profound impact on me because it was the first time I had seen menstruation portrayed as something that could positively bond women together. My body was changing in a way that I couldn't control, but this was the first time that I felt that maybe this wasn't such a bad thing. In fact, this scene struck me with such force that when the movie came out on video, I immediately hired it just to watch that one scene over.

For women and girls around the world, it's vitally important that we develop narratives about menstruation which counter the dominant cultural and religious discourses. And there is good news here. After all, the only thing more powerful than a taboo is breaking one.

Thankfully, feminists, women's health professionals, artists, individual women and even some advertising executives are already doing this work. And since I don't like to acknowledge a problem without also acknowledging those who are trying to fix it, let's take a look at a few examples.

In 2010, the tampon and pad company Kotex produced a bitingly satirical video that parodied the conventional pad advertisements on TV. The clip formed part of a wider campaign called 'Break the Cycle', which aimed to challenge the stigma around menstruation. The clip begins with a woman on a couch saying, 'How do I feel about my period? Ah, we are like this.' She then crosses her fingers indicating tight friendship. She continues: 'I love it. It makes me feel really pure. Sometimes I just want to run on the beach. I like to twirl, maybe in slow motion. And usually by the third day, I just want to dance. The ads on TV are really helpful, because they use that blue liquid, and I'm like, 'Oh! That's what is supposed to happen!' The video quickly went viral, and dozens of articles were subsequently written about the unhelpful ways in which menstruation is discussed and depicted in the public arena.

Others are doing their bit to challenge the stigma through more radical means. The US artist Vanessa Tiegs and the German artist Petra Paul are known for collecting their menstrual flow and using it to paint intriguing pieces of art. While some have labelled their work more 'biohazard' than art, they have managed to stimulate international discussions about the menstrual taboo.

Even vampire-themed texts, which have historically been read as allegories about monstrous menstruation, are beginning to play around with the stigma. In the original *Buffy the Vampire Slayer* movie, for example, Buffy's superpower strength is intrinsically linked to her menstrual cycle and every time a vampire is near she experiences light period cramps. This operates as an inbuilt alarm system to alert her to the danger around her. While this 'ability' was dropped for the series of the show by the same name, its inclusion in the movie represents an interesting break with conventional portrayals of menstruation in vampire-themed texts.

Moving away from art and popular culture, community workers and not-for-profit organisations in the developing world are doing some amazing work to address the social exclusion of menstruating women. For example, in Rwanda, Sustainable Health Enterprises (SHE) has partnered with existing local women's networks to offer microloans to women who then use the money to manufacture and distribute affordable, quality and eco-friendly sanitary pads. Not only does this provide the community with access to low-cost sanitary goods, but the model also offers women financial independence and increased economic security. Already this model has proved effective in increasing the school attendance of girls who may otherwise have stayed at home during their period.

But perhaps the most important work is the work that is being done by ordinary women in everyday settings. In households, workplaces, schoolyards and online, girls and women are breaking a powerful taboo by talking about their experiences. Sisters, mothers, daughters and friends are blogging and speaking out about the menstrual stigma. They are developing new ways of thinking and talking about women's bodies and, in the process, are fighting back against outmoded patriarchal attitudes. These women and girls are changing the future for all of us. They are our destroyers.

The Politics of Exclusion

Stella Young

Destroy the joint? Shit, I'd be happy just to be allowed in the joint.

Alan Jones's comment last year that 'women are destroying the joint' was laughable to most. To me, as a disabled woman, it was particularly so.

Take a moment to think about Australian women with disabilities who have a profile in any area of public life. Are you thinking? Still thinking, aren't you?

I had to think pretty hard myself, and so I did what any modern woman would: I asked Twitter.

The name mentioned most in the overwhelming response I received was Louise Sauvage, a retired paralympic athlete who now coaches wheelchair racing. Sauvage's list of achievements is long and impressive: she competed in four Paralympic Games, winning thirteen medals; has coached in two; and has been inducted into the International Paralympic Committee's Hall of Fame.

Many of us in disability circles know that Sauvage is also one of many disabled people who've attempted to tackle discrimination among airlines. In 2006, she lobbied Virgin Blue to scrap their policy of requiring all wheelchair users to travel with a carer, whether they actually needed one or not. She also tackled Qantas about their two wheelchair policy, which mandates a maximum of two wheelchair users on any particular flight.

Louise Sauvage certainly deserves her status as a household name, but can you think of any others who are women with disabilities? Kelly Vincent may spring to mind for some. In 2010, aged just 21, Vincent was the youngest person to be elected to South Australian Parliament, and the first in any parliament in Australia to be a wheelchair user.

Women with disabilities are largely invisible in Australian society, but it's not because there just aren't that many of us. People with disabilities make up roughly 20% of the Australian population, and disability is slightly more prevalent among women. So why is it that when asked to think of a high-profile disabled woman, we struggle?

It has often been said that women with disabilities experience a double disadvantage: we experience the same gender inequality as non-disabled women, and it's compounded because we're also discriminated against on the basis of disability. Granted, men with disabilities also experience discrimination, and gender can be a disempowering construct for disabled men as well, but the outcomes for women with disabilities show that this double disadvantage is very real.

Women with disabilities are less likely to be educated than non-disabled women. In 1982, the year I was born, the Victorian Government announced a major review of the education system for children with disabilities. The report was completed in 1984 and included the principle that 'every child has a right to be educated in a regular school'.

As a result of that report, I had the great privilege of being educated in a mainstream state primary school and secondary college. If I'd been born ten years earlier, my life would have looked very different. The educational outcomes for people with disabilities in previous generations are shockingly inconsistent, simply because there was no standard curriculum across special schools. Many of them focused on physical and medical treatment rather than academic education.

Our current education system actually doesn't do a great deal better. Despite the fact that 'every child has [had] a right to be educated in a regular school' for almost 30 years now, many disabled people are still educated in segregated environments. Even when parents want to send their child to a mainstream school rather than a special school, they're often hampered by a lack of support – even if that support is as minor as toileting assistance. So they're faced with two impossible options: a mainstream school with a meaningful curriculum but not enough support, or a special school where their child's physical needs will be met, but where they won't get the skills they need to compete in the labour market or enter tertiary education.

A prime example of this can be seen in Victorian special schools. After a wide and thorough search, I have been unable to find a single one that offers VCE. Glenallen School in Melbourne's eastern suburbs say that they are a specialist school for students 'who have a physical disability and/or significant health impairment'. It is widely regarded as one of the better special schools in Victoria, but even there, students cannot complete VCE.

From what friends who attended special schools tell me, students in such schools spend more time learning how to make cups of tea and tie their shoelaces than they do learning how to read and write.

The word *special*, as it is applied to disability, too often means *a bit shit.*

According to a report by the Australian Bureau of Statistics in 2011, there is a large disparity in educational outcomes between Australians with a disability and those without. In 2009, 25% of people with disabilities between the ages of fifteen and 64 completed Year 12, compared to 55% of people without a disability. This trend also continues after high school, with 58% of 25- to 44-year-olds with a disability having no post-school qualification, compared to 28% of people in the same age bracket without disabilities.

Interestingly, there's little discrepancy between the educational outcomes of girls and boys with disabilities. Unfortunately, the same cannot be said for workforce participation.

Compared to other OECD countries, Australia has one of the lowest workforce participation rates for people with disabilities. We rank 21st out of 29 OECD nations; 39.8% of people with disabilities are employed, compared to 79.4% of people who don't have disabilities.

Labour force participation rates in Australia also indicate that women with disabilities are less likely to be employed than men with disabilities. In 2003, 46.9% of women with disabilities were employed, compared to 59.3% of men with disabilities. When they are employed, women with disabilities experience the same kinds of gender discrimination as non-disabled women; they earn less, they spend more on healthcare, and they are more likely to live in poverty.

The barriers facing us in education and the workforce are attitudinal and physical. This brings us back to Kelly Vincent, the first wheelchair user to hold a seat in a state parliament. South Australian Parliament House, like many historic buildings, has a striking façade. According to the website, it's 'a classically designed building with majestic marble columns, Corinthian capitals and keystone portrayals of nineteenth-century governors, presidents and speakers'. It also doesn't have any wheelchair access at the main entrance.

When Kelly Vincent was first elected, she had to enter her workplace through two heavy iron gates and a large wooden door which, despite displaying a wheelchair access symbol bold as brass, was so heavy that even able-bodied people struggled to open it. After she complained, the door was automated, and plans are afoot to automate the gates as well. Unfortunately, these renovations aren't expected to be completed until the end of 2013, a good three years after Vincent's election.

If you're already shocked that Vincent had to use an alternative entrance to enter the building in the first place, consider this: until the usual accessible entrance is complete – remembering that it is still not the same one her parliamentary colleagues use – she gets in through the carpark. The alternative? Staying at home. Not taking the extraordinary opportunity she's been afforded for all her hard work and skill.

If I had a dollar for every time I've entered a building via the bins, the carpark, or both, I'd be able to fund the reno at SA parliament myself. Of course, getting in is better than not.

But an alternative entrance is more than that. It's a daily reminder that you're not really supposed to be there. That you're not entitled to public space in the same way non-disabled people are.

While completing my Diploma of Education at Melbourne University, I did a three-week teaching round in a school with no disabled toilets. The only way to deal with not being able to go to the toilet in your workplace is simply not to consume liquid at work, or in the hours before you arrive. I had to kick my morning coffee habit pretty quickly. If I started to get a dehydration headache towards the afternoon, I'd take tiny sips of water, but I didn't dare have any more than that. Last period Year 8 English was tough enough without a bladder full to bursting.

Looking back, it's easy to wonder why I didn't complain. Why didn't I tell the placement coordinators that it wasn't acceptable for me to spend three weeks in a school with no disabled toilets? Well, because I considered myself lucky to be there in the first place. It was incredibly difficult for the university to find me a placement. I almost missed out on that first round because finding a school with access – even the most basic kind that allowed me to get into the building – and that was willing to take a student teacher in a wheelchair – let's not pretend that attitudes aren't just as problematic as access – was incredibly difficult.

I felt, as I often do, that I was there because other people had allowed it, not because I actually deserved to be.

We are conditioned, as disabled people, to feel grateful.

The invisibility of women with disabilities happens because we are not represented in public life. In Australia in particular, more than half of people with disabilities live near or below the poverty line. Women with disabilities are more likely than men with disabilities to be affected by poverty.

It's very hard to be out and about in the community if you're poor. You might not have a mobility aid that suits your needs. You might be limited to using taxis (a very expensive option for daily travel) because the public transport in your area is inaccessible to you. Or you might just feel, because of the access and attitudinal barriers you know are out there, that you are not allowed a place in your community.

The media compounds this invisibility. When is the last time you saw a disabled character on television or in film where that character's impairment was not part of the storyline? Disability, when it does appear, is generally used as a device. Take Stefan Dennis's Paul Robinson from *Neighbours* – he's the resident bad guy. It's no accident that he's also the resident amputee. Well, not really, because that would require the Australian television industry to employ a real live disabled person and if history is anything to go by, that's not about to happen any time soon.

A friend of mine once remarked that when he was growing up, he thought that he was either going to die before he reached adulthood, or he'd grow up to be a non-disabled person. The lack of disabled people on screen taught him that people like him only existed inside the walls of the hospital he visited regularly, and his special school. He had no idea disabled people came in adult form because he'd simply never seen any.

Perhaps one of the more frustrating areas of exclusion for me as a disabled woman is from mainstream feminism. Disabled women have traditionally been treated as a side issue by the women's movement. Sometimes our issues aren't considered at all. Sometimes they are, but we're not really asked for our own perspectives on what these issues are and how we could address them.

Karen Pickering, a fellow feminist and friend of mine, runs a popular monthly feminist event in Melbourne called Cherchez La Femme. After asking me to speak at one event, I had to decline and point out that her venue was upstairs at a pub. Not only could I not speak at her event, I couldn't even attend. Horrified that her event wasn't accessible to me and to other women with mobility impairments, she immediately started looking for another home. She found one. It was lovely. It was step-free, which solved some of the access issues. Unfortunately, it didn't have a disabled toilet. At least back in my teaching round days, there wasn't the temptation of wine.

Again, she was horrified. 'I really want to own that failure and make it a priority to fix it,' Pickering said. 'It's something concrete I can do as an event organiser to make mainstream feminism accessible to more people; I won't book venues without proper access. I learned this the hard way, by letting my friend down! I was mortified to discover I was part of the problem and that for all my words about inclusivity and intersectionality, my actions weren't backing that up. I'm resolved to change that.'

Cherchez La Femme is by no means an isolated case. I was asked to speak at Women Say Something in Sydney last year, but was ultimately unable to because there was no way to negotiate access to the stage in their venue. Women of Letters, a monthly literary event curated by Marieke Hardy and Michaela McGuire, which celebrates a diverse range of strong female voices, was formerly held at Melbourne's Thornbury Theatre, an entirely inaccessible venue. It's recently found a new home at the much more accessible Regal Ballroom just down the road, but it wasn't a quick and easy process.

'We're embarrassed to say that it took three years for Women of Letters to move to a wheelchair accessible venue,' McGuire said. 'Frankly, I don't think it's something we even considered during our first six months at the Bella Union, and I'm quite sure we were far too carried away by the beauty of the art deco ceiling at the Thornbury Theatre to notice that not everybody was going to be able to climb those marble stairs.'

Hardy and McGuire raised their concerns but, of course, installing an elevator in the foyer of a heritage-listed building is no easy task.

'We waited patiently for some time, but concluded that we were going to have to enforce change ourselves, and not just hope for it to happen. We spent six months scouting for a venue that met all of our requirements, and finally found our new home at the Regal Ballroom. We were sad to part with the Thornbury Theatre, but are proud that our event can finally be accessible to everyone.'

Neither Pickering, Hardy nor McGuire set out to exclude disabled women in the choice of venues for their events; they simply didn't think of it. And that's the thing. Exclusion of disabled women is rarely malicious. The problem of invisibility is simply so great that it doesn't occur to people to include us until we're sitting outside tapping on the windows.

Indeed, the very Destroy the Joint movement created in the wake of Jones's fatuousness inadvertently excludes disability from their approach. A website was set up where people could take a pledge that stated:

> I want an Australia where girls and women, where men and boys, can take part in our society without enduring discrimination, sexism and violence.
>
> I want an Australia where we respect each other; an Australia where no person experiences hate because of their gender, race, religion or sexuality.
>
> And I will challenge anyone who uses sex, race, religion or sexual orientation to incite hatred or to demean or vilify any of us. I will not stand by and let others do so without speaking up.

The omission of disability as a reason many people experience hate and exclusion is striking, so I raised it with the creators of the pledge. Disappointingly, they said, 'we can't include everything'. Well, of course we can. People with disabilities make up 20% of the population. More than half of us are women. If that doesn't rate a mention, I don't know what does.

Again, the exclusion is not malicious. But it is harmful. It reinforces the invisibility and exclusion that women with disabilities already face. It's yet another thing to overcome.

Whenever I hear a story, and I frequently do, of a person with disability achieving something 'against the odds' or 'overcoming obstacles', the intention is usually to portray disability itself as the odds and obstacles. This simply isn't true.

Living with disability is nothing compared to living with exclusion.

Again, we can't very well destroy the joint if we're not allowed in.

It is a shame that in the wake of Jones's comments, little attention has been paid to the issue that drew his ire in the first place. Jones quoted Prime Minister Julia Gillard as saying 'we know societies only reach their full potential if women are politically participating'.

To make that truly possible for all Australian women is what we must focus on. It's much more deserving of our time than some philistine on the radio.

Markers of Change

Senator Penny Wong

Progressives are always on the lookout for signs of change. Activists, feminists, reformers; we watch in hope for indicators that things have improved.

Unfortunately, for those of us who are impatient, this process is a little like watching the tide change. We watch, look away and only observe the difference the next time. And change often requires a reference point to be discernible: an event, a moment or a response from which to invite comparison in much the same way as landmarks enable us to perceive the changing of the tide. These are the markers of change.

The destroying the joint discussion, which became a movement of sorts, was one such marker. Not the comment, because in many ways it was unremarkable; a throwaway putdown like we've heard before, enhanced in its notoriety due only to the profile of the speaker. It was the response engendered that was remarkable.

When I first heard of the comment, I thought 'same old, same old'. A repetition of what our society had sadly begun to become inured to: a backdrop of ongoing personal and gendered vitriol directed towards the nation's prime minister, sending a message that it was once again acceptable to speak of women in this way.

Mad Men had come to Australian politics.

In fact, the nature of contemporary public debate to that point had itself been a marker. The boundaries of what was acceptable to say or to condone had been shifted and shifted again; where a senior political leader could speak of 'making an honest woman' of their opponent with little controversy, and tastelessly use an anti-rape slogan without embarrassment. These were warnings then that we had achieved far less than we had thought or hoped.

But as the Twitterverse took off following the now infamous statement, and word spread via Facebook and on blogs and more, the hashtag *destroythejoint* signalled *enough.*

It was a spontaneous outburst, a declaration that multiplied in minutes and grew over days and weeks in myriad different voices. Some humorous, some serious, some satirical; many different strategies all highlighting the absurdity of the assertion and coming together with little practical coordination but a great deal of shared principle. Many contributions also demonstrated aspects of the Australian character that we so value: a feistiness, an irreverence and an overriding belief in a fair go.

This was the sort of citizen power that social media potentially enables but which usually dissipates through fragmentation. Here, we saw a version of online collectivism.

And, for many, it was more: an underlying frustration

with our society's dominant voices that erupted in an online roar of 'You don't speak for me!' Because, for many of the advocates of the *#destroythejoint* message, these voices (whether of politician or talkback host) are disconnected from the experiences and beliefs of so many Australians.

In the ensuing days and weeks the power of the *#destroythejoint* trend or movement, howsoever described, surprised many. It upset the status quo and modelled a spontaneous activism that variously inspired or irritated. It was a change marker. It was a declaration that many Australians had had enough. Enough not just of acts of sexism, but of their acceptability. It was a declaration that offensive statements against women should not and would not continue to go unremarked, and it demonstrated the capacity of a social media campaign to disrupt the dominant paradigm.

But while the experience was so inspirational in many ways, it was for me also bookmarked by realisation. This episode for me ends in the aftermath of the now famous speech by the prime minister and my realisation yet again that we still have so much more to do.

Just as markers can demonstrate progress, so too they lay bare the status quo.

When Prime Minister Julia Gillard rose to her feet on the floor of the House of Representatives that day, few would have expected the speech that followed. A speech that was itself powerful, but vastly magnified by its resonance. It was heard by many women not as a speech about the prime minister, but as a speech about them. These were words that reflected their own experiences: a comment ignored, a snub disregarded, a cheek turned.

In the ensuing days, the prime minister's speech was not only viewed by women and men all over the world, it became a point of engagement for many Australians, and particularly young women, for whom politics often holds little relevance.

For many, it was a parliamentary articulation of the values that motivate them and, landing as it did in the context of an online campaign, gave the speech a significance of even greater intensity.

In a year that had been mired in conflict and negativity and division, both this speech and the *#destroythejoint* campaign spoke to a hope of something more – of a nation defined by both equality and opportunity, in which difference did not lead to belittlement.

It was a speech that also sparked furious debate. Interestingly, one of the themes in the discussion was reprised with much criticism of the mainstream media for missing its significance. This exemplified once again a disconnect between parts of our community and our institutional voices, a disconnect that can no longer be airily dismissed by references to a Twitter echo chamber because the echo can now be heard in too many places.

It's also a disconnect which derives from perceptions of relevance. Because while, for the Parliament House Press Gallery, the speech was primarily assessed in terms of political tactics and strategy, to many others, this frame was not relevant. This wasn't about day-to-day politicking but a deeper resonance in Prime Minister Gillard's words, words that gave voice to women's experience. For so many Australians – men and women – this was its significance.

Perhaps even more noteworthy was the divergence that became increasingly apparent in the public's response. As commentator Susie O'Brien wrote: 'While men wondered what all the fuss was about, many women around the nation cheered.'[1]

Some of this could be observed in the partisan sphere, with predictable responses accusing the prime minister of playing the victim, unable to 'stand the heat' and using gender as 'a shield against criticism'.

But the more important response was not from political players but from the community, and increasingly it was apparent to me that both men and women did indeed wonder 'what all the fuss was about'. Leaving aside the small minority whose views were clouded by their own prejudice, others were simply puzzled by the response. This spoke to me of the divergent experiences that so influence our understanding of the world; that even when we try, it is often a stretch for us to understand the experience of others.

Perhaps the men, and some women, who made clear that they didn't understand 'what the fuss was about' had not experienced or observed the sort of behaviour the prime minister's speech spoke to. Or, if they had witnessed sexism and misogyny, it did not carry the same emotional weight for them.

This serves as a reminder of the divergent realities that co-exist within our community; that we still often cannot see how different things are for another.

The most powerful descriptor of this I know was in an Eva Sallis lecture during which she said: 'The Aboriginal Australians I know live in a different Australia from the one I live in.'[2] While the distinction she speaks of is race rather than gender, it remains apposite. We live in the same Australia, we share many values, but our experiences and therefore our perceptions of reality can be so different. If we are to understand across these differences, we have to be capable of more than tolerance. We have to try to imagine another's experience and to do so with imagination, compassion and respect.

And we have to counter those voices whose intent is to divide. The retrograde trend which culminated in these events was enabled and permitted by our silence and by our acceptance of sexism and misogyny.

If we aspire to a national unity built on bringing people together, we must remember the importance of giving voice to these different realities.

And that complacency can become complicity if we do not speak out.

The University and the Beast: A Fairy Tale

Krissy Kneen

In February 2011, Krissy Kneen enrolled in a PhD in creative writing, looking at pornographic expression through literature. In September 2011, after a brief but emotionally devastating struggle with the university over the content of her creative component (published as Triptych *by Text Publishing in 2011) she was no longer enrolled in her studies. In 2012, she wrote the following story. It is, she says, a work of fiction.*

WEEK FIVE

Sarah Dainler thought the strawberry cream cake in the cabinet looked like a vagina. It was something to do with the way they had sliced it, taking away a slightly convex piece of the cake, the freshly revealed pink sponge within and the too-soft icing slipping over the swollen crust of it like some giant beast's ejaculate. The strawberries on top were part of the sex play: toying with your food. She had just finished reading Linda Jaivin's *Eat Me* and she supposed the supermarket scene had added to her interpretation of the image. She had begun to see sex everywhere, which was probably exactly what you were supposed to do when you were writing your PhD on the power of perversity in pornographic literary fiction.

'Hey.' James folded himself into the chair opposite her. James was her supervisor and, perversely, Sarah seemed to be the only woman on campus who was not overwhelmed by his boyish good looks. She looked at his sweet open face, the large intelligent eyes, took in his strong square shoulders, a hint of aftershave, masculine spicy. His presence in the café was no more or less sexually charged than her interaction with the strawberry sponge cake only moments before.

'Hey,' she said, closing her laptop and resting her hands on the top of it as if her fingers were still poised over the keyboard. She had been on a roll.

'How's it going?' He pointed to her computer with his chin, an oddly endearing gesture.

'I got hold of *Irene's Cunt*.'

'Great. Good work.'

'There's just so much. How do you narrow this kind of stuff down?'

'That's the trick. I still think you should look at the bacchanal.'

'Soon. Promise.'

James nodded. The waitress hovered beside their table. When James looked towards her, she blushed. Sarah wondered what it would be like to wield that kind of sexual power. The staff had always taken her for granted and she had been writing in this café every second day for a month.

He ordered a coffee for himself and raised an eyebrow at the cold cup beside her laptop.

'Sure,' she said. 'You can't have enough caffeine, right?'

When the waitress hurried self-consciously away, James leaned forward.

'Sarah. I just have to flag something with you.'

She felt her heart skip. She had handed in her initial notes on her exegesis along with the first of her pornographic novellas. She was new to this kind of research. The story was good. She was sure of that, but the essay was a bit lumpy, perhaps a little under-cooked.

'The head of department wants to read what you've written.'

'The essay.'

'No. Not the essay, that's fine. It's the pornography. There's some concern about the – content.'

'The story?'

'I'm not saying you should worry or anything.'

'Worry?'

'It is not like your writing is gratuitous. You have a clearly described reasoning behind your research.'

'What do you mean worry?'

'I mean don't. I have to pass the fiction on to him, but it'll be fine. I've got a masters student writing about a serial killer. He goes into intricate detailed explanations of how to remove a person's lower bowel. If he can get away with that … '

The waitress arrived with their coffees, spilling some. James moved to help her wipe it up. Their fingers touched. Sarah noticed how the waitress's hands were shaking. She looked around the café. There was a man sitting at the table next to them. He was short and nondescript and he kept wiping the palms of his hands against his jeans. He could easily be a serial killer and yet no waitress would start to tremble setting his coffee cup down beside him. Such is the power of sex, Sarah supposed.

WEEK TEN

On Friday the froth on the top of her cappuccino disappeared, not a slow bubble-by-bubble bursting, but all at once. One minute there was froth and the next minute it was gone leaving an oily smear of chocolate clinging to the hot meniscus. She had been working on the second novella. A sex scene. That was the thing with pornographic literature. There was very little of it that was not an actual sex scene. She liked writing it in the university café, the illicitness of the act, subversive. She liked the effort it took to keep her bored expression when a woman was opening her legs under the careful tapping of her fingers. She liked rubbing her eyes as if exhausted, picking up her coffee, sipping a little before turning her attention back to the protagonist whose fingers were sticky with the juices of her lover, her mouth a glisten of emissions from half a page of cunnilingus. Sarah sighed and feigned a yawn as her dark-haired heroine took hold of one of her breasts, greasing it with the slipperiness of her lover's cunt and pushed it into the orifice as one might push a butternut pumpkin into the yielding folds of a woman's labia, marvelling at the way the orifice expands to accommodate the ripe globe of the fruit. The breast would be just the beginning. The woman would slide her whole body, an inch at a time, into the ever-expanding cunt of her lover until by the end of the story she had disappeared entirely.

One breast and then a second. Her girl had pushed forward with her tongue, licking down the squeezed-tight globes of her own cleavage, her tongue slipping into the soft yielding wetness of flesh. It was then that the froth on the top of her cappuccino began to hum quietly. Sarah stopped typing. She touched the edge of her cup and, yes, there was a slight vibration. Sarah frowned. She sat back, staring, puzzled, at the cup. Nothing else was vibrating, just her cappuccino. Then the froth was gone. Burst. All at once.

Sarah looked around. Nothing had changed. Her computer was still open, the woman in her story paused in the middle of a perverse act. The woman behind the coffee maker was frothing milk, sliding the metal jug up and down on the hot breath of the wand. The cake of the day, this time chocolate, still gaped lewdly, dripping brown icing in a predictably suggestive manner down its sliced black heart.

Sarah pushed the cup away from her. She closed the laptop.

WEEK TWELVE

When boys write about sex it is literature. When girls write about sex it is erotica. This seemed clear enough. She rested her copy of *Wish* by Peter Goldsworthy reverentially at the edge of the table. The consummation of the sex act between an ape and a man. There was nothing explicit about the moment of interspecies sex. Unspeakable. Words could not describe it according to Goldsworthy, and yet she knew this was not true. Words could of course describe it. In her case, the acts involved a woman and an octopus, a dog, a small pony. Words could in fact describe anything. That was the wonder of the written word, the world transformed and yet still potent.

Her supervisor, James, had left a packet of mints on the table. She supposed this was on purpose, a small gesture of his support, a sweetener to take away the bitter taste of their conversation.

They wanted her to remove the creative component of her thesis. In short they wanted her to stop writing pornography.

When men like Frank Moorhouse, Ian McEwan, Rod Jones, Nabokov, when these great men of literature write about sex it is elevated to something transcendent. The mind overcoming the content of the work.

'Call it erotica perhaps?' James seemed agitated, shifting a little on his seat, his usual calm broken by the weight of the information he had to convey. She could smell a slight acidity emanating from him, a nervous sweat perhaps. He was not wearing his signature spicy cologne.

She had three options it seemed. Remove the creative component from her PhD so that she was effectively analysing rather than creating pornographic literature. Remove the word 'pornography' from her study entirely, veiling the naked sexuality of her work under the softer, more feminine word 'erotica' and, with it, remove any reference to perversity including the bestial sex at the heart of her latest novella. Or, three, move to a different department where she would be thrown from hand to hand like the hot potato that she so clearly was, till someone dropped her, eventually, after years of struggle.

She could still smell the distinct odour of distress. It had seeped into the chair, permeated the cushion that he had been leaning against, rubbed into the laminate of the table. As her supervisor they were in this together. Her transgressions would be his transgressions. She was still on scholarship here but those days were numbered. The Dean had made it perfectly clear.

University Funds Pornography was not a newspaper headline that they were happy to wear.

She had planned her day, a meeting with James, some readings on the bacchanal that he was so insistent that she research, finishing the second story, a cold glass of wine at the university bar. She looked into her empty coffee cup as if the dark stains on the bottom were a sign of something. A tempest perhaps, the dark clouds of a storm brewing. She had been so excited about receiving her scholarship. A PhD would be hard work but she was dedicated, smart, fearless. She would tackle the very hardest questions in her study, she would wade into the cesspit of literary sexuality, taking on the great men of letters who disguised their actual names and clothed themselves in the upraised skirts of prostitutes to romp in the filth of unfettered sexuality. She would show them all that a woman could be just as perverse and yet a hundred times more ethical than they could be. She would level the playing field with detonations of foul language and lewd acts.

Now she sat, staring impotently into a coffee cup. All the virile sexuality of her undertaking seemed to have gone suddenly flaccid in the space of one short conversation.

'You want another cup of coffee now?' It was the waiter, the sweet young one with the curls and the much older boyfriend who would pick him up on his motorcycle when his shift ended. She knew the staff a little now. She had written 50 000 words at this particular table. They knew how many coffees she would order, they knew to make her a salad at 12.15. She had imagined she would spend the next two years here, sitting in this corner, secretly detailing the exact shape and scent of a woman's genitals, struggling over the perfect descriptors for the pearly whiteness of ejaculate, Googling 'horse penis' using her iPhone hotspot so that she wouldn't contravene the university rules about inappropriate content on their wifi network.

She looked at the screen in front of her. The protagonist had fallen in love with her dog. The dog loved her back, so much so that he was poised above her, his penis a little wriggly pink finger of flesh, she was a virgin, but she was in love and even the pain of the consummation would, with a few careful canine thrusts, transform into sexual pleasure.

The Dean wanted her to cease and desist. There had been a directive. She must remove the bestial content from her manuscript or the university would remove their support for her project despite the rigorous questioning of pornographic expression and perversity, despite the great men of letters who had been here before her. Despite de Sade and Bataille and even Felix Salter, who was the writer of *Bambi* as well as one of the many fake prostitute memoirs that had been circulated illicitly in hand-bound volumes throughout the ages. Cease and desist.

'Or are you finished? Should I get you the bill?'

She took a deep breath and plucked her copy of *Wish* from the edge of the table before it tipped over and plummeted to the floor.

'Yeah. Another coffee would be great thanks. And maybe, in an hour or so —'

'The salad. I've already saved you a serve of the parmesan, rocket and roast pumpkin.'

'Excellent.' She tried to smile. She raised her fingers above the keyboard. One thrust of those neat little canine hips and the girl would be a virgin no more. Sarah bit her bottom lip. She began to type.

WEEK SIXTEEN

Sarah stood outside L block and her hands were trembling. She had been ambushed. She knew it. It was too late now to storm back into the Dean's office and demand the support of someone, anyone, student services, a counsellor, a lawyer, even the simple courtesy of having her own supervisor present. She held her hands up in front of her, stretched out to catch the dapple of sunlight on her fingers. It was, indeed, a beautiful day. A group of young women walked passed her clutching folders and library books. One of them laughed, a sweet sound. It was easy to imagine this girl running with her friends in the playground at high school less than a year ago. Sarah felt terribly old. Too old certainly to be treated like a naughty child. The Dean had used soothing words. It sounded for a moment as though they were praising her for her boldness, taking on difficult areas of research, too difficult certainly for the limited skills of their time-poor staff. She looked into her hands, the light and shade of them, and was almost surprised by the drops of water that had begun to spatter her fingers. Rain, she thought, and looked up at a sky bereft of clouds. It was only when she felt the droplets of water slide down her cheeks and gather at the edge of her jaw line that she realised she was upset.

She had two weeks. Two weeks to find a new supervisor, a new department, a new topic of research. Two weeks to abandon and rewrite a 50 000-word document from scratch without the calm, smart, sweet support of James. They had fired her supervision, fired her whole department it seemed, but when she stopped, trying to calm her breathing and looked at it another way, it was easy to see that in reality they had just fired her. Ultimately, she would be the only one without a job, without a scholarship, without a future at the university.

Her bag was inordinately heavy. She opened it, glanced at the stack of books in there. *The 120 Days of Sodom*. She was suddenly too exhausted to carry the de Sade another step. She lifted the heavy volume out of her bag and placed it on the footpath. Lighter. Certainly, she could turn now and walk a little way down the hill. The next book to be abandoned was Goldsworthy's *Wish*. A book about bestiality by an award-winning author that had been hailed as literature, transformed into a stageplay, when she herself had been silenced so dismissively. She placed the book on the bench at the bus stop, wondering vaguely if the sweet image of an ape's hairy fingers on the cover would tempt some child into reading the transgressions stored inside.

She picked up pace, her boots slamming against the pavement as she made her way down the hill. She reached into her bag and pulled out *Irene's Cunt*, tossing it casually into the doorway of a chemist as if it were their mail. *Lolita*, the lovely *Lolita*, found a new home on a table outside the burger place; she deposited *The Story of the Eye* under the windscreen wiper of some student's shiny red Mini Coupé. She was running now, a rain of paperbacks thundering down onto the pavement behind her, Henry Miller, Kawabata, Sacher-Masoch, Devereaux. All these men of perverse letters abandoned in her furious downhill stride.

She stopped outside the café where she had been working so diligently for the first four months. They were minding her computer while she ducked up the hill for the meeting with the head of school. Her laptop was resting on top of the cake cabinet.

The Dean had read the first of her perverse narratives. The second was almost finished, silently waiting in her Word documents to be unleashed on the unsuspecting reading public. If they thought the first story was disturbing, too dangerous for their program of study, too wild and furious to be unleashed on the world, then what would they think of the second, darker, more sexually transgressive story? Or the third, which was only the germ of an idea in her brain, but which was gestating day by day, growing larger and more wriggly, causing her head to throb with its dark and dangerous potential.

'How'd your meeting go?'

Sweet young man. Genuine smile. He hadn't yet noticed the snail-trail of dried tears staining her skin with their salt, the tremor in her fingers, the incredible lightness of her bag, which only moments ago had been weighed down with the legacy of great men. She was free of it all now. Free to walk out into the world unburdened by her obligations to the university. She was no longer a student here. She no longer had deadlines and dead white males to reference. She stood in the café unfettered for the first time. And, for the first time she heard it. The throbbing, a pulse. She wondered if the waiter could hear it too.

'You OK?'

She stared at him, trying to hear his voice through the suddenly thunderous pulse in her head. Was she OK? Did he really want to know if she was OK? Or was this, like so many words we speak, yet another politeness. Did he actually want to know what was wrong and what she could possibly do to right it once more?

Her laptop was vibrating. She looked past him to where it was perched on the cabinet and she was certain this was where the pulsing was emanating from. The little heartbeat of a light on the top of the laptop pulsed, a warning that although the lid was closed, the computer was still turned on, the content of her story still open on the desktop. The terribly dangerous sexuality of her fiction throbbing there like the ticking of a bomb as it counts down to detonation.

She heard a rattle of crockery and glanced to the table beside the door. A hiss and the froth disappeared off the top of the coffee. The same sudden absence of froth. The same thing that had happened to her own coffee only a few weeks before. She saw the man lift the cup and peer into it, confused. She watched as his chocolate slice began to bubble, to melt down to a dark, almost black puddle, which slid over the edge of his plate and onto the table.

A sound like ice melting, a cracking, surfaces dividing. Sarah watched as a sharp line etched the surface of the kitchen cabinet. The cakes dripped their cream onto the plates, the sponge peeled back.

'Are you OK?'

The waiter hadn't noticed. Perhaps it wasn't happening at all, perhaps it was just in her head that the pastries were reshaping themselves, the hills and valleys of fruit glaze realigning. The strudel gaped, the puff-pastry parted, the sticky sweetness oozed out to the surface.

He put out his hand to touch her elbow. She must have looked quite pale, perhaps he thought she would faint. His fingers touched her bare skin and he flinched away again, shaking his hand as if it had been snapped at by some wild beast.

'— the fuck?'

And the cabinet exploded. The barista pulling a coffee at the machine beside it shrieked. The waiter held his still stinging fingers up to cover his face. Glass shards shot out and thumped into the feature wall with its row of books, ripping through the leather and sending slivers of paper scattering like feathers. She heard the clatter of her laptop as it fell through the suddenly shattered cabinet and came to rest, the screen flipping open, in the middle of a black forest cake. She saw the document still open on the screen, her words, her sex words, the power of them, her own ideas so charged that they had frightened a whole department, leading to her expulsion from these halls of learning. The throbbing seemed louder now. She pressed the palms of her hands against her head. There was blood on her cheek, glass shrapnel perhaps, or maybe just the terrible sound tearing at the thin membranes in her ears. She held her hands in front of her face, blood now dappling the skin where there had been sunlight.

'Oh god,' said the sweet young waiter, holding out his hands to her, too afraid to touch, 'are you all right?' She didn't hear it but she saw the words, lip-read them, and her own voice when it came was a bellow, a roar, a rush of air that hit him hard in the chest and sent him tumbling back against the door to the male toilets.

'No!' she said. 'No! No! No!'

The fault lines spread out from her feet. She hadn't stamped but it was as if she had raised a giant heavy boot and crashed it down against the floorboards. The concrete cracked, the doorframe buckled, cars trembled, pitched sideways, scraped along the now crumbling bitumen of the road. The fissures stretched out towards L Block, Z block, A block, the whole alphabet of the university began to shake, the students held on to their desks, ducked underneath them, threw themselves into stairwells, plummeted from windows. The buildings shuddered and then, one by one they began to fall.

Sarah lifted her hands from her face.

A terrible silence had settled around her. People ran, screaming, along the footpath. She could see them, but the sound had been turned off. They were like a movie played on mute. Their terror now seemed almost comical.

She stepped towards the cabinet. Her computer was open, jammed into the prised-apart orifice of a dark and creamy cake. She reached in, avoiding the shards of glass and the profiteroles that had burst open like cysts. Her story was still there. She balanced the thing on her arm and hit command and S.

Saved. Her story was safe.

She felt a shudder in the ground, another building toppling, these inviolable halls, nothing but rubble now. She closed the laptop and cradled it against her chest like a baby. She slipped a thumb in her mouth, it was wet with the remnants of the cake: thick, sticky, and oh so sweet.

Contributors

Steph Bowe is the author of young adult novels *Girl Saves Boy* and *All This Could End*. Steph has appeared at various festivals, including the Melbourne and Brisbane writers festivals, the National Young Writers Festival and the Emerging Writers Festival. In 2010, Steph won Express Media's award for Outstanding Achievement by a Writer Under 25. She was born in Melbourne in 1994 and now lives in Queensland with her family. Find her at stephbowe.com.

Dr Leslie Cannold is a writer and writing mentor, public speaker and public ethicist at the Gender, Leadership and Social Sustainability Research Unit at Monash University in Melbourne. In 2011, Leslie was honoured as Australian Humanist of the Year. Her books include the award-winning *The Abortion Myth* and *What, No Baby?* Her latest book is a historical novel, *The Book of Rachael*. Find her at cannold.com.

Dr Abby Cathcart is a senior lecturer in the School of Management at Queensland University of Technology. Abby currently researches in the area of customised work, employee voice and cross-cultural group working and she lectures in Management and Organisational Behaviour as well as Cross Cultural Communication. In 2011, Abby received an *Australian Learning and Teaching Council* Award for Excellence in the priority area of teaching large classes, and a citation for her work in Assessment and Feedback.

Destroy the Joint, an online community of more than 26 000 people, seeks gender equality in Australia by shining a spotlight on sexism and misogyny. The DtJ community changed the way Australians think: from companies to cafés; from t-shirt manufacturers to radio stations; from church-run organisations to telecommunications companies. In 2013, DtJ won the NAB Women's Agenda 'Agenda Setter' Award, decided by popular vote. DtJ's administrators are Wendy French, El Gibbs, Jennie Hill, Sally McManus, Amanda McNulty, Jenna Price and Jill Tomlinson.

Catherine Deveny is a comedian, author, social commentator, broadcaster and regular columnist with *The Age*. Along with fellow contributors Jane Caro and Leslie Cannold, Catherine co-founded *No Chicks No Excuses* – a website dedicated to redressing the lack of female voices in public life. Catherine is a proud ambassador for *Dying with Dignity Victoria* and *International Day of People with Disability*. Her first novel and seventh book is called *The Happiness Show*. Find her at catherinedeveny.com.

Monica Dux is a writer, social commentator, author of *Things I Didn't Expect (when I was expecting)* and co-author of *The Great Feminist Denial.* She can be heard regularly on ABC radio and 3RRR, and has been published widely, especially on women's issues. Monica is a founding board member of the Stella Prize, an annual literary prize that celebrates Australian women's writing. Find her at monicadux.com.au.

Lily Edelstein is a 17-year-old student, artist and feminist. When she gets jaded about problematic advertising and pop culture, Lily watches *Buffy the Vampire Slayer* and makes satirical art and zines. The perils of ignorance and inequality disturb her, and she is working on a body of horror-themed feminist pieces, because girls do more than 'check on the mysterious noise in the middle of the night (in their underwear)'.

Clementine Ford is a freelance writer, broadcaster and troublemaker based in Melbourne. She enjoys cups of tea on stormy summer afternoons, men with beards and the collected works of Nancy Mitford. You can read more of her work at clementineford.com.au or follow her on Twitter @clementine_ford.

Catherine Fox is a journalist, author and public speaker with a particular interest in women and the workforce, workforce trends, management and career. Catherine worked for the *Australian Financial Review* until November 2012, and has written three books. Her latest is *Seven Myths about Women and Work.* She is on several advisory boards, including the Defence

Force Gender Equality Advisory Board, and lives in Sydney with her husband and three daughters.

Nina Funnell is a freelance writer, social commentator and feminist activist. She sits on various boards and councils and in 2010 was awarded the Australian Human Rights Community (Individual) award for her advocacy work around sexual assault. Nina has recently written her first book, co-authored with Dannielle Miller. It is a non-fiction work aimed at teen girls on the subject of ethical dating and respectful relationships, and will be published in 2014.

Corinne Grant is best known for her work on television shows *Rove Live* and *The Glasshouse*. In addition to this, she has appeared on everything from *Spicks and Specks* to *Dancing With The Stars* to *Good News Week*. She is a weekly columnist for the online magazine *The Hoopla*, and her first book is called *Lessons in Letting Go: Confessions of a Hoarder*. Corinne is an ambassador for the National Breast Cancer Foundation and the Asylum Seekers Resource Centre. Find her at corinnegrant.com.au.

Wendy Harmer is an author and broadcaster. She has written five books for adults, two plays, three one-woman stage shows and a libretto for the Australian Opera. Her bestselling children's book series 'Pearlie in the Park' has been translated into ten languages. She is the editor-in-chief of the daily online women's magazine *The Hoopla* (www.thehoopla.com.au). Find her at www.wendyharmer.com or follow her on Twitter @wendy_harmer.

Susan Johnson is the author of seven novels and two works of non-fiction, including a memoir of motherhood, illness and writing, *A Better Woman*. She was shortlisted for the 1991 Victorian Premier's Literary Award for her novel *Flying Lessons*. Her latest novel is *My Hundred Lovers*. She currently works as a journalist at *Qweekend* magazine in Brisbane, and is an Adjunct Professor in Creative Writing at QUT. Read more of her work at abetterwoman.net.

Krissy Kneen works at Avid Reader Bookshop in Brisbane. She is the author of the sexual memoir *Affection*, the pornographic narrative *Triptych*, and *Steeplechase*. She has had short fiction published in www.nerve.com, *Griffith Review* and *Best Women's Erotica 2013*. Her fiction has been banned and removed from the iBook store and her blog, www.furious-vaginas.com, is banned in China.

Michelle Law is a Brisbane writer. Her work has appeared in *Women of Letters*, *Growing up Asian in Australia* and *Meanjin*. She is an AWGIE award-winning screenwriter and is currently working on a documentary, short film and TV comedy series. Her brother once told her 'on average, you will cop roughly 50 672% more abuse [on social media] by mere virtue of having a vagina'. She is still trying to grow a penis. Follow her on Twitter @ms_michellelaw.

Dr Carmen Lawrence has served at both State and Federal levels. She was the WA Minister for Education and Aboriginal Affairs and was the first woman Premier and Treasurer of a state government. She shifted to Federal politics in 1994 and was elected National President of the Labor Party in 2004. She retired from politics in 2007 and is now Director of the Centre for the Study of Social Change at the University of Western Australia and Chair of the Australian Heritage Council.

Melissa Lucashenko is an Australian writer of European and Goorie heritage. Her first novel, *Steam Pigs*, won the Dobbie Literary Award for Australian women's fiction and was shortlisted in the New South Wales Premier's Literary Awards and regional Commonwealth Writers' Prize. *Steam Pigs* was followed by the Aurora Prize-winning *Killing Darcy*, and *Hard Yards*, which was shortlisted for the 2001 *Courier-Mail* Book of the Year. Melissa's latest novel is *Mullumbimby*. Melissa lives between Brisbane and the Bundjalung nation.

Paula McDonald is Professor and ARC Future Research Fellow in the Queensland University of Technology Business School. Her research addresses work in its social context – in particular, gendered forms of workplace discrimination and harassment, work-life boundaries, and young people's early employment experiences. Paula has published over 40 journal articles and three international edited books: *Women and Representation in Local Government: International Case Studies* (with Barbara Pini); *Young People and Work* (with Robin Price, Janis Bailey and Barbara Pini) and *Men, Wage Work and Family* (with Emma Jeanes).

Emily Maguire is the author of four novels and two non-fiction books. Her articles and essays on feminism, sex and culture have been published widely including in *The Monthly*, *The Weekend Australian* and *The Age*. She is a 2010 *Sydney Morning Herald* Best Young Australian Novelist and the recipient of the 2011 New South Wales Writer's Fellowship. Her latest book is the novel *Fishing for Tigers*. Find her at emilymaguire.com.au.

Dannielle Miller is co-founder and CEO of Enlighten Education, a provider of in-school workshops for teen girls on body image, self-esteem and empowerment. She is the author of *The Butterfly Effect* and *The Girl with the Butterfly Tattoo – A Girl's Guide to Claiming her Power*, and is currently co-writing a book with Nina Funnell which will offer girls an up-front guide to ethical dating and relationships. Find her at danniellemiller.com.

Jennifer Mills is the author of two novels, *Gone* and *The Diamond Anchor*, and a collection of short stories, *The Rest is Weight*. Her work has received wide critical acclaim and won numerous awards both nationally and internationally. In 2012, she was named a *Sydney Morning Herald* Best Young Australian Novelist. She is currently the fiction editor at *Overland*. Find her at jenjen.com.au and on Twitter at @millsjenjen.

Christine Milne grew up on a dairy farm and after university taught in north-west Tasmania. She led the successful campaign against the Wesley Vale pulp mill and was elected to the Tasmanian parliament in 1989. Christine was the first woman to lead a political party in Tasmania in 1993. She was elected to the Senate in 2004 and as leader of the Greens in 2012. She is a United Nations Global 500 Laureate.

Tara Moss is the author of nine novels, a journalist, blogger, sometime model, UNICEF patron for Breastfeeding and a doctoral student at Sydney University. Since 1999, she has written nine bestselling novels and has been published in eighteen countries in twelve languages. Her writing has appeared in the *Australian Literary Review*, *Sydney Morning Herald*, *The Hoopla*, *Sun Herald*, and *Daily Life*. Visit her at taramoss.com.

Jenna Price is a wife and mother of two daughters and a son, now all adults. She worked as a journalist for 25 years and is now a journalism and social media academic at the University of Technology, Sydney. She writes a weekly column for *The Canberra Times* and contributes to *The Drum*, *Crikey* and *The Conversation*. She has been a member of various feminist groups since she was seventeen.

Yvette Vignando is the publisher of parenting website happychild.com.au, and dedicated to work that supports children's social and emotional wellbeing and their human rights. She appears regularly on Channel 9 as a parenting commentator and is known for speaking, writing and advocating for the importance of emotional intelligence being taught in schools. Formerly a lawyer, and still an executive coach for senior managers, she has never been accused of destroying the joint.

Penny Wong was born in Malaysia and moved to Australia when she was eight years old. Penny was elected to the Senate in 2001 and was appointed Minister for Climate Change and Water in 2007, a portfolio that was later expanded to include Energy Efficiency. In 2010, she was appointed Minister for Finance and Deregulation. Penny is the first woman to be elected by the Labor Caucus to hold the senior position of Deputy Leader of the Government in the Senate. Penny and her partner, Sophie, have a young daughter.

Stella Young is a comedian, disability advocate and editor of ABC's *Ramp Up* website, an online space for news, discussion and opinion about disability in Australia. With a particular interest in issues facing young people and women with disabilities, Stella holds a degree in journalism and a Diploma of Secondary Education. Prior to joining the ABC, Stella worked in public programs at Melbourne Museum, where she taught kids about bugs, dinosaurs and other weird and wonderful things. Find her at stellayoung.com and on Twitter @stellajyoung.

Notes

LESLIE CANNOLD

1 *The Global Gender Gap Report* 2011, World Economic Forum, http://www.weforum.org/reports/global-gender-gap-report-2011.

2 Windsor, G, 'Writers and Reviewers', *Island Magazine* No. 27, Winter 1986: 15–18.

3 McCann, Dr J and Wilson, J, *Representation of Women in Australian Parliaments*, Australian Parliamentary Library, 7 March 2012.

4 Irving, R, 'Career Trajectories of Women in Policing in Australia', *Trends & Issues in Crime and Criminal Justice*, No. 370, Australian Institute of Criminology, February 2009.

5 Stevenson, C, 'The Blokeyness Index: Blokes Win the Gender War in Australia's 4th Estate', *The King's Tribune*, 6 December 2012, http://www.kingstribune.com/index.php/magazines/december-2012/item/1659-the-blokeyness-index-blokes-win-the-gender-war-in-australia-s-4th-estate.

6 Wikipedia, 'Arab Spring', http://en.wikipedia.org/wiki/Arab_Spring#cite_ref-ASPO-H-01_23-0.

LILY EDELSTEIN

1 'It Happens All The Time', *Rookie*, 21 May 2012, http://rookiemag.com/2012/05/it-happens-all-the-time/.

TARA MOSS

1 'Homicide Trends in the United States, 1980–2008', US Justice Department, November 2011, http://bjs.ojp.usdoj.gov/content/pub/pdf/htus8008.pdf.

2 'Men Fare Worse than Women in Education, Health and Crime', Australian Bureau of Statistics media release, 27 July 2012, http://www.abs.gov.au/ausstats/abs@.nsf/Lookup/by%20Subject/4125.0~Jul%202012~Media%20Release~Men%20fare%20worse%20than%20women%20in%20education,%20health%20and%20crime%20(Media%20Release)~6152.

3 Women in National Parliaments, http://www.ipu.org/wmn-e/world.htm.

4 'Gender Pay Gap Statistics', Australian Bureau of Statistics, http://www.wgea.gov.au/Information_Centres/Resource_Centre/Statistics/Gender_Pay_Gap_Fact_Sheet_May_2012.pdf.

5 'Gender Indicators, Australia – Superannuation', Australian Bureau of Statistics, January 2012, http://www.abs.gov.au/ausstats/abs@.nsf/Lookup/by+Subject/4125.0~Jan+2012~Main+Features~Superannuation~1230.

6 'Silenced: Gender Gap in Election Coverage', *4thEstate.net*, http://www.4thestate.net/female-voices-in-media-infographic/.

7 Greer, G, 'Why the World Doesn't Need an Annie Warhol or a Francine Bacon', *The Guardian*, 17 January 2010, http://www.guardian.co.uk/artanddesign/2010/jan/17/germaine-greer-elles-pompidou.

8 'Should More Famous Women be Depicted as Statues?', BBC News, 23 August 2012, http://www.bbc.co.uk/news/entertainment-arts-19356833.

9 'Seen But Not Heard: How Women Make Front Page News', Women in Journalism, 15 October 2012, http://womeninjournalism.co.uk/wp-content/uploads/2012/10/Seen_but_not_heard.pdf.

10 'The Count', VIDA – Women in Literary Arts, http://www.vidaweb.org/the-count.

11 Moss-Racusin, CA; Dovidio, JF; Brescoll, VL; Graham, MJ; and Handelsman, J, 'Science Faculty's Subtle Gender Biases Favor Male Students', http://www.pnas.org/content/early/2012/09/14/1211286109.

12 Rothfield, P and Hadland, D, 'What's the Buzz: Phil Rothfield and Darren Hadland look at the Best and Fairest of 2012', *The Daily Telegraph*, 23 December 2012, http://www.dailytelegraph.com.au/sport/nrl/whats-the-buzz-phil-rothfield-and-darren-hadland-look-at-the-best-and-fairest-of-2012/story-e6frexnr-1226542468659.

CARMEN LAWRENCE

1 Lubchenco, J. 'Entering the Century of the Environment: A New Social Contract for Science', *Science*, 279 (1998), 492.
2 Lytle, MH, *The Gentle Subversive: Rachel Carson, Silent Spring and the Rise of the Environmental Movement.* New York, Oxford University Press, 2007, 133.
3 'Rachel Carson's Warning', *The New York Times*, 2 July 1962, 28.
4 Wright, J, 'The Individual in a New Environmental Age', in *Because I was Invited,* Melbourne, Oxford University Press, 1975, 251.
5 ibid.
6 Dasgupta, P, 'Nature's Role in Sustaining Economic Development', *Philosophical Transactions of the Royal Society*, vol. 365, no. 1537, 2010, 6.
7 ibid.
8 Schor, J, *Plenitude: The New Economics of True Wealth.* Melbourne, Scribe, 2010.
9 Judt, T, *Ill Fares the Land.* London, Allen Lane, 2010, 1.
10 McNeill, JR, *Something New Under the Sun: An Environmental History of the Twentieth Century World.* New York, Norton, 2000, 336.
11 Krugman, P, 'The Finite World', *The New York Times*, 26 December 2010, http://www.nytimes.com/2010/12/27/opinion/27krugman.html.
12 Stiglitz, JE, 'A Cool Calculus of Global Warming', *Project Syndicate*, 2009, http://www.project-syndicate.org/commentary/a-cool-calculus-of-global-warming.
13 Orrell, D, *Economyths: Ten Ways That Economics Gets It Wrong*, Sydney, Allen & Unwin, 2010, 214.
14 Bok, D, *The Politics of Happiness: What Government Can Learn from the New Research on Well-Being.* Princeton, Princeton University Press, 2009.
15 West Australian Aboriginal Child Health Survey, *Kalinga Research Network Report*, 2004.
16 Conner, L; Albrecht, G; Higginbotham, N; Freeman, S; and Smith, W, 'Environmental Change and Human Health in Upper Hunter Communities of New South Wales, Australia', *EcoHealth 1* (Suppl. 2), 47–58, 2004, 47.
17 Nitschke, M; Tucker, G; Bi, P, 'Morbidity and Mortality During Heatwaves in Metropolitan Adelaide', *Medical Journal of Australia*, 187(11–12); 662–665, 2007.
18 Sherwood, S and Huber, M, 'An Adaptability Limit to Climate Change Due to Heat Stress', *Proceedings of the National Academy of Science*, 107 (21), 9552–9555, 2010, 9952.
19 Rehdanz, K and Maddison, D, 'Climate and Happiness', *Ecological Economics*, 52(1), 111–125, 2005.

20 Smyth, R; Nielsen, I; Zhai, Q; Liu, T; Liu, Y; Tang, CY; Wang, Z; Wang, Z; and Zhang, J, 'Environmental Surroundings and Personal Well-being in Urban China', *Monash Department of Economics Discussion Paper* 32/08, 2008.
21 Kasser, T, *The High Price of Materialism*, Cambridge, MA, MIT Press, 2002.
22 Reed, K, '15 Questions with Jane Goodall', *The Harvard Crimson*, 7 May 2010, www.thecrimson.com.
23 Schultz, PW; Gouveia, VV; Cameron, LD; Tankha, G; Schmuck, P; and Franek, M, 'Values and their Relationship to Environmental Concern and Conservation Behavior', *Journal of Cross-Cultural Psychology*, July 2005, vol. 36, no. 4, 457–475, 2005.
Zelezny, LC; Chua, PP; and Aldrich, C, 'Elaborating on Gender Differences in Environmentalism', *Journal of Social Issues*, 56, 443–457, 2000.

EMILY MAGUIRE

1 Alan Jones, on air interview with Senator Barnaby Joyce, 31 August 2012, transcript: http://nationals.org.au/News/LatestNews/tabid/94/articleType/ArticleView/articleId/7723/Senator-Barnaby-Joyce--Interview-with-Alan-Jones-on-2GB.aspx.
2 World Bank, 'Gender Equality and Development', *World Development Report 2012*, http://go.worldbank.org/6R2KGVEXP0.
3 Ballington, Julie, *Equality in Politics: A Survey of Women and Men in Parliaments*, Inter-Parliamentary Union, 2008, http://www.ipu.org/pdf/publications/equality08-e.pdf.
4 World Bank, *Toward Gender Equality in East Asia and the Pacific*, 2012 http://siteresources.worldbank.org/EASTASIAPACIFICEXT/Resources/226300-1339798342386/eap-gender-full-conference.pdf.
5 UNDP, *Power, Voice and Rights: A Turning Point for Gender Equality in Asia and the Pacific*, Macmillan, 2010, http://hdr.undp.org/en/reports/regional/asiathepacific/RHDR-2010-AsiaPacific.pdf.
6 WRAP, *Promoting Gender Equity in the Pacific: Recommendations for Pacific Island Forum Leaders*, 2011, http://www.ifuw.org/pgwnet/docs/2011-promoting-gender-equality-WRAP.pdf.
7 Srivastava, N, 'Exposing Violence against Women: A Campaign in Uttar Pradesh', *Economic and Political Weekly*, 34(8), 20 February 1999, 453–454.
8 Ashoka India, 'Madhavi Kukreja', Ashoka Fellow Profile, http://india.ashoka.org/fellow/madhavi-kuckreja.
9 Moore, U, 'The Rise of Afghanistan's Fearless Young Feminists', 6 July 2011, *UN Dispatch* http://www.undispatch.com/the-rise-of-afghanistan%E2%80%99s-fearless-young-feminists.

10 Akbar, N, 'Women Take a Stand in Kabul', *The New York Times*, 22 November 2011, http://kristof.blogs.nytimes.com/2011/11/22/women-take-a-stand-in-kabul/.
11 Schlaffer, E, 'A Powerful Voice for Libyan Women: Interview with Alaa Murabit', *Women Without Borders*, 4 May 2012, http://www.women-without-borders.org/news/296/.
12 The Voice of Libyan Women, *2011– July 2012 Project Report*, http://www.vlwlibya.org/resources/VLW-2011-July-2012.pdf.
13 Hviid, S (Translated by Andrew Bell), 'Abuse of Religion Libya's Women's Major Challenge', *WoMen Dialogue*, 14 August 2012, http://www.womendialogue.org/magazine/abuse-religion-greatest-challenge-women-libya.
14 Gorani, A, 'On the Record: Women in South Kordofan', *Open Democracy*, 14 November 2011, http://www.opendemocracy.net/5050/amel-gorani/on-record-women-in-south-kordofan.
15 Ru'ya, 'South Kordofan Regional Background', *Ruya Blog*, http://ruyaassociation.blogspot.com.au/p/regional-background.html.
16 Gorani, loc. cit.
17 Gorani, loc. cit.
18 'UN Security Council R 1325 – Karen Women Have to be Part of the Peace Process', *Karen News*, March 5 2012, http://karennews.org/2012/03/un-security-council-r-1325-karen-women-have-to-be-part-of-the-peace-process.html/.
19 Phyu Phyu Sann and Akila Radhakrishnan, 'License to Rape: How Burma's Military Employs Systematic Sexualized Violence,' *Women Under Siege*, 15 March 2012, http://www.womenundersiegeproject.org/blog/entry/license-to-rape-how-burmas-military-employs-systematic-sexualized-violence.
20 Women's League of Burma, 'Background', *Women of Burma* http://womenofburma.org/aboutus/.
21 Women's League of Burma, 'Programs', *Women of Burma* http://womenofburma.org/aboutus/programs/.

YVETTE VIGNANDO

1 'Radio Broadcaster Alan Jones Blames "Cyber Bullying" for Commercials Being Pulled from Show', *The Australian*, 8 October 2012, http://www.theaustralian.com.au/media/radio-broadcaster-alan-jones-blames-cyber-bullying-for-commercials-being-pulled-from-show/story-e6frg996-1226490322476.
2 Sheikh, S, 'When Bullies Play Victim', *Sydney Morning Herald*, 8 October 2012, http://www.smh.com.au/opinion/politics/when-bullies-play-victim-20121008-278ki.html.
3 Partridge, E. 'Alan Jones Apologises to Prime Minister', *The Age*,

30 September 2012, http://www.theage.com.au/national/alan-jones-apologises-to-prime-minister-20120930-26t5j.html.
4 Alan Jones's Twitter page: https://twitter.com/2GB_AlanJones.
5 4012.0 Australian Social Trends, June 2011, http://www.abs.gov.au/ausstats/abs@.nsf/lookup/4102.0main+features60jun+2011.

JENNA PRICE

1 'Prime Minister Gillard Responds to Allegations', *7.30 Report*, Australian Broadcasting Corporation, 23 August 2012, www.abc.net.au/7.30/content/2012/s3574703.htm.
2 Lewis, H, '"You Should Have Your Tongue Ripped Out": The Reality of Sexist Abuse Online', 3 November 2011, *New Statesman*, www.newstatesman.com/blogs/helen-lewis-hasteley/2011/11/comments-rape-abuse-women.

CATHERINE FOX

1 2012 Census of Women in Leadership, Workplace Gender Equality Agency, www.wgea.gov.au.
2 Liswood, L, *The Loudest Duck: Moving Beyond Diversity While Embracing Differences to Achieve Success at Work*, Wiley, 2009.
3 Fine, C, *Delusions of Gender: How Our Minds, Society and Neurosexism Create Difference*, WW Norton & Company, 2010.
4 Lucas, C, 'Want to Rise to the Top? Be their Friend', *Sydney Morning Herald*, 3 January 2013, http://www.smh.com.au/national/want-to-rise-to-the-top-be-their-friend-20130102-2c5n6.html.
5 Australian Bureau of Statistics, www.abs.gov.au.
6 Household, Income and Labour Dynamics in Australia (HILDA) survey 2012, www.melbourneinstitute.com/hilda.
7 University Graduates, Department of Education, Employment and Workplace Relations November 2012, cited in Saunders, M, *Creating a Positive Cycle: Critical Steps to Achieving Gender Parity in Australia* Bain/Chief Executive Women Research Report 2013.
8 Workplace Gender Equality Agency *Gender Pay Gap: The Facts* February 2012.

CATHERINE DEVENY

1 Spender, D, *Man-Made Language*, Routledge & Kegan Paul, 1980.
2 Stevenson, C, 'The Blokeyness Index: Blokes Win the Gender War in Australia's 4th Estate', *The King's Tribune*, 6 December 2012, http://www.kingstribune.com/index.php/magazines/december-2012/item/1659-the-blokeyness-index-blokes-win-the-gender-war-in-australia-s-4th-estate.

Chrys Stevenson's blog can be found at http://thatsmyphilosophy.wordpress.com/.

See also The Geena Davis Institute on Gender in Media (http://www.seejane.org/), which Clementine Ford referenced in her fabulous piece 'Why Women Aren't Essential Characters in Movies', *Daily Life*, 25 September 2012, http://www.dailylife.com.au/news-and-views/dl-opinion/why-women-arent-essential-characters-in-movies-20120924-26ged.html.

And read Jane Douglas's letter to me on gaslighting: http://puttingheroarin.wordpress.com/2012/09/14/an-open-letter-to-catherine-deveny/.

WENDY HARMER

1 Rayner, J, 'Gillard Takes a Calculated Risk in Leaving Jones Adrift', *The Conversation*, 2 October 2012, http://theconversation.edu.au/gillard-takes-a-calculated-risk-in-leaving-alan-jones-adrift-9905.

2 ibid.

3 Muller, S, 'And Now from the FM Boys (Club)', *The Hoopla*, 1 March 2012, http://thehoopla.com.au/hear-fm-boys/.

4 ibid.

PAULA MCDONALD AND ABBY CATHCART

1 Sexual harassment is defined by the federal *Sex Discrimination Act 1984* (Cth) ('SDA') as 'an unwelcome sexual advance, or an unwelcome request for sexual favours ... or other unwelcome conduct of a sexual nature ... in circumstances in which a reasonable person ... would have anticipated that the person harassed would be offended, humiliated or intimidated' (Section 28A). SH is covered by both the federal *Sex Discrimination Act 1984* (SDA) and by state-based anti-discrimination legislation.

2 Bristol, J; Chakravarty, A; Charmers, A; Edgerton, W; Freeman, H; Gilmore, R; Hunshaw, C; Mayer, M; Muste, A; Pickett, C; Rustin, B; Whitney, N, *Speak Truth to Power: A Quaker Search for an Alternative to Violence*, American Friends Service Committee, 1955.

CLEMENTINE FORD

1 Smart, H, 'Comedy: The Boys' Club Asserts Itself, Feminist Killjoys Destroy the Vibe', *Hoyden About Town*, 16 November 2012, http://hoydenabouttown.com/20121116.12590/comedy-the-boys-club-asserts-itself-feminist-killjoys-destroy-the-vibe/.

2 Gough, D, 'Comedy Audience Heckles Rape Survivor', *The Age*, 15 November 2012, http://www.theage.com.au/entertainment/

comedy/comedy-audience-heckles-rape-survivor-20121115-29ek0.html.

3 Butler, K, 'No Joke, Freedom of Speech is Worth Debating', *Crikey*, 28 November 2012, http://www.crikey.com.au/2012/11/28/no-joke-freedom-of-speech-is-worth-debating/.

NINA FUNNELL

1 In July 2000, the Howard Government sparked outrage by including the GST (Goods and Services Tax) on pads and tampons, stating that they were not necessities, but 'luxury items' for women. The government currently rakes in about $25 million a year from the GST on female hygiene products; however, in 2012, Coles cut 10% off the price of these items to offset the cost to women, saving us ladies about $6 million a year. Good on you, Coles.

2 Kandel, N, MBBS, MA; Raj Bhandari, A, LLB, MBA; Lamichanne, J, MA, '"Chhue, Chhaupadi and Chueekula Pratha" – Menstrual Sheds: Examples of Discriminatory Practices against Women in the Mid- and Far-Western Regions of Nepal: Considering Women as "Impure" or "Unclean" During Menstruation and Post-Partum Periods', http://drnirmal.tripod.com/Journal1.pdf.

3 Guru Nanak, the founder of Sikhism, condemned the practice of treating menstruating women as impure, instead stating that the menstrual cycle is a fundamental, God-given process necessary for life. In Sikhism, no restrictions are placed on menstruating women and menstrual blood is not considered a pollutant.

4 The word *hysteria* derives from the Greek word for womb, *hystera*, hence we get other words like *hysterectomy*.

5 Hunter, K, 'Do Either of these Words Offend You?', *MamaMia*, 17 July 2012, http://www.mamamia.com.au/news/this-ad-uses-the-word-vagina-is-it-offensive/.

6 Longhurst, R, *Bodies: Exploring Fluid Boundaries*, 132–133, Routledge, 2000.

PENNY WONG

1 O'Brien, S, 'Gillard Stood Up for Women Everywhere', *Herald Sun*, 15 October 2012, http://www.heraldsun.com.au/opinion/gillard-stood-up-for-women-everywhere/story-e6frfhqf-1226495406677.

2 Sallis, E, 'Australian Dream; Australian Nightmare. Some Thoughts on Multiculturalism and Racism', *The Dymphna Clark Memorial Lecture*, 31 March 2007, http://australiansall.com.au/archive/post/australian-dream-australian-nightmare-some-thoughts-on-multiculturalism-and-racism/.

Acknowledgements

Without Alexandra Payne from UQP this collection would never have happened. She had the idea, worked with me on the list of possible contributors and has been there gently chivvying me (and one or two of the contributors) when we have fallen behind. My name may be on the cover, but this is really Alexandra's achievement and her baby. Thanks also to our fabulous copyeditor Kylie Mason and the tenacious and energetic Susan Hornbeck who has made sure anyone who remains unaware of the existence of this book must live under a rock.

I also want to acknowledge the simply amazing rollcall of brilliant and committed women who have – at ridiculously short notice – written such wonderful and varied responses to the phenomenon that has become Destroying the Joint, in all its incarnations. Thank you each and every one.

Finally, I must thank Alan Jones. Say what you like about shock jocks, they dominate their microphones for a reason. He speaks what far too many others think – that's why he rates. If such attitudes exist (and they do) it is better they be aired publicly, particularly as – thanks to Twitter and other forms of social media – those of us who disagree now have the means to argue back.